Revelation
What John Knew

Rev. Barbara M. Schobl-Legee

Olympus Story House
www.olympusstoryhouse.com

Table Of Contents

Table Of Contents

Foreword

John the Revelator was exiled to the isle of Patmos in approximately 95 A.D. [1] Now, there is some debate about who this John was. John, the brother of James, the sons of Zebedee, was martyred at the hand of Herod in Acts 12:2, so it was not him. There is some speculation that the young man in Mark 14:51 – 52 was John, a young man of approximately 13 or 14 years of age, who was referred to as an "apostle." Some think that this young man was the John Jesus talked to from the cross and said, "Behold thy mother!" This was "the disciple whom Jesus loved." This same John could have been the writer of Revelation – or not. There is always the chance of it being written by a pseudo-epigrapher.

If it was this young lad, then, given that Christ died in either 30 A.D. or 33 A.D. (those were two years when Earthquakes were recorded in Jerusalem and those same two years debated by scholars as to the year of Jesus' death), then in 95 A.D., John would have been between 74 and 79 years old.

Other theologians say that the young man was John Mark—the Mark who wrote the Gospel of Mark—and that the author of Revelation was John the Apostle. If that were the case, Revelation had to be written during the reign of Domitian, and if John was twenty years old when he started following Jesus, then he would have been between 80 and 85 years old. Still, it is possible.

Other theologians say the author of Revelation was neither of these two, but someone else named John, or someone who used the name John.

No matter who this John was, to better understand his perspective, we need to know the history of the time and what the early Christians believed. The closest we can get to this latter point is by looking at the writings of early Christians, some of which are still extant. One of the best sources is the Ante-Nicene Fathers. Also, there is one early commentary on Revelation that is extant, which was written by Victorinus around 280 A.D. Even then, I believe some of his thoughts were not like those of the earlier Christians, and particularly not like

---

[1] Revelation 1:9

the Jewish Christians (those who were Jewish and then believed Jesus was the Messiah). It is akin to playing a game where people stand in a circle, and the first one tells a story and whispers it to the next one, and so forth around the circle until it returns to the one who originally told the story. By the time it goes full circle, it is hardly recognizable, if at all. For example:

Justin Martyr wrote, c. 160 A.D., "There was a certain man with us, whose name was John, one of the apostles of Christ, who prophesied by a revelation that was made to him. He prophesied that those who believed in our Christ would dwell a thousand years in Jerusalem." [2]

Compare this to the writings just one hundred years later:

Dionysius of Alexandria wrote, c. 262 A.D., "I do not deny that this person was called John, therefore, and that this was the writing of someone named John. I also acknowledge that it was the work of some holy and inspired man. However, I could not so easily acknowledge that the author was one of the apostles. I cannot so easily acknowledge that it is the same person who wrote the Gospel that bears the title, 'According to John,' and the author of the general epistle. Rather, from the character of both those works and the forms of expression in them. . . I draw the conclusion that the authorship is not his. For the evAngelist nowhere else affixes his name [to his works]. He never proclaims himself either in the Gospel or in the epistle." [3]

Whoever he was, this John was most certainly a Jew. He was extremely knowledgeable in the Holy Scriptures (Old Testament). God would not have shown these images to anyone but a "prophet" (a prophet speaks the word of God through the Scriptures or through a Rhema Word). Some explanation of these confusing scenes would have been necessary. I believe that John would have recognized the historical aspect of some of these images, and others he would have recognized enough to know to whom the event was going to happen and by whom it was going to be committed, even though he did not know exactly how it was going to transpire.

As to the date of the writing of Revelation, Victorinus wrote, c. 280 A.D., "The date that the Apocalypse was written must be remembered. For at that time, Caesar Domitian reigned. But before him there had been Titus (his brother), Vespasian, Otho, Vitellius, and Galba. These are the five who have fallen. One remains – Domitian – under whom the Apocalypse was written. 'The other has not yet come.' This refers to Nerva. 'And when he is come, he will be for a short time.'" Nerva did

[2] The Ante-Nicene Fathers, translated by David W. Bercot (Dry Run, PA, Scroll Publishing) Vol. 1, 240,
[3] Ibid., Vol. 6, 83

not even reign for two full years. 'And the beast that you saw is of the seven.' Nero reigned before those kings. . . Now [in saying] that one of the heads was, as it were, slain to death . . . he speaks of Nero." [4]

To translate the above, Victorinus is talking about the kings, five of whom had fallen, and one is, and the other had not yet come (Revelation 17:10). Domitian became emperor in 81 A.D. and was assassinated in 96 A.D. It was during this time that John wrote Revelation. The closest guess is that John was exiled to Patmos in 95 A.D. and wrote Revelation in that year's span prior to Domitian's death. Once Domitian had died, Trajan released John.

Once released, John would have taken this letter to the seven Churches and then, if possible, to other Churches.

For the record, I believe this John, the author of the Book of Revelation, was John the Apostle—the same person who wrote the Gospel of John and the three letters of John.

Another thing the reader needs to be aware of is that Jesus talked on several diverse levels, all at the same time. For instance, when Jesus was recorded in Matthew and Mark as saying:

Matthew 21:21 Jesus answered and said unto them, Verily I say unto you, If ye have faith, and doubt not, ye shall not only do this which is done to the fig tree, but also if ye shall say unto this mountain, Be thou removed, and be thou cast into the sea; it shall be done.

Mark 11:23 For verily I say unto you, That whosoever shall say unto this mountain, Be thou removed, and be thou cast into the sea; and shall not doubt in his heart, but shall believe that those things which he saith shall come to pass; he shall have whatsoever he saith.

Jesus was not just talking about their faith. He was discussing having the new religion that would arise after His death and resurrection cast among the Gentiles. You will understand more about that statement as you read Revelation – What John Knew.

---

[4] CHURCH FATHERS: Commentary on the Apocalypse (Victornius) - New Advent, https://www.newadvent.org/fathers/0712.htm.

Introduction

Revelation Chapter 1

Revelation 1:1 The Revelation of Jesus Christ, which God gave unto him, to shew unto his servants things which must shortly come to pass; and he sent and signified it by his Angel unto his servant John:

Two verses later, John says, "For the time is at hand." In Revelation 22:6, it is written, ". . . the things which must shortly be done." Then, again, in Revelation 22:10, ". . . for the time is at hand." This is four times that John was told it would not be a long time. God usually emphasizes something by mentioning it three times. John would have recognized four as a sense of totality or completeness as it related to creation. [5]

He also knew this Greek word, which was translated into "Revelation," is found only once in the Gospels, in Luke 2:32 *A light to lighten the Gentiles, and the glory of Israel,* where *"to lighten"* should be translated *"for revelation."* It is used in the sense that Jesus is the light of the world, dispelling the darkness under which the Gentiles were covered. This word is used thirteen times in Paul's writings and three times in First Peter. It has the following connotations:

1. The unveiling of something hidden, gives knowledge to those who see it.

2. Christian insight into spiritual truth.

3. The second coming of the Lord in which His glory will be revealed.

Revelation 1:2 Who bare record of the word of God, and of the testimony of Jesus Christ, and of all things that he saw.

1 Corinthians 1:6 Even as the testimony of Christ was confirmed in you:

And what is this testimony of Christ?

John would later write in Revelation 19:10, ". . .for the testimony of Jesus is the spirit of prophecy."

Revelation 1:3 Blessed is he that readeth, and they that hear the words of this prophecy, and keep those things which are written therein: for the time is at hand.

---

[5] John J. Davis, *Biblical Numerology A Basic Study of the use of Numbers in the Bible* (Grand Rapids, Michigan, Baker Book House, 1968) 122

1

John might have been aware of Luke's writing, in Luke 11:28, "But he said, Yea rather, blessed are they that hear the word of God and keep it."

These words mean an official, public reading in a congregational setting.

This is the second time we have been told that things must soon come to pass or that the time is at hand.

Revelation 1:4 John to the seven Churches which are in Asia: Grace be unto you, and peace, from him which is, and which was, and which is to come; and from the seven Spirits which are before his throne;

The Churches in Asia were in the area which is now known as Turkey. Seven was known as the perfect number. [6] If you search "spirit," you will find more than seven spirits mentioned. Since Christ was perfect, the spirits had to be perfect, too.

Jesus Christ established His Church as a new institution on Earth. This new institution was to play a central part in Christ's "Revealing."

Victorinus said of Verse 4, "He is, because He endures continually; He was, because with the Father He made all things; and, He is to come, because assuredly He will come to judgment."

Who, or What are the seven spirits which are before His throne? John would have known that there are a lot more than seven spirits mentioned in the Bible. As we research the Bible, we find the seven spirits in Isaiah 11:2:

Isaiah 11:2 And the spirit of the LORD shall rest upon him, the spirit of wisdom and understanding, the spirit of counsel and might, the spirit of knowledge and of the fear of the LORD;

Here, we see seven spirits:

The Spirit of the LORD
The Spirit of wisdom
The Spirit of understanding
The Spirit of Counsel
The Spirit of Might
The Spirit of Knowledge
The Spirit of the fear of the LORD

If we look for spirit throughout the Bible, we find:

Exodus 28:3 And thou shalt speak unto all that are wise hearted, whom I have filled with the spirit of wisdom, that they may make Aaron's garments to consecrate him, that he may minister unto me in the priest's office.

---

[6] Ibid.

2

Exodus 31:3 And I have filled him with the <u>spirit of God</u>, in wisdom, and in understanding, and in knowledge, and in all manner of workmanship,

Numbers 5:14 And the <u>spirit of jealousy</u> come upon him, and he be jealous of his wife, and she be defiled: or if the spirit of jealousy come upon him, and he be jealous of his wife, and she be not defiled:

Deuteronomy 34:9 And Joshua the son of Nun was full of the <u>spirit of wisdom</u>; for Moses had laid his hands upon him: and the children of Israel hearkened unto him, and did as the LORD commanded Moses.

Job 20:3 I have heard the check of my reproach, and the <u>spirit of my understanding</u> causeth me to answer.

Isaiah 4:4 When the Lord shall have washed away the filth of the daughters of Zion, and shall have purged the blood of Jerusalem from the midst thereof by the <u>spirit of judgment</u>, and by the spirit of burning.

Isaiah 11:2 And the <u>spirit of the LORD</u> shall rest upon him, the <u>spirit of wisdom and understanding</u>, the <u>spirit of counsel and might</u>, the <u>spirit of knowledge and of the fear of the LORD</u>;

Isaiah 29:10 For the LORD hath poured out upon you the <u>spirit of deep sleep</u>, and hath closed your eyes: the prophets and your rulers, the seers hath he covered.

Isaiah 61:3 To appoint unto them that mourn in Zion, to give unto them beauty for ashes, the oil of joy for mourning, the garment of praise for the <u>spirit of heaviness</u>; that they might be called trees of righteousness, the planting of the LORD, that he might be glorified.

Ezekiel 1:20 Whithersoever the spirit was to go, they went, thither was their spirit to go; and the wheels were lifted up over against them: for the <u>spirit of the living creature</u> was in the wheels.

Zechariah 12:10 And I will pour upon the house of David, and upon the inhabitants of Jerusalem, the <u>spirit of grace and of supplications</u>: and they shall look upon me whom they have pierced, and they shall mourn for him, as one mourneth for his only son, and shall be in bitterness for him, as one that is in bitterness for his firstborn.

John 14:17 Even the <u>Spirit of truth</u>; whom the world cannot receive, because it seeth him not, neither knoweth him: but ye know him; for he dwelleth with you, and shall be in you.

Acts 16:16 And it came to pass, as we went to prayer, a certain damsel possessed with a <u>spirit of divination</u> met us, which brought her masters much gain by soothsaying:

This spirit of divination is an evil spirit.

Romans 1:4 And declared to be the Son of God with power, according to the <u>spirit of holiness</u>, by the resurrection from the dead:

Romans 8:2 For the law of the <u>Spirit of life in Christ Jesus</u> hath made me free from the law of sin and death.

Romans 8:15 For ye have not received the <u>spirit of bondage</u> again to fear; but ye have received the <u>Spirit of adoption</u>, whereby we cry, Abba, Father.

Romans 11:8 (According as it is written, God hath given them the <u>spirit of slumber</u>, eyes that they should not see, and ears that they should not hear;) unto this day.

1 Corinthians 4:21 What will ye? shall I come unto you with a rod, or in love, and in the <u>spirit of meekness</u>?

2 Corinthians 4:13 We having the same <u>spirit of faith</u>, according as it is written, I believed, and therefore have I spoken; we also believe, and therefore speak;

Galatians 6:1 Brethren, if a man be overtaken in a fault, ye which are spiritual, restore such an one in the <u>spirit of meekness</u>; considering thyself, lest thou also be tempted.

Ephesians 1:13 In whom ye also trusted, after that ye heard the word of truth, the gospel of your salvation: in whom also after that ye believed, ye were sealed with that holy <u>Spirit of promise</u>,

Ephesians 1:17 That the God of our Lord Jesus Christ, the Father of glory, may give unto you the <u>spirit of wisdom and revelation in the knowledge of him</u>:

2 Thessalonians 2:8 And then shall that Wicked be revealed, whom the Lord shall consume with the <u>spirit of his mouth</u>, and shall destroy with the brightness of his coming:

2 Timothy 1:7 For God hath not given us the <u>spirit of fear</u>; but <u>of power</u>, and <u>of love</u>, and <u>of a sound mind</u>.

Hebrews 10:29 Of how much sorer punishment, suppose ye, shall he be thought worthy, who hath trodden under foot the Son of God, and hath counted the blood of the covenant, wherewith he was sanctified, an unholy thing, and hath done despite unto the <u>Spirit of grace</u>?

1 Peter 4:14 If ye be reproached for the name of Christ, happy are ye; for the <u>spirit of glory and of God</u> resteth upon you: on their part he is evil spoken of, but on your part he is glorified.

1 John 4:6 We are of God: he that knoweth God heareth us; he that is not of God heareth not us. Hereby know we the <u>spirit of truth</u>, and the <u>spirit of error</u>.

Revelation 11:11 And after three days and an half the <u>Spirit of life from</u> God entered into them, and they stood upon their feet; and great fear fell upon them which saw them.

Revelation 19:10 And I fell at his feet to worship him. And he said unto me, See thou do it not: I am thy fellowservant, and of thy brethren *that have the testimony of Jesus: worship God: for the testimony of Jesus is the <u>spirit of prophecy</u>.*

So, we see if we go by every spirit which is mentioned in the Bible as coming from God or from the Lord (and both of those are spirits mentioned, also), then we have many more than seven spirits with which we need to deal. What we must consider is that seven is the perfect Heavenly number. The Book of Revelation is the Revelation or revealing of Jesus Christ. Seven is the number that means perfect, and Jesus Christ was, is, and will always be perfect. Therefore, this must be part of revealing Jesus Christ as being perfect.

Revelation 1:5 And from Jesus Christ, who is the faithful witness, and the first begotten of the dead, and the prince of the kings of the Earth. Unto him that loved us, and washed us from our sins in his own blood,
1 Corinthians 15:20 But now is Christ risen from the dead, and become the firstfruits of them that slept.

This says, "of them that slept," because the Jews, especially the Pharisees, believed people "slept" until the physical, bodily resurrection. The Sadducees did not believe in a resurrection. That is why they were sad, you see. But to sleep was a euphemism for being dead. Jesus was the first to be physically resurrected – He was the first, or first fruit.

Jesus was not only God's "first begotten," He was God's "only begotten son." But Christ was the first to be resurrected – "the first begotten of the dead." The rest of the Christians will follow in resurrection.

John later wrote, in Revelation 20:6, "*Blessed and holy is he that hath part in the first resurrection: on such the second death hath no power, but they shall be priests of God and of Christ, and shall reign with him a thousand years.*" We, as Christians, have our part in Christ's resurrection, it being the first.

Revelation 1:6 And hath made us kings and priests unto God and his Father; to him be glory and dominion for ever and ever. Amen.

John wrote again, in Revelation 5:10, "*And has made us unto our God kings and priests: and we shall reign on the Earth.*"

As Christ makes us kings and priests to God, we can overcome Satan and have power through prayer. But ALL glory and dominion belong to God forever. Be aware that kings and priests are to have humble dignity—not arrogance.

Elsewhere in Revelation, it says:

Revelation 5:10 And hast made us unto our God kings and priests: and we shall reign on the Earth.

See Revelation 20:6: *Blessed and holy is he that hath part in the first resurrection: on such the second death hath no power, but they shall be priests of God and of Christ, and shall reign with him a thousand years.*

Revelation 1:7 Behold, he cometh with clouds; and every eye shall see him, and they also which pierced him: and all kindreds of the Earth shall wail because of him. Even so, Amen.

Matthew had written, in Matthew 24:30, "*And then shall appear the sign of the Son of man in Heaven: and then shall all the tribes of the Earth mourn, and they shall see the Son of man coming in the clouds of Heaven with power and great glory.*" This verse is in three parts:

1. to begin the Revelation: *And then shall appear the sign of the Son of man in Heaven*; the Tribulation:
2. and then shall all the tribes of the Earth mourn;
and last,
3. the Rapture: *and they shall see the Son of man coming in the clouds of Heaven with power and great glory.*

The mourners of John's day wailed at funerals, so this verse agrees completely with Matthew. John was also aware of Zechariah 12:10, "*And I will pour upon the house of David, and upon the inhabitants of Jerusalem, the spirit of grace and of supplications: and they shall look upon me whom they have pierced, and they shall mourn for him, as one mourneth for his only son, and shall be in bitterness for him, as one that is in bitterness for this firstborn.*"

Revelation 1:8 I am Alpha and Omega, the beginning and the ending, saith the Lord, which is, and which was, and which is to come, the Almighty.

John knew Isaiah 44:6, "Thus saith the LORD the King of Israel, and his redeemer the LORD of hosts; I am the first, and I am the last; and beside me there is no God."

Revelation 1:9 I John, who also am your brother, and companion in tribulation, and in the kingdom and patience of Jesus Christ, was in the isle that is called Patmos, for the word of God, and for the testimony of Jesus Christ.

John was the brother to all other Christians (and to us) and the former companion of those to whom he was writing. They were all going through the tribulation of persecution for being Christians. John had been exiled to the island of Patmos, off the coast of Greece, because of his preaching of the Gospel.

He also knew what Luke had written in Acts:

Acts 14:22 Confirming the souls of the disciples, and exhorting them to continue in the faith, and that we must through much tribulation enter into the kingdom of God.

Notice it says, "through much tribulation."

John would recognize Deuteronomy 4:30 – 31, *"When thou art in tribulation, and all these things are come upon thee, even in the latter days, if thou turn to the LORD thy God, and shalt be obedient unto his voice, (For the LORD thy God is a merciful God;) he will not forsake thee, neither destroy thee, nor forget the covenant of thy fathers which he sware unto them."*

We must remember this verse in all our times of trouble and tribulation!

Revelation 1:10 I was in the Spirit on the Lord's day, and heard behind me a great voice, as of a trumpet,

Some have interpreted this "Lord's Day" as the day of the Lord's second coming. But why would Christ show John all that was to be before He came back if He came back that day? This had to be a Sunday, called the Lord's Day, and not to be confused with the Sabbath. The Sabbath was Saturday—the last day of the week. The first day of the week was called the Lord's Day because Christ arose on that day of the week.

Revelation 1:11 Saying, I am Alpha and Omega, the first and the last: and, What thou seest, write in a book, and send it unto the seven Churches which are in Asia; unto Ephesus, and unto Smyrna, and unto Pergamos, and unto Thyatira, and unto Sardis, and unto Philadelphia, and unto Laodicea.

John was not the first prophet to be told to write the words He gave them:

Jeremiah 36:2 Take thee a roll of a book, and write therein all the words that I have spoken unto thee against Israel, and against Judah, and against all the nations, from the day I spake unto thee, from the days of Josiah, even unto this day.

The seven Churches were close together on a mail route for that day. They represent the Churches that existed at that time and the spiritual representation of the progression of the Church through the ages. We have the Book of Ephesians, which was written to the Church at Ephesus. The only time Smyrna, Pergamos, Sardis, and Philadelphia are mentioned is in Revelation. Thyatira is mentioned in Acts 16:14. When Paul went to Philippi, the chief city in that part of Macedonia, he mentioned Lydia, a seller of purple from Thyatira. Laodicea is mentioned four times in Colossians.

Revelation 1:12 And I turned to see the voice that spake with me. And being turned, I saw seven golden candlesticks;

Irenaeus wrote, c. 180 A.D., "The Church preaches the truth everywhere, and she is the seven-branched candlestick that bears the light of Christ." [7] This is confirmed by Revelation 1:20, "*. . . the seven candlesticks which thou sawest are the seven Churches.*"

Revelation 1:13 And in the midst of the seven candlesticks one like unto the Son of man, clothed with a garment down to the foot, and girt about the paps with a golden girdle.

John would have recognized the long robe of the high priest—the only one who was allowed in the Holy of Holies. Revelation 1:20 says the candlesticks are the seven Churches. Christ is in the midst – the middle – of the seven Churches. He is the Shepherd of those Churches.

Revelation 1:14 His head and his hairs were white like wool, as white as snow; and his eyes were as a flame of fire;

Victorinus wrote, c. 280 A.D., "His eyes were as a flame of fire. God's precepts are those which minister light to believers, but to unbelievers burning." [8]

Revelation 1:15 And his feet like unto fine brass, as if they burned in a furnace; and his voice as the sound of many waters.

John would have recognized Daniel's vision, "*Daniel 10:5-6 Then I lifted up mine eyes, and looked, and behold a certain man clothed in linen, whose loins were girded with fine gold of Uphaz: His body also was like the beryl, and his face as the appearance of lightning, and his eyes as lamps of fire, and his arms and his feet like in colour to polished brass, and the voice of his words like the voice of a multitude.*"

The sound of God's voice was described in Ezekiel 43:2: "*and, behold, the glory of the God of Israel came from the way of the east: and his voice was like a noise of many waters: and the Earth shined with his glory.*"

The Old Testament speaks of His voice as the voice of great waters. Have you ever been by a rushing river, particularly where it joins another river? The noise is deafening.

---

[7] Ante-Nicene Fathers, Translated by David W. Bercot, Editor, (Dry run, PA, Scroll Publishing) Vol. 1, 548

[8] CHURCH FATHERS: Commentary on the Apocalypse (Victorinus) - New Advent, https://www.newadvent.org/fathers/0712.htm.

Revelation 1:16 And he had in his right hand seven stars: and out of his mouth went a sharp twoedged sword: and his countenance was as the sun shineth in his strength.

Jesus had told his disciples, in Matthew 10:34, *"Think not that I am come to send peace on Earth: I came not to send peace, but a sword." John would also have recognized this sword as the word of God. Paul, who wrote to the Ephesians and ministered in Asia, wrote, in Hebrews 4:12, "For the word of God is quick, and powerful, and sharper than any twoedged sword, piercing even to the dividing asunder of soul and spirit, and of the joints and marrow, and is a discerner of the thoughts and intents of the heart."*

John also wrote in Revelation 19:15, *"And out of his mouth goeth a sharp sword, that with it he should smite the nations: and he shall rule them with a rod of iron: and he treadeth the winepress of the fierceness and wrath of Almighty God."*

As for those stars, we go back to Revelation 1:20 *The seven stars are the Angels of the seven Churches:*

Revelation 1:17 And when I saw him, I fell at his feet as dead. And he laid his right hand upon me, saying unto me, Fear not; I am the first and the last:

Irenaeus wrote, c. 180 A.D., "When John could not endure the sight (for he says, 'I fell at his feet as dead'), . . . the Word revived him. Christ reminded him that it was He upon whose bosom he had leaned at supper." [9]

But John would have recognized this experience as being the same type Daniel had, in Daniel 10:16 – 19: *"And, behold, one like the similitude of the sons of men touched my lips: then I opened my mouth, and spake, and said unto him that stood before me, O my lord, by the vision my sorrows are turned upon me, and I have retained no strength. 17) For how can the servant of this my lord talk with this my lord? for as for me, straightway there remained no strength in me, neither is there breath left in me. 18) Then there came again and touched me one like the appearance of a man, and he strengthened me, 19) And said, O man greatly beloved, fear not: peace be unto thee, be strong, yea, be strong. And when he had spoken unto me, I was strengthened, and said, Let my lord speak; for thou hast strengthened me."*

Revelation 1:18 I am he that liveth, and was dead; and, behold, I am alive for evermore, Amen; and have the keys of hell and of death.

---

[9] Ante-Nicene Fathers, Translated by David W. Bercot, Editor, Vol. 1, 491

John knew that Jesus was alive, but was dead, but is alive forever. The literal translation of this verse is:

Yea (*or therefore*) life and became a corpse; behold I am life into the end. Amen; and hold the key: hell and death.

The translators added a few words to make it more readable and understandable.

Notice a subtle but significant difference: I am alive forevermore vs. I am alive into the end. Jesus said, in John 14:6, "I am the way, the truth, and the life; no man comes to the Father but by me."

Revelation 1:19 Write the things which thou hast seen, and the things which are, and the things which shall be hereafter;

This was a simple command from Christ. John is the scribe. John has seen what God, Christ, and the Angels have already shown him. The things that are are the things that have already happened. The things that shall be hereafter are the things that John will be shown to be happening from that point forward until the end of time.

Revelation 1:20 The mystery of the seven stars which thou sawest in my right hand, and the seven golden candlesticks. The seven stars are the Angels of the seven Churches: and the seven candlesticks which thou sawest are the seven Churches.

Victorinus wrote, c. 280 A.D., "those seven stars are the seven Churches. . .. This does not mean that they themselves are the only Churches – or even the main Churches. Rather, what he says to one, he says to all. For they are in no respect different." [10]

---

[10] CHURCH FATHERS: Commentary on the Apocalypse (Victurinus) - New Advent, https://www.newadvent.org/fathers/0712.htm.

The Letters to the Seven Churches

Revelation Chapters 2 – 3

Theologians agree that the seven Asian Churches were on a "mail route" for that day. It was also customary to take an epistle from Church to Church and read it at each location. In this way, each Church received the same word and doctrine. As we saw in the Forward, this helped to do away with an oral tradition that could cause opposite opinions within just one hundred years. It has been almost two thousand years since Christ died. Look at all the differing opinions of doctrine and how many different Churches there are—each with a slightly different doctrine. Sometimes, there is even a slight difference in doctrine within the same denomination.

When Jesus told John what to write to each Church, He explained that they had let their community's ways affect their Church's actions. They were not only in the world, but they had also become of the world!

From this point, we are going to cover things differently. We will examine the whole letter to one Church and then discuss what John knew.

EPHESUS

Revelation 2:1 Unto the Angel of the Church of Ephesus write; These things saith he that holdeth the seven stars in his right hand, who walketh in the midst of the seven golden candlesticks;

Revelation 2:2 I know thy works, and thy labour, and thy patience, and how thou canst not bear them which are evil: and thou hast tried them which say they are apostles, and are not, and hast found them liars:

Revelation 2:3 And hast borne, and hast patience, and for my name's sake hast laboured, and hast not fainted.

Revelation 2:4 Nevertheless I have somewhat against thee, because thou hast left thy first love.

Revelation 2:5 Remember therefore from whence thou art fallen, and repent, and do the first works; or else I will come unto thee quickly, and will remove thy candlestick out of his place, except thou repent.

Revelation 2:6 But this thou hast, that thou hatest the deeds of the Nicolaitans, which I also hate.

Revelation 2:7 He that hath an ear, let him hear what the Spirit saith unto the Churches; To him that overcometh will I give to eat of the tree of life, which is in the midst of the paradise of God.

Ephesus means *desirable*. Paul wrote to the Church at Ephesus and praised her for her soundness of faith. They did not *lose* their first love; they *left* their first love. This is *leaving* salvation, not *losing* salvation. Then, were they ever saved to start with? God knows—not man.

They were to return to their first works – telling the Gospel – or Christ would "remove their candlestick out of its place." Jesus always used what the people in the city would understand. Not much is known about the original city of Ephesus until the seventh century B.C. when it became a thriving city. The Lydian King Croesus rebuilt the Temple of Artemis. In 356 B.C., the Temple burned down. When it was rebuilt (again), it was estimated to be four times larger than the Parthenon. The temple was later destroyed, never to be rebuilt. [11]

In 334 B.C., Alexander the Great defeated the Persians, and one of his generals renamed the city Arsineia. That general, Lysimachus, moved Ephesus two miles away and built a new harbor and defensive walls. In 281 B.C., that city was renamed Ephesus. [12]

So, when the letter to the Ephesians was read, they knew exactly what the Angel was telling John. Cities do not move easily. First, the original must be destroyed. Then, it takes a long time to relocate and build, and there is a lot of tribulation.

Victorinus also wrote that the Nicolaitans were ministers under Nicolaus, who taught that meat that had been offered to various idols could be exorcised and eaten. Then, after eight days, the sin of fornication would be absolved. Nicholaus also taught the hierarchy of the Church. There were to be different "layers" of pastors, preachers, and teachers. Then, there was to be someone like a supervisor over several Churches, then someone over them for several districts [3], etc., until you got to the one man who was over all others—and it was not Jesus and God.

Christ considers this sin of following the Nicolaitans such an offense that He offers to those who overcome the gift of being able to eat of the tree of life. Since this doctrine was being taught, there were obviously pagan temples in Ephesus. By teaching this doctrine, Nicolaus had left his "first love"—the Gospel of Christ.

---

[11] https://www.history.com/topics/ancient-greece/ephesus
[12] Ibid.

It is no wonder Paul wrote to the Corinthians about this practice. He said that every man knew there was but one God. If they see us eat the meat offered to idols, their conscience is weak and, therefore, defiled. On the other hand, we are made no worse nor better whether we eat meat or not. However, if a weak individual sees us eat the meat, it may be an obstacle to them, and that would be a sin against the brethren who are weak and, therefore, a sin against Christ. [13]

SMYRNA

Revelation 2:8 And unto the Angel of the Church in Smyrna write; These things saith the first and the last, which was dead, and is alive;
Revelation 2:9 I know thy works, and tribulation, and poverty, (but thou art rich) and I know the blasphemy of them which say they are Jews, and are not, but are the synagogue of Satan.
Revelation 2:10 Fear none of those things which thou shalt suffer: behold, the devil shall cast some of you into prison, that ye may be tried; and ye shall have tribulation ten days: be thou faithful unto death, and I will give thee a crown of life.
Revelation 2:11 He that hath an ear, let him hear what the Spirit saith unto the Churches; He that overcometh shall not be hurt of the second death.

Revelation 2:8 And unto the Angel of the Church in Smyrna write; These things saith the first and the last, which was dead, and is alive;
God was the first – He made all things. God will be the last – He will judge all things.
This also speaks to Jesus' resurrection. We will find that the Angel who spoke with John gave information in each letter to which the individual community could relate. In Smyrna's case, it was the "resurrection." According to the Israel Bible Center's course on Revelation, Smyrna was sacked and destroyed in the sixth century B.C. However, Alexander the Great and his successors re-established the city, and Smyrna rose to prominence during the Roman period.
Smyrna still exists as Izmir, Turkey. [14]

Revelation 2:9 I know thy works, and tribulation, and poverty, (but thou art rich) and I know the blasphemy of them which say they are Jews, and are not, but are the synagogue of Satan.

---

[13] 1 Corithians Chapter 8
[14] https://Churchofchristarticles.com/blog/david-hersey/smyrna-the-suffering-Church/

Jesus told the Church at Smyrna that, though they thought they were poverty-stricken, they were laying up treasures in Heaven.

Again, this relates to Jesus, who left the glory and riches of Heaven to come to Earth as a mortal man to be the sacrifice for man. The blood of bulls, goats, and sheep cannot atone for man.

The only true Jews were those following Christ, those who recognized their Messiah. The Jews were God's people, and some thought and taught that one could "convert" by being circumcised. Some taught that to become a Christian, one first converted to Judaism by being circumcised, learning all the law and feasts, etc., and then accepting Christ as your Savior and becoming baptized. [15] This was not what Jesus came for.

When it comes to "the synagogue of Satan," "synagogue" was a generic Greek term that meant "assembly" or "gathering" of any people. There were pagan temples to Zeus, Athena, Cybele, Hermes, Hestia, Dionysus, Eros, and Hercules. [16] It could very well be that some of the members of those temples converted to Judaism or even just adopted the lifestyle of the Jews, but were not faithful to the one true God. If you are not faithfully worshipping God, then you are worshipping Satan and would, therefore, be of "the synagogue of Satan."

Revelation 2:10 Fear none of those things which thou shalt suffer: behold, the devil shall cast some of you into prison, that ye may be tried; and ye shall have tribulation ten days: be thou faithful unto death, and I will give thee a crown of life.

In prophecy, a day is a year, as described in:

Ezekiel 4:4-6 Lie thou also upon thy left side, and lay the iniquity of the house of Israel upon it: according to the number of the days that thou shalt lie upon it thou shalt bear their iniquity. For I have laid upon thee the years of their iniquity, according to the number of the days, three hundred and ninety days: so shalt thou bear the iniquity of the house of Israel. And when thou hast accomplished them, lie again on thy right side, and thou shalt bear the iniquity of the house of Judah forty days: I have appointed thee each day for a year.

This same prophetic time is described in:

Numbers 14:34 After the number of the days in which ye searched the land, even forty days, each day for a year, shall ye bear your iniquities, even forty years, and ye shall know my breach of promise.

A month in prophecy is 30 days, which equates to 30 years in the natural. To prove this, let us look at Hosea:

[15] https://www.gotquestions.org/Judaizers.htm
[16] https://Churchofchristarticles.com/blog/david-hersey/smyrna-the-suffering-Church/

Hosea 5:7 They have dealt treacherously against the LORD: for they have begotten strange children: now shall a month devour them with their portions.

Hosea started his prophecies in 785 B.C. and continued until 725 B.C. This portion had to be written sometime around 770 B.C., because, in 740 B.C., the kingdom of Israel fell to the Neo-Assyrian Empire. This was the first time Israel had been attacked and lost. The Neo-Assyrian Empire was the most powerful nation on Earth. They were what is modern-day Iraq.

In verse ten, Christ warned that some people could be imprisoned for 10 years for preaching the gospel. Now, because John wrote this book at the end of Domitian the Emperor's reign, as Justinus and Irenaeus wrote, this should refer to the persecution which was done by the emperor Trajan, who began to persecute the Christian Church in the tenth year of his reign. The persecution continued until Adrian, the emperor, had succeeded him: The space of time is precisely ten years. This crown of life was their eternal, immortal, spiritual life.

Izmir is not known for its Christian Church. Muhammedism has taken it over. John could not have known about Muhammedism or Islam. It would be another 3-400 years before Muhammed lived.

Revelation 2:11 He that hath an ear, let him hear what the Spirit saith unto the Churches; He that overcometh shall not be hurt of the second death.

All who accept Jesus as their personal Savior will not be hurt by the second death, which is complete and final separation from God— the death of the soul.

PERGAMOS

Revelation 2:12 And to the Angel of the Church in Pergamos write; These things saith he which hath the sharp sword with two edges;

Revelation 2:13 I know thy works, and where thou dwellest, even where Satan's seat is: and thou holdest fast my name, and hast not denied my faith, even in those days wherein Antipas was my faithful martyr, who was slain among you, where Satan dwelleth.

Revelation 2:14 But I have a few things against thee, because thou hast there them that hold the doctrine of Balaam, who taught Balac to cast a stumblingblock before the children of Israel, to eat things sacrificed unto idols, and to commit fornication.

Revelation 2:15 So hast thou also them that hold the doctrine of the Nicolaitans, which thing I hate.

Revelation 2:16 Repent; or else I will come unto thee quickly, and will fight against them with the sword of my mouth.

Revelation 2:17 He that hath an ear, let him hear what the Spirit saith unto the Churches; To him that overcometh will I give to eat of the hidden manna, and will give him a white stone, and in the stone a new name written, which no man knoweth saving he that receiveth it.

Revelation 2:12 And to the Angel of the Church in Pergamos write; These things saith he which hath the sharp sword with two edges;

Pergamum means "thoroughly married."

The Angel with the sharp, two-edged sword is Christ, as we saw in Revelation 1:16.

Revelation 2:13 I know thy works, and where thou dwellest, even where Satan's seat is: and thou holdest fast my name, and hast not denied my faith, even in those days wherein Antipas was my faithful martyr, who was slain among you, where Satan dwelleth.

The word translated "seat" is the Greek word *thronos* - which means a stately seat or throne and indicates the power the person who sat in that seat wielded. Christ's sword in verse twelve is in comparison to the pagan god's power. Since there were many pagan temples, there were many seats or "thrones."

The Christians were persecuted by Emperor Trajan but held fast to their faith.

Antipas was a bishop in Pergamum and had been ordained by the Apostle John. In fear of Antipas, the demons, it was said, appeared to the pagan priests in their dreams and told them that their great fear of Antipas was making them leave the city. The priests stirred up the multitude, and they began to persecute Antipas, pressing him to deny Christ and worship idols. Antipas said to them, "When your so-called gods, lords of the universe are frightened of me, a mortal man, and must flee from this city, do you not recognize that, by this, your faith is an aberration?" [17] Antipas told them the Christian faith was the only true and saving faith, but the people became infuriated like wild beasts and dragged the aged Antipas before the temple of Artemis, where an ox, cast in bronze, stood. They heated the ox and threw Antipas inside. Inside the red-hot ox, St. Antipas glorified God with thanksgiving, like Jonah in the whale and the Three Children in the

---

[17] https://img.sermonindex.net/modules/articles/article_pdf.php?aid=4241

burning fiery furnace. [18] Antipas prayed for his flock and the whole world until he died, and his soul joined the Angels in the Kingdom of Christ. He died suffering and was crowned with unfading glory in the year 92 A.D. [19]

Revelation 2:14 But I have a few things against thee, because thou hast there them that hold the doctrine of Balaam, who taught Balac to cast a stumblingblock before the children of Israel, to eat things sacrificed unto idols, and to commit fornication.

The Balaam doctrine consisted of idolatry and sexual immorality. This fornication is spiritual adultery – worshipping other idols. For the people of Pergamos, it meant Baal worship.

Revelation 2:15 So hast thou also them that hold the doctrine of the Nicolaitans, which thing I hate.

While the Ephesians hated the deeds of the Nicolaitans, the Church at Pergamos had those who believed in the doctrine of the Nicolaitans among their members. They probably partook of the burned offerings and engaged in sexual immorality.

Revelation 2:16 Repent; or else I will come unto thee quickly, and will fight against them with the sword of my mouth.

The sword of God's or Jesus' mouth was His word. God and Jesus (the Elohim) had spoken the universe into existence. They had breathed life into Adam. They spoke with the voice of many waters. They spoke with thunderings. God told them, "I brought you into this world, and I can take you out!"

Revelation 2:17 He that hath an ear, let him hear what the Spirit saith unto the Churches; To him that overcometh will I give to eat of the hidden manna, and will give him a white stone, and in the stone a new name written, which no man knoweth saving he that receiveth it.

Victorinus wrote, c. 280 A.D., "The hidden manna is immortality. The white gem is adoption as a son of God. The new name written on the stone is 'Christian.'" [20]

In Exodus 16, Manna was the bread from Heaven with which God fed the Israelites to prove whether they walked in His law. Moses also

---

[18] https://www.orthodox.net/menaion-april/11-the-hieromartyr-antipas-bishop-of-pergamum-in-asia.html

[19] Ibid.

[20] CHURCH FATHERS: Commentary on the Apocalypse (Victorinus) - New Advent, https://www.newadvent.org/fathers/0712.htm.

told Aaron to put an omer of manna in a pot and place it before the Testimony to keep it. Because of this, Victorinus noted that the hidden manna represented immortality. Jesus is the bread from Heaven; anyone who eats it will not die. [21]

In the Greek courts, a white pebble meant acquittal in a court of law. Jesus will undoubtedly acquit us of our sins; after all, He has already paid the price for our sins. The white stone was also used to give to honored guests, with the host's name inscribed on it.

In Pergamos, a white stone set at the city's entrance had the names of prominent people inscribed on it. Victorinus wrote that this stone represents the adoption to be the sons of God; the new name written on the stone is "Christian." The only ones who will know the name "Christian" and all that it means are those who received Christ.

In Revelation 3:12, *Christ says He will write upon us His new name.*

Revelation 3:12 Him that overcometh will I make a pillar in the temple of my God, and he shall go no more out: and I will write upon him the name of my God, and the name of the city of my God, which is new Jerusalem, which cometh down out of Heaven from my God: and I will write upon him my new name.

This agrees with 1 Peter 2:5 *Ye also, as lively stones, are built up a spiritual house, an holy priesthood, to offer up spiritual sacrifices, acceptable to God by Jesus Christ.*

Pergamos is the modern-day Berghama, Turkey.

THYATIRA

Revelation 2:18 And unto the Angel of the Church in Thyatira write; These things saith the Son of God, who hath his eyes like unto a flame of fire, and his feet are like fine brass;

Revelation 2:19 I know thy works, and charity, and service, and faith, and thy patience, and thy works; and the last to be more than the first.

Revelation 2:20 Notwithstanding I have a few things against thee, because thou sufferest that woman Jezebel, which calleth herself a prophetess, to teach and to seduce my servants to commit fornication, and to eat things sacrificed unto idols.

Revelation 2:21 And I gave her space to repent of her fornication; and she repented not.

---

[21] John 6:48-51

Revelation 2:22 Behold, I will cast her into a bed, and them that commit adultery with her into great tribulation, except they repent of their deeds.

Revelation 2:23 And I will kill her children with death; and all the Churches shall know that I am he which searcheth the reins and hearts: and I will give unto every one of you according to your works.

Revelation 2:24 But unto you I say, and unto the rest in Thyatira, as many as have not this doctrine, and which have not known the depths of Satan, as they speak; I will put upon you none other burden.

Revelation 2:25 But that which ye have already hold fast till I come.

Revelation 2:26 And he that overcometh, and keepeth my works unto the end, to him will I give power over the nations:

Revelation 2:27 And he shall rule them with a rod of iron; as the vessels of a potter shall they be broken to shivers: even as I received of my Father.

Revelation 2:28 And I will give him the morning star.

Revelation 2:29 He that hath an ear, let him hear what the Spirit saith unto the Churches.

Revelation 2:18 And unto the Angel of the Church in Thyatira write; These things saith the Son of God, who hath his eyes like unto a flame of fire, and his feet are like fine brass;

Thyatira was a city of trade guilds, and finding work without being a guild member was impossible. To be a guild member, one had to be a temple member. Their followers ate burnt offerings and engaged in sexual immorality. It was taught that no Christian could belong to one of the guilds. [22] Without belonging to a guild, one could not work. Without work, one could not feed their family.

Revelation 2:19 I know thy works, and charity, and service, and faith, and thy patience, and thy works; and the last to be more than the first.

The Church at Thyatira represented works of faith. John knew that one is not saved by their works, but they produce works because of their faith.

Their last works were better than the first. This is what we should all strive for. When others had *left their first love*, these were growing wiser and better. It should be the desire of all Christians that their last works may be their best works.

---

[22] https://www.biblestudytools.com/encyclopedias/isbe/thyatira.html, public domain

Revelation 2:20 Notwithstanding I have a few things against thee, because thou sufferest that woman Jezebel, which calleth herself a prophetess, to teach and to seduce my servants to commit fornication, and to eat things sacrificed unto idols.

One of the temples at Thyatira was dedicated to Sambethe, and at this shrine was a prophetess, by some supposed to represent the Jezebel of Revelation 2:20, who enticed the people to worship pagan gods, just as the Jezebel of the Old Testament had enticed others to worship Baal.

Tertullian wrote, c. 203 A.D., "If you doubt, unravel the meaning of what the Spirit says to the Churches. . .. He reproaches the Thyatirenes (sic) for fornication and for eating things sacrificed to idols." [23]

We first see Jezebel in 1 Kings: 16:31. Now, Ahab should have known that his wife did not worship God. Her father's name meant *with* Baal. [24] Ahab knew Baal was a false god, but his wife led him to worship him, and he became a wicked king.

Revelation 2:21 And I gave her space to repent of her fornication; and she repented not.

Christ offers repentance to all. In the Holy Scriptures, in the Books of Kings, is the story of Jezebel, who was married to King Ahab. Elijah, the prophet, was the sole prophet of God left after Jezebel killed all the other prophets of God. Elijah called four hundred fifty of Jezebel's prophets together and had them build an altar to their god, Baal. Elijah took two bullocks and slaughtered them for sacrifice. Baal's prophets called upon him all morning. When there was no answer to light the sacrifice's fire, they jumped onto the altar. At noon, Elijah started mocking them, "Cry aloud: for he is a god; either he is talking, or he is pursuing, or he is in a journey, or peradventure he sleepeth, and must be awaked." [25] They started crying louder and louder and cutting themselves until they bled profusely. When noonday was past, they kept prophesying until the time of the evening sacrifice. Then, Elijah called the people to the altar he had built to God. He told the prophets of Baal to pour water over the sacrifice and on the wood. Three barrels of water later, with the altar and the trench around it full of water, Elijah called on the name of God, and the fire of the LORD fell, consumed the sacrifice, the wood, the stones, the dust, and licked up the water that was in the trench.

---

[23] CHURCH FATHERS: Commentary on the Apocalypse (Victorinus) - New Advent, https://www.newadvent.org/fathers/0712.htm.

[24] https://www.abarim-publications.com/Meaning/Ethbaal.html

[25] 1 Kings 18:27

When the people saw what had happened, they fell on their faces to worship God. Elijah then told the people to take the prophets of Baal and kill them with a sword.

Jezebel heard about it from her husband, Ahab, and she told Elijah that he would be like the other prophets of God by the same time the next day. Now Elijah, who had just brought fire down from God and killed four hundred fifty prophets of Baal, ran from one little woman! But this was the time for Jezebel to repent. Elijah had proven Baal was a false god, and Jezebel did not repent. She was still in spiritual "fornication" with a false god. Later, Elijah prophesied that dogs would eat Jezebel and that practically nothing would be left of her. [26] She heard of the prophecy, put on her make-up, and walked over to the window, where she fell out onto the street by the gate, and the dogs did, indeed, eat her, leaving nothing but her skull and a foot.

Revelation 2:22 Behold, I will cast her into a bed, and them that commit adultery with her into great tribulation, except they repent of their deeds.

Revelation 2:23 And I will kill her children with death; and all the Churches shall know that I am he which searcheth the reins and hearts: and I will give unto every one of you according to your works.

Verses 22 and 23 show the punishment for non-repentance. The "children" are the people she teaches with her false religion. That is spiritual adultery. We are God's children, and if we follow another god (little "g"), it is adultery. God will judge each of us according to our deeds.

Galatians 2:16 Knowing that a man is not justified by the works of the law, but by the faith of Jesus Christ, even we have believed in Jesus Christ, that we might be justified by the faith of Christ, and not by the works of the law: for by the works of the law shall no flesh be justified.

And:

James 2:13 For he shall have judgment without mercy, that hath shewed no mercy; and mercy rejoiceth against judgment.

Revelation 2:24 But unto you I say, and unto the rest in Thyatira, as many as have not this doctrine, and which have not known the depths of Satan, as they speak; I will put upon you none other burden.

Verse 24 can be seen in:

Acts 15:28-29 For it seemed good to the Holy Ghost, and to us, to lay upon you no greater burden than these necessary things; That ye abstain from meats offered to idols, and from blood, and from things

---

[26] 2 Kings 9:10

strangled, and from fornication: from which if ye keep yourselves, ye shall do well. Fare ye well.

We must witness verbally and non-verbally to all—especially to the Jezebelites.

Several of the communities chastised in this Chapter of Revelation apparently were guilty of eating meat offered to idols. God did not like this practice. Even Paul, in his first recorded letter to the Corinthians, warned Jesus' followers:

1 Corinthians 8:4-13 As concerning therefore the eating of those things that are offered insacrifice unto idols, we know that an idol is nothing in the world, and that there is none other God but one. 5) For though there be that are called gods, whether in Heaven or in Earth, (as there be gods many, and lords many,) 6) But to us there is but one God, the Father, of whom are all things, and we in him; and one Lord Jesus Christ, by whom are all things, and we by him. 7) Howbeit there is not in every man that knowledge: for some with conscience of the idol unto this hour eat it as a thing offered unto an idol; and their conscience being weak is defiled. 8) But meat commendeth us not to God: for neither, if we eat, are we the better; neither, if we eat not, are we the worse. 9) But take heed lest by any means this liberty of yours become a stumblingblock to them that are weak. 10) For if any man see thee which hast knowledge sit at meat in the idol's temple, shall not the conscience of him which is weak be emboldened to eat those things which are offered to idols; 11) And through thy knowledge shall the weak brother perish, for whom Christ died? 12) But when ye sin so against the brethren, and wound their weak conscience, ye sin against Christ. 13) Wherefore, if meat make my brother to offend, I will eat no flesh while the world standeth, lest I make my brother to offend.

We need to stand fast in our faith and not compromise our beliefs.

Matthew 10:22 And ye shall be hated of all men for my name's sake: but he that endureth to the end shall be saved.

Revelation 2:25 But that which ye have already hold fast till I come.
We must hold onto our faith, no matter our tribulation.

Revelation 2:26 And he that overcometh, and keepeth my works unto the end, to him will I give power over the nations:

Hebrews 12:1 Wherefore seeing we also are compassed about with so great a cloud of witnesses, let us lay aside every weight, and the sin which doth so easily beset us, and let us run with patience the race that is set before us,

We see we are to run our race to the end of our mortal lives and to keep His works, not our works. Why are we to run this race and to keep going until the end?

Exodus 9:16 And in very deed for this cause have I raised thee up, for to shew in thee my power; and that my name may be declared throughout all the Earth.

We are to show forth God's power – not by ourselves. Without Him, we can do nothing. [27]

Revelation 2:27 And he shall rule them with a rod of iron; as the vessels of a potter shall they be broken to shivers: even as I received of my Father.

John recognized this as a fulfillment of:

Psalm 2:1 - 9 Why do the heathen rage, and the people imagine a vain thing? 2) The kings of the Earth set themselves, and the rulers take counsel together, against the LORD, and against his anointed, saying, 3) Let us break their bands asunder, and cast away their cords from us. 4) He that sitteth in the Heavens shall laugh: the Lord shall have them in derision. 5) Then shall he speak unto them in his wrath, and vex them in his sore displeasure. 6) Yet have I set my king upon my holy hill of Zion. 7) I will declare the decree: the LORD hath said unto me, Thou art my Son; this day have I begotten thee. 8) Ask of me, and I shall give thee the heathen for thine inheritance, and the uttermost parts of the Earth for thy possession. 9) Thou shalt break them with a rod of iron; thou shalt dash them in pieces like a potter's vessel.

But here we see that Christ has given us the power and the rule. All we must do is to keep His works until the end.

Revelation 2:28 And I will give him the morning star.

Who or what is this morning star? The one who overcomes will have Christ! Revelation 22:16 confirms this:

Revelation 22:16 I Jesus have sent mine Angel to testify unto you these things in the Churches. I am the root and the offspring of David, and the bright and morning star.

Victorinus wrote that the morning star represented the first resurrection. "The morning star drives away night and announces the light, that is, the beginning of day." [28] The night it was driving away was living under the law; the beginning of day was living under God's grace.

Revelation 2:29 He that hath an ear, let him hear what the Spirit saith unto the Churches.

---

[27] John 15:5
[28] CHURCH FATHERS: Commentary on the Apocalypse (Victorinus) - New Advent, https://www.newadvent.org/fathers/0712.htm.

23

Revelation 1:3 tells us that if we hear this prophecy and keep the things in it, we shall be blessed. And we are to listen to what He says—not only to this Church, but to ALL the Churches.

SARDIS

Revelation 3:1 And unto the Angel of the Church in Sardis write; These things saith he that hath the seven Spirits of God, and the seven stars; I know thy works, that thou hast a name that thou livest, and art dead.

Revelation 3:2 Be watchful, and strengthen the things which remain, that are ready to die: for I have not found thy works perfect before God.

Revelation 3:3 Remember therefore how thou hast received and heard, and hold fast, and repent. If therefore thou shalt not watch, I will come on thee as a thief, and thou shalt not know what hour I will come upon thee.

Revelation 3:4 Thou hast a few names even in Sardis which have not defiled their garments; and they shall walk with me in white: for they are worthy.

Revelation 3:5 He that overcometh, the same shall be clothed in white raiment; and I will not blot out his name out of the book of life, but I will confess his name before my Father, and before his Angels.

Revelation 3:6 He that hath an ear, let him hear what the Spirit saith unto the Churches.

Revelation 3:1 And unto the Angel of the Church in Sardis write; These things saith he that hath the seven Spirits of God, and the seven stars; I know thy works, that thou hast a name that thou livest, and art dead.

At Sardis, the Church appeared prosperous and busy, as shown by the bath gymnasium that remains standing today—but Christ knew their hearts and knew that they were not doing works to show their faith.

They were like the scribes and Pharisees that Jesus called "like unto whited sepulchers" but full of dead men's bones (Matthew 23:27).

Revelation 3:2 Be watchful, and strengthen the things which remain, that are ready to die: for I have not found thy works perfect before God.

There were some things they were doing right, but even those were "dying". Resting on grace alone dies when it becomes stagnant. Doing works for the love of the cross is salvation. But we are not saved by works of righteousness, but by God's mercy, according to:

24

Titus 3:5 Not by works of righteousness which we have done, but according to his mercy he saved us, by the washing of regeneration, and renewing of the Holy Ghost;
and
Ephesians 2:8-9 tells us, *"For by grace are ye saved through faith: and that not of yourselves: it is the gift of God: not of works, lest any man should boast."*

Revelation 3:3 Remember therefore how thou hast received and heard, and hold fast, and repent. If therefore thou shalt not watch, I will come on thee as a thief, and thou shalt not know what hour I will come upon thee.

The people at Ephesus, and most likely Sardis, had received the word from Christ's apostle. Therefore, they had heard it directly from God.

They needed to be watchful – In Revelation 3: 3, Christ warns them that He will come as a thief, and a thief never lets one know when he is coming.

Revelation 3:4 Thou hast a few names even in Sardis which have not defiled their garments; and they shall walk with me in white: for they are worthy.

"A few" still had the Spirit and were not dead. The white garments signified righteousness and salvation. Even in the modern Church, a few hold to the true doctrines of Christ.

Revelation 3:5 He that overcometh, the same shall be clothed in white raiment; and I will not blot out his name out of the book of life, but I will confess his name before my Father, and before his Angel.

We see this in:

Matthew 10:32 Whosoever therefore shall confess me before men, him will I confess also before my Father which is in Heaven.

If we confess Christ before men, he will confess us before His Father. But we must overcome temptation and change our sinful ways. Then, we must remain in our walk with Him. John would have known this from the Holy Scriptures:

Ezekiel 33:12 - 20 Therefore, thou son of man, say unto the children of thy people, The righteousness of the righteous shall not deliver him in the day of his transgression: as for the wickedness of the wicked, he shall not fall thereby in the day that he turneth from his wickedness; neither shall the righteous be able to live for his righteousness in the day that he sinneth. 13) When I shall say to the righteous, that he shall surely live; if he trust to his own righteousness, and commit iniquity, all his righteousnesses shall not be remembered; but for his iniquity that he hath committed, he shall die for it. 14) Again, when I say unto the wicked, Thou shalt surely die; if he turn from his sin, and do that which is lawful and right; 15) If the wicked restore the pledge, give again that he had robbed, walk in the statutes of life, without committing iniquity; he shall surely live, he shall not die. 16) None of his sins that he hath committed shall be mentioned unto him: he hath done that which is lawful and right; he shall surely live. 17) Yet the children of thy people say, The way of the Lord is not equal: but as for them, their way is not equal. 18) When the righteous turneth from his righteousness, and committeth iniquity, he shall even die thereby. 19) But if the wicked turn from his wickedness, and do that which is lawful and right, he shall live thereby. 20) Yet ye say, The way of the Lord is not equal. O ye house of Israel, I will judge you every one after his ways.

Revelation 3:6 He that hath an ear, let him hear what the Spirit saith unto the Churches.

Again, we need to have that spiritual ear, hear and obey Christ's words, sacrifice what we consider pleasure, repent, and hear Him.

This Church was to be laid in ruins, as it remains.

PHILADELPHIA

Revelation 3:7 And to the Angel of the Church in Philadelphia write; These things saith he that is holy, he that is true, he that hath the key of David, he that openeth, and no man shutteth; and shutteth, and no man openeth;

Revelation 3:8 I know thy works: behold, I have set before thee an open door, and no man can shut it: for thou hast a little strength, and hast kept my word, and hast not denied my name.

Revelation 3:9 Behold, I will make them of the synagogue of Satan, which say they are Jews, and are not, but do lie; behold, I will make them to come and worship before thy feet, and to know that I have loved thee.

Revelation 3:10 Because thou hast kept the word of my patience, I also will keep thee from the hour of temptation, which shall come upon all the world, to try them that dwell upon the Earth.

Revelation 3:11 Behold, I come quickly: hold that fast which thou hast, that no man take thy crown.

Revelation 3:12 Him that overcometh will I make a pillar in the temple of my God, and he shall go no more out: and I will write upon him the name of my God, and the name of the city of my God, which is new Jerusalem, which cometh down out of Heaven from my God: and I will write upon him my new name.

Revelation 3:13 He that hath an ear, let him hear what the Spirit saith unto the Churches.

Revelation 3:7 And to the Angel of the Church in Philadelphia write; These things saith he that is holy, he that is true, he that hath the key of David, he that openeth, and no man shutteth; and shutteth, and no man openeth;

Victorinus wrote, "This Church was of the best. The habits of the Saints are set forth; of those who are lowly in the world, and unskilled in the Scriptures, and who hold the faith immovably, and are not at all broken down by any chance, or withdrawn from the faith by any fear." [29]

Throughout history, God has shut and opened things. No one else could do what He could do or undo what He had done. He opened Sarah's womb to have Isaac. He shut up Hannah's womb and later opened it.

Revelation 3:8 I know thy works: behold, I have set before thee an open door, and no man can shut it: for thou hast a little strength, and hast kept my word, and hast not denied my name.

This open door was Christ. He had opened the door for the Gospel to be preached and would not let anyone else shut it. Most theologians agree that Philadelphia was a border town and reached many areas because other people traveled through there. They were probably small in number but kept true to God's word, loved their neighbors, and spread the Gospel. This is the remnant of those who genuinely love Christ. Better yet:

Colossians 4:3 Withal praying also for us, that God would open unto us a door of utterance, to speak the mystery of Christ, for which I am also in bonds:

This Church knew the truth about the cross of Christ—who He was—and that is why it was the missionary Church.

Acts 14:27 And when they were come, and had gathered the Church together, they rehearsed all that God had done with them, and how he had opened the door of faith unto the Gentiles.

John might have known the original passage came from Isaiah:

---

[29] CHURCH FATHERS: Commentary on the Apocalypse (Victorinus) - New Advent, https://www.newadvent.org/fathers/0712.htm.

Isaiah 22:22 And the key of the house of David will I lay upon his shoulder; so he shall open, and none shall shut; and he shall shut, and none shall open.

Revelation 3:9 Behold, I will make them of the synagogue of Satan, which say they are Jews, and are not, but do lie; behold, I will make them to come and worship before thy feet, and to know that I have loved thee.

The synagogue of Satan was the Jewish people, who said they loved God but, in fact, rejected Him because they rejected His Son. Christ said He would make them come and worship before THY feet—the Christians' feet. This may mean either the completed Jews or those who recognize Him at His second coming as the Messiah.

Revelation 3:10 Because thou hast kept the word of my patience, I also will keep thee from the hour of temptation, which shall come upon all the world, to try them that dwell upon the Earth.

When we see the word *world*, we must be careful. There are several different Greek words that are translated into world, but which can have different meanings. When we see the word *Earth*, this is one of the meanings of a word that can be translated into either *world* or Earth and means the whole globe. The word world here, in Revelation 3:10, is the word *oikoumene* (*oy-kou-men'-ay*) and means specifically the area of land which was the Roman Empire. [30] John knew this. The hour of temptation was to come on only those lands which the Romans controlled in John's time; but it would try the inhabitants over the whole globe (*Earth – ge [ghay]*). [31] The time of temptation for the Middle East affects the whole Earth. We must remember that Jerusalem is still God's city. All the times He became angry with His people, sent them into exile and brought them home, He still loved them. The New Jerusalem is His bride. Nations are either friends with Israel or enemies of Israel. The time of tribulation may break some of the bonds of friendship. We must be incredibly careful about our relationship with God's people as a nation. We, as Christians, are grafted into that olive tree—being the Jewish nation, as Paul discussed in Romans 11:16-32:

For if the firstfruit be holy, the lump is also holy: and if the root be holy, so are the branches. 17) And if some of the branches be broken off, and thou, being a wild olive tree, wert graffed in among them, and with them partakest of the root and fatness of the olive tree; 18) Boast not against the branches. But if thou boast, thou bearest not the root, but

---

[30] Strong's Hebrew and Greek Dictionaries, Published 1890, public domain
[31] Ibid.

the root thee. 19) Thou wilt say then, The branches were broken off, that I might be graffed in. 20) Well; because of unbelief they were broken off, and thou standest by faith. Be not highminded, but fear: 21) For if God spared not the natural branches, take heed lest he also spare not thee. 22) Behold therefore the goodness and severity of God: on them which fell, severity; but toward thee, goodness, if thou continue in his goodness: otherwise thou also shalt be cut off. 23) And they also, if they abide not still in unbelief, shall be graffed in: for God is able to graff them in again. 24) For if thou wert cut out of the olive tree which is wild by nature, and wert graffed contrary to nature into a good olive tree: how much more shall these, which be the natural branches, be graffed into their own olive tree? 25) For I would not, brethren, that ye should be ignorant of this mystery, lest ye should be wise in your own conceits; that blindness in part is happened to Israel, until the fulness of the Gentiles be come in. 26) And so all Israel shall be saved: as it is written, There shall come out of Sion the Deliverer, and shall turn away ungodliness from Jacob: 27) For this is my covenant unto them, when I shall take away their sins. 28) As concerning the gospel, they are enemies for your sakes: but as touching the election, they are beloved for the fathers' sakes. 29) For the gifts and calling of God are without repentance. 30) For as ye in times past have not believed God, yet have now obtained mercy through their unbelief: 31) Even so have these also now not believed, that through your mercy they also may obtain mercy. 32) For God hath concluded them all in unbelief, that he might have mercy upon all.

While we will all experience tribulation while living on Earth, the hour of temptation is the outpouring of God's wrath upon the unbelievers. He will keep us from that.

To rephrase Revelation 3:10, using another translation from Greek, the verse would read, "In that you have maintained the motive of my waiting, I also will guard you from loss from the time of experience of evil, which is expected to come over the whole land (specifically, the Roman Empire), to discipline those that dwell on the Earth."

But we are to be of good cheer – Christ has overcome the world.

Other verses which show we will be going through the tribulation are:

Deuteronomy 4:30 When thou art in tribulation, and all these things are come upon thee, even in the latter days, if thou turn to the LORD thy God, and shalt be obedient unto his voice;

Deuteronomy 4:31 (For the LORD thy God is a merciful God;) he will not forsake thee, neither destroy thee, nor forget the covenant of thy fathers which he sware unto them.

John 16:33 These things I have spoken unto you, that in me ye might have peace. In the world ye shall have tribulation: but be of good cheer; I have overcome the world.

Acts 14:22 Confirming the souls of the disciples, and exhorting them to continue in the faith, and that we must through much tribulation enter into the kingdom of God.

Romans 2:9 Tribulation and anguish, upon every soul of man that doeth evil, of the Jew first, and also of the Gentile;

Revelation 1:9 I John, who also am your brother, and companion in tribulation, and in the kingdom and patience of Jesus Christ, was in the isle that is called Patmos, for the word of God, and for the testimony of Jesus Christ.

Revelation 2:10 Fear none of those things which thou shalt suffer: behold, the devil shall cast some of you into prison, that ye may be tried; and ye shall have tribulation ten days: be thou faithful unto death, and I will give thee a crown of life.

And do you agree that God is the same yesterday, today, and forever? If so, I offer the following:

Noah – saved from wrath – the destruction of the world.

Rahab – saved from wrath – the destruction of Jericho. (OK, I will admit she may have been different. She may have been one of those living in sin and initially causing problems in the community, but she found God through His prophets and was saved – which is a picture of people being saved just before the destruction of the world.); and, finally,

Lot and his family – saved from wrath – the destruction of Sodom and Gomorrah.

All those people had to go through the tribulation of living with sinful people. Lot lived with people who wanted him to send his company outside to them so they could have their sexual pleasures with them. He was a righteous man and was saved from destruction, the wrath of God, not the tribulation.

God – the same yesterday, today, and forever.

Revelation 3:10 Because thou hast kept the word of my patience, I also will keep thee from the hour of temptation, which shall come upon all the world, to try them that dwell upon the Earth.

In verse ten, the Greek word used here and translated as "temptation" is *peirasmos* (pi-ras-mos'). The word temptation was only used once in the Old Testament, and that in:

Psalm 95:8 Harden not your heart, as in the provocation, and as in the day of temptation in the wilderness.

This passage describes the children wandering in the desert for 40 years, while they were on that 11-day trip from Egypt to the Promised Land. They were being tested and tried and found not to be worthy to enter the promised land.

In the New Testament, this same word temptation is found in twenty different verses, starting with the Model Prayer, Matthew 6:13a, "And lead us not into temptation, but deliver us from evil:"

Matthew 26:41 tells us to watch and pray that we do not enter into temptation, for the spirit is willing, but the flesh is weak. This is the same temptation that Jesus endured and conquered when Satan tempted Him after His forty-day fast.

Luke 8:13, in the parable of the Sower, tells us that the seed that falls onto rock are we who rejoice when we hear and receive the word but have no root, so we believe for a time, and during the time of temptation, fall away.

In Luke 22, Jesus tells the apostles that they stayed with Him during His time of temptation so they would sit on thrones to judge the twelve tribes of Israel.

In that same chapter, Jesus admonishes them to pray that they do not enter into temptation. When He caught them sleeping, He again told them to pray, or they would enter into temptation—the testing and trial.

Paul tells us in 1 Corinthians10:13, *"There hath no temptation taken you but such as is common to man: but God is faithful, who will not suffer you to be tempted above that ye are able; but will with the temptation also make a way to escape, that ye may be able to bear it."*

This verse fits perfectly with Revelation 3:10, which says Christ will keep us from the hour of temptation and provide us with a way to escape so that we might bear it.

James tells us to count it all joy when we fall into temptation, knowing that the trying of our faith works patience. We are to let patience have her perfect work so we will be perfect and want nothing.

James says ten verses later, *"Blessed is the man that endureth temptation: for when he is tried, he shall receive the crowns of life, which the Lord hath promised to them that love Him."*

1 Peter 4:12 Beloved, think it not strange concerning the fiery trial which is to try you, as though some strange thing happened unto you:

1 Peter 4:13 But rejoice, inasmuch as ye are partakers of Christ's sufferings; that, when his glory shall be revealed, ye may be glad also with exceeding joy.

2 Peter 2:9 tells us that the Lord knows how to deliver the godly out of temptation and to reserve the unjust unto the day of judgment to be punished.

Finally:

1 Corinthians15:52 In a moment, in the twinkling of an eye, at the last trump: for the trumpet shall sound, and the dead shall be raised incorruptible, and we shall be changed.

This was a confirmation of:

Isaiah 26:19 Thy dead men shall live, together with my dead body shall they arise. Awake and sing, ye that dwell in dust: for thy dew is as the dew of herbs, and the Earth shall cast out the dead.

But there's good news:

2 Corinthians 1:7 And our hope of you is stedfast, knowing, that as ye are partakers of the sufferings, so shall ye be also of the consolation.

2Tim. 2:12 If we suffer, we shall also reign with him: if we deny him, he also will deny us:

And, finally, Luke quotes Jesus:

Luke 18:8 I tell you that he will avenge them speedily. Nevertheless when the Son of man cometh, shall he find faith on the Earth?

This question presumes a negative answer, meaning no faith will be left on Earth when Christ returns.

Revelation 3:11 Behold, I come quickly: hold that fast which thou hast, that no man take thy crown.

Christ promises to come quickly for His people. While we are here, we are to hold fast to our faith, which includes testing the teachers. Prove their teachings against the rest of the Scriptures.

Revelation 3:12 Him that overcometh will I make a pillar in the temple of my God, and he shall go no more out: and I will write upon him the name of my God, and the name of the city of my God, which is new Jerusalem, which cometh down out of Heaven from my God: and I will write upon him my new name.

John knew a reference to Isaiah:

Isaiah 62:2 And the Gentiles shall see thy righteousness, and all kings thy glory: and thou shalt be called by a new name, which the mouth of the LORD shall name.

Pillars were used in Christ's time on Earth to inscribe the names of prominent people. We will not go out of Heaven, and He will write three names on us: The name of His God, New Jerusalem, and His new name.

In Revelation 2:17, we saw where Christ was giving a white stone with a new name written on it.

Revelation 3:13 He that hath an ear, let him hear what the Spirit saith unto the Churches.

Once again, we are admonished to use our spiritual ears and obey what Christ says. To have these spiritual ears, we must pray. 1 Thess. 5:17 tells us to pray without ceasing.

LAODICEA

Revelation 3:14 And unto the Angel of the Church of the Laodiceans write; These things saith the Amen, the faithful and true witness, the beginning of the creation of God;

Revelation 3:15 I know thy works, that thou art neither cold nor hot: I would thou wert cold or hot.

Revelation 3:16 So then because thou art lukewarm, and neither cold nor hot, I will spue thee out of my mouth.

Revelation 3:17 Because thou sayest, I am rich, and increased with goods, and have need of nothing; and knowest not that thou art wretched, and miserable, and poor, and blind, and naked:

Revelation 3:18 I counsel thee to buy of me gold tried in the fire, that thou mayest be rich; and white raiment, that thou mayest be clothed, and that the shame of thy nakedness do not appear; and anoint thine eyes with eyesalve, that thou mayest see.

Revelation 3:19 As many as I love, I rebuke and chasten: be zealous therefore, and repent.

Revelation 3:20 Behold, I stand at the door, and knock: if any man hear my voice, and open the door, I will come in to him, and will sup with him, and he with me.

Revelation 3:21 To him that overcometh will I grant to sit with me in my throne, even as I also overcame, and am set down with my Father in his throne.

Revelation 3:22 He that hath an ear, let him hear what the Spirit saith unto the Churches.

Revelation 3:14 And unto the Angel of the Church of the Laodiceans write; These things saith the Amen, the faithful and true witness, the beginning of the creation of God;

Amen means "So be it." Here, we see Jesus as the "So be it." He is part of the Trinity, God incarnate, and He is there when God speaks the universe into existence.

Jesus is the faithful and true witness. He was the witness on Earth as to who God the Father was, is, and will be. He was the faithful and true witness because He and the Father were one, are one, and will be one.

Jesus was at the beginning of God's creation (Genesis 1:1) and was there (John 1:1-4) when God the Father said, "Let there be light." Jesus was, is, and will be the "So be it."

Revelation 3:15 I know thy works, that thou art neither cold nor hot: I would thou wert cold or hot.

Victorinus wrote, c. 280 A.D., "By saying 'they are neither cold nor hot,' He means they are neither unbelieving nor believing. Rather, they try to be all things to all men." [32]

Laodicea also had a warm spring where they got their water. Then, they built an aqueduct from Colossae to bring them fresh, cool water. This was supposed to be a "transferred blessing". But by the time the water got there in the summer, it, too, was warm.

Revelation 3:16 So then because thou art lukewarm, and neither cold nor hot, I will spue thee out of my mouth.

This Church was not – and is not – on fire for God! This is the only Church for which Christ had no commendation – everything was wrong! They were so lacking in spiritual works that God wanted to "spew" them out of His mouth. This Greek word, emeo, means to vomit forcefully. [33]

Revelation 3:17 Because thou sayest, I am rich, and increased with goods, and have need of nothing; and knowest not that thou art wretched, and miserable, and poor, and blind, and naked:

John would have recognized this from Jeremiah:

Jeremiah 5:3 O LORD, are not thine eyes upon the truth? thou hast stricken them, but they have not grieved; thou hast consumed them, but they have refused to receive correction: they have made their faces harder than a rock; they have refused to return.

Jeremiah 5:4 Therefore I said, Surely these are poor; they are foolish: for they know not the way of the LORD, nor the judgment of their God.

Revelation 3:18 I counsel thee to buy of me gold tried in the fire, that thou mayest be rich; and white raiment, that thou mayest be clothed, and that the shame of thy nakedness do not appear; and anoint thine eyes with eyesalve, that thou mayest see.

---

[32] CHURCH FATHERS: Commentary on the Apocalypse (Victorinus) - New Advent, https://www.newadvent.org/fathers/0712.htm.

[33] Strong's Hebrew and Greek Dictionaries, Published 1890, public domain

You may have heard that Gold tried in the fire is where it is heated and has the impurities scraped off and then you can see your reflection in what is left. However, after researching refining gold, you do NOT want to place your face over the gold—dangerous fumes come off it in the refining process. [34] However, if the amount of gold is large enough, once it is fully refined and all the chemicals have been neutralized, then you can see your image in the gold. God wants us to be refined so He can see His image in us.

Laodicea was a very wealthy area. They had produced black wool and, therefore, were in the clothing industry. But here, God was telling them they were naked—their sins were exposed for God to see. They needed to repent and have their sins covered by the blood of Jesus— the blood that washes white as snow.

White is the color of purity and righteousness. The nakedness we are to cover is our guilt of sin. Victorinus stated, ". . . this Church declared they are rich men placed in positions of dignity, believing they were rich, among whom the Scriptures are discussed in their bedchamber while the faithful are outside." He went on to say. "this discussion was understood by no one, even though these prominent men said they knew all things and that they alone were endowed with the confidence of learning, but they ceased from God's labor." [35]

The Laodiceans had also produced an eye salve. The city had bankers and other businessmen living there, and there was also a medical center. But all these things did not make the Church at Laodicea rich spiritually. The eye salve did not allow them to see the spiritual things of God. They needed the eye salve Jesus was offering.

Revelation 3:19 As many as I love, I rebuke and chasten: be zealous therefore, and repent.

Despite all that was wrong with Laodicea, and although Christ had no commendation for her, he still loved her. The modern, self-righteous Church should repent. The modern Church talks down to "brothers" and "sisters" in Christ, proclaiming to be "more than conquerors" <u>NOW</u> rather than in the life to come.

John 3:16 For God so loved the world, that he gave his only begotten Son, that whosoever believeth in him should not perish, but have everlasting life.

He tries to correct us because He wants us to repent so we can spend eternity with Him. Some modern movements use this verse to

---

[34] https://www.wikihow.com/Refine-Gold
[35] CHURCH FATHERS: Commentary on the Apocalypse (Victorinus) - New Advent, https://www.newadvent.org/fathers/0712.htm.

show that God loves everyone—which He does—and this means that everyone is going to Heaven. He will accept you just the way you are. You do not need to do anything.

It is amazing how Satan will use God's word and twist it! There's just enough truth in that to make people believe this false doctrine.

Revelation 3:20 Behold, I stand at the door, and knock: if any man hear my voice, and open the door, I will come in to him, and will sup with him, and he with me.

Christ stands at the door. He will not barge in where He is not wanted. If we will but open the door, accept Christ as our Savior, and obey His will, He will come in and give us the hidden manna (bread of life) and the living water.

Revelation 3:21 To him that overcometh will I grant to sit with me in my throne, even as I also overcame, and am set down with my Father in his throne.

Christ overcame Satan's temptations. Every time Satan tried to twist God's word, Jesus quoted scripture. He also overcame sin in the world by dying on the cross and then rising to sit at the right hand of God, His Father.

It **is** strange that Jesus says He will grant us to sit in His throne since He said otherwise:

Matthew 20:23 And he saith unto them, Ye shall drink indeed of my cup, and be baptized with the baptism that I am baptized with: but to sit on my right hand, and on my left, is not mine to give, but it shall be given to them for whom it is prepared of my Father.

Matthew 19:28 And Jesus said unto them, Verily I say unto you, That ye which have followed me, in the regeneration when the Son of man shall sit in the throne of his glory, ye also shall sit upon twelve thrones, judging the twelve tribes of Israel.

So, here are what appears to be conflicting statements from Jesus:

1. Revelation 3:21, where He says to him who overcomes, He will grant to sit with Him in His throne;

2. To sit on His right or His left hand is given only by the Father; and,

3. Those who followed Him in the regeneration when He will sit in the throne of His glory, shall also sit upon twelve thrones, judging the twelve tribes of Israel.

But is it conflicting?

We will sit in His throne with Him because we are the body of Christ:

Romans 12:5 So we, being many, are one body in Christ, and every one members one of another.

1 Corinthians 12:27 Now ye are the body of Christ, and members in particular.

Ephesians 5:30 For we are members of his body, of his flesh, and of his bones.

Colossians 1:18 And he is the head of the body, the Church: who is the beginning, the firstborn from the dead; that in all things he might have the preeminence.

That covers number one. For number two, where to sit is the Father's to give,

*Psalm 110:1 **A Psalm of David**. The LORD said unto my Lord, Sit thou at my right hand, until I make thine enemies thy footstool.*

Here, David was speaking of The Lord, meaning the Father, saying unto David's Lord, meaning the Messiah, "Sit thou at my right hand until make thine enemies thy footstool." This verse was quoted several times in the New Testament. Of course, the Old Testament, or what they called the Holy Scriptures, was the only scripture they had. They (the disciples) were in the process of writing the New Testament, whether they knew it or not.

Also, Jesus reigns until He delivers the kingdom to God. Jesus must reign until God has put all enemies under Jesus' feet.

1 Corinthians 15:24-28 Then cometh the end, when he shall have delivered up the kingdom to God, even the Father; when he shall have put down all rule and all authority and power. For he must reign, till he hath put all enemies under his feet. The last enemy that shall be destroyed is death. For he hath put all things under his feet. But when he saith all things are put under him, it is manifest that he is excepted, which did put all things under him. And when all things shall be subdued unto him, then shall the Son also himself be subject unto him that put all things under him, that God may be all in all.

For number three, the apostles sit on twelve thrones. The only places we see them sitting upon thrones are in Matthew 19:28 and again in Luke 22:30. Both scriptures discuss the same incident where Jesus was talking to His disciples.

Matthew 19:28 And Jesus said unto them, Verily I say unto you, That ye which have followed me, in the regeneration when the Son of man shall sit in the throne of his glory, ye also shall sit upon twelve thrones, judging the twelve tribes of Israel.

Luke 22:30 That ye may eat and drink at my table in my kingdom, and sit on thrones judging the twelve tribes of Israel.

The next place is in Revelation, where we see not only the twelve disciples but also the twelve patriarchs sitting on twenty-four seats.

Revelation 4:4 And round about the throne were four and twenty seats: and upon the seats I saw four and twenty elders sitting, clothed in white raiment; and they had on their heads crowns of gold.

These seats are located around the throne where God sits. However, the word translated as "seats" is the Greek word thron'-os, which, of course, is "throne." [36] The twelve disciples are among those seated here. The others, we assume, are the twelve patriarchs. God has ordained that these twenty-four sit around about the throne.

Revelation 3:22 He that hath an ear, let him hear what the Spirit saith unto the Churches.

Once again, we are to have spiritual ears and really hear—and heed—what the Spirit says to us. Those who want to hear God's voice should read God's word (the Bible) and pray, pray, and pray.

We have the same "transferred blessing" concept today as they did at Laodicea. The River movement claims they can transfer a blessing. There are also those who always want to take a "wait and see" attitude—to see which way the religious and political winds are blowing. When I first started studying Revelation and God revealed His word, I was told I could not repeat some of that information—I would offend people and some entire groups of people. I was told I needed to be "politically correct." My response was that this information needed to be told—God's word convicts. Political correctness is lukewarm, and it has also proven to be leading to the death of this country. But God will spew these lukewarm individuals and groups out of His mouth!

There are some things John did not know about these verses, and that is how theologians would interpret them later. They would try to bring these Churches through several "Church ages" up to the present. You can see where they had ground on which to stand, but these types of Churches are present in every "Church age."

---

[36] Strong's Hebrew and Greek Dictionaries, Published 1890, public domain

The Throne Room

Revelation Chapter 4

Chapter 4 is known as "The Throne Room Chapter." John would have recognized these images from the Holy Scriptures he had studied.

Revelation 4:1 After this I looked, and, behold, a door was opened in Heaven: and the first voice which I heard was as it were of a trumpet talking with me; which said, Come up hither, and I will shew thee things which must be hereafter.

Victorinus wrote: "The New Testament is announced as an open door in Heaven. Since the door is shown to be opened, it is obvious that previously it had been closed to men. And it was laid fully open when Christ ascended with His body to the Father into Heaven. A door must be opened in Heaven before anyone can go in." [37]

John would simply have recognized this as his invitation to join Christ, in the spirit, in Heaven.

Some theologians believe that this is the rapture, but John would not have recognized it as such:

1 Corinthians 15:52 In a moment, in the twinkling of an eye, at the last trump: for the trumpet shall sound, and the dead shall be raised incorruptible, and we shall be changed.

There have been no trumpets at this point – only God's voice as a trumpet – and there are seven trumpets to come, so how can this be the rapture since it is to take place at the last trump?

As for the open door:

Colossians 4:3 Withal praying also for us, that God would open unto us a door of utterance, to speak the mystery of Christ, for which I am also in bonds:

John also knew the Heavens were opened for Ezekiel to see God:

Ezekiel 1:1 Now it came to pass in the thirtieth year, in the fourth month, in the fifth day of the month, as I was among the captives by the river of Chebar, that the Heavens were opened, and I saw visions of God.

---

[37] CHURCH FATHERS: Commentary on the Apocalypse (Victorinus) - New Advent, https://www.newadvent.org/fathers/0712.htm.

Revelation 4:2 And immediately I was in the spirit: and, behold, a throne was set in Heaven, and one sat on the throne.

John knew he was "in the spirit" and not in the flesh. This would have been an "out-of-body experience."

Revelation 4:3 And he that sat was to look upon like a jasper and a sardine stone: and there was a rainbow round about the throne, in sight like unto an emerald.

Compare this with verses from Ezekiel, which John would have recognized:

Ezekiel 1:26 And above the firmament that was over their heads was the likeness of a throne, as the appearance of a sapphire stone: and upon the likeness of the throne was the likeness as the appearance of a man above upon it.

Ezekiel 10:1 Then I looked, and, behold, in the firmament that was above the head of the cherubims there appeared over them as it were a sapphire stone, as the appearance of the likeness of a throne.

Revelation 4:4 And round about the throne were four and twenty seats: and upon the seats I saw four and twenty elders sitting, clothed in white raiment; and they had on their heads crowns of gold.

Clement of Alexandria wrote, c. 195 A.D., "And although here upon Earth a spiritual man is not honored with the chief seat, he will sit down on the twenty-four thrones, judging the people, as John says in the Apocalypse." [38]

Much speculation has been made as to who the twenty-four elders are. Some say they are the twelve patriarchs and the twelve disciples, minus Judas Iscariot, and then add Paul. Others believe this is the original twelve apostles, and this is borne out by:

Matthew 19:28 And Jesus said unto them, Verily I say unto you, That ye which have followed me, in the regeneration when the Son of man shall sit in the throne of his glory, ye also shall sit upon twelve thrones, judging the twelve tribes of Israel.

Revelation 4:5 And out of the throne proceeded lightnings and thunderings and voices: and there were seven lamps of fire burning before the throne, which are the seven Spirits of God.

John knew the thunderings were judgments of God, from:

1 Samuel 2:10 The adversaries of the LORD shall be broken to pieces; out of Heaven shall he thunder upon them: the LORD shall judge

---

[38] Ante-Nicene Fathers, Vol. 2, Page 504, as translated by David W. Bercot, Editor

the ends of the Earth; and he shall give strength unto his king, and exalt the horn of his anointed.

Revelation 4:6 And before the throne there was a sea of glass like unto crystal: and in the midst of the throne, and round about the throne, were four beasts full of eyes before and behind.

Victorinus wrote, c. 280 A.D., "'A sea of glass like crystal.' This represents the gift of baptism that He sheds forth through his Son at the time of repentance." [39] John would have recognized other representations for this image, however. The actual image would have been "the sea" from the building of Solomon's temple:

1 Kings 7:23-39 And he made a molten sea, ten cubits from the one brim to the other: it was round all about, and his height was five cubits: and a line of thirty cubits did compass it round about. 24) And under the brim of it round about there were knops compassing it, ten in a cubit, compassing the sea round about: the knops were cast in two rows, when it was cast. 25) It stood upon twelve oxen, three looking toward the north, and three looking toward the west, and three looking toward the south, and three looking toward the east: and the sea was set above upon them, and all their hinder parts were inward. 26) And it was an hand breadth thick, and the brim thereof was wrought like the brim of a cup, with flowers of lilies: it contained two thousand baths. 27) And he made ten bases of brass; four cubits was the length of one base, and four cubits the breadth thereof, and three cubits the height of it. 28) And the work of the bases was on this manner: they had borders, and the borders were between the ledges: 29) And on the borders that were between the ledges were lions, oxen, and cherubims: and upon the ledges there was a base above: and beneath the lions and oxen were certain additions made of thin work. 30) And every base had four brasen wheels, and plates of brass: and the four corners thereof had undersetters: under the laver were undersetters molten, at the side of every addition. 31) And the mouth of it within the chapiter and above was a cubit: but the mouth thereof was round after the work of the base, a cubit and an half: and also upon the mouth of it were gravings with their borders, foursquare, not round. 32) And under the borders were four wheels; and the axletrees of the wheels were joined to the base: and the height of a wheel was a cubit and half a cubit. 33) And the work of the wheels was like the work of a chariot wheel: their axletrees, and their naves, and their felloes, and their spokes, were all molten. 34) And there were four undersetters to the four corners

---

[39] CHURCH FATHERS: Commentary on the Apocalypse (Victorinus) - New Advent, https://www.newadvent.org/fathers/0712.htm.

of one base: and the undersetters were of the very base itself. 35) And in the top of the base was there a round compass of half a cubit high: and on the top of the base the ledges thereof and the borders thereof were of the same. 36) For on the plates of the ledges thereof, and on the borders thereof, he graved cherubims, lions, and palm trees, according to the proportion of every one, and additions round about. 37) After this manner he made the ten bases: all of them had one casting, one measure, and one size. 38) Then made he ten lavers of brass: one laver contained forty baths: and every laver was four cubits: and upon every one of the ten bases one laver. 39) And he put five bases on the right side of the house, and five on the left side of the house: and he set the sea on the right side of the house eastward over against the south.

John also would have recognized a "sea" as a nation, particularly a gentile nation.

Isaiah 60:5 Then thou shalt see, and flow together, and thine heart shall fear, and be enlarged; because the abundance of the sea shall be converted unto thee, the forces of the Gentiles shall come unto thee.

While verse six mentions four beasts, verse seven describes them.

Revelation 4:7 And the first beast was like a lion, and the second beast like a calf, and the third beast had a face as a man, and the fourth beast was like a flying eagle.

Victorinus wrote, c. 280 A.D., "The four living creatures are the four Gospels. . . .. The lion designates Mark, in whom is heard the voice of the lion roaring in the desert. And in the figure of a man, Matthew strives to declare to us the genealogy of Mary, from whom Christ took flesh. . . .. Therefore, his announcement sets forth the image of a man. Luke, in narrating the priesthood of Zachariah as he offers a sacrifice for the people, . . . bore the likeness of a calf. John the evAngelist is like an eagle speeding on uplifted wings to greater heights. For he writes about the Word of God. As an evAngelist, Mark thus begins: 'The beginning of the Gospel of Jesus Christ, as it is written in Isaiah the prophet.' 'The voice of one crying in the wilderness.' This has the figure of a lion. And Matthew, 'The book of the generation of Jesus Christ, the son of David, the son of Abraham.' This is the form of a man. But Luke begins, 'There was a priest by the name of Zechariah. . . .. This is the likeness of a calf. But John begins, 'In the beginning was the Word, and the Word was with God, and the Word was God.' Here he resembles the likeness of a flying eagle." [40]

---

[40] CHURCH FATHERS: Commentary on the Apocalypse (Victorinus) - New Advent, https://www.newadvent.org/fathers/0712.htm.

Contrast this with Irenaeus' writing, "The cherubim, too, had four faces, and their faces were representations of the dispensation of the Son of God. For it says, 'The first living creature was like a lion.' This symbolizes Christ's effectual working. His leadership, and his royal power. The second one was like a calf, signifying His sacrificial and priestly order. 'The third had, as it were, the face of a man.' This is a clear depiction of His coming as a human being. 'The fourth was like a flying eagle.' This points out the gift of the Spirit, who hovers with His wings over the Church. Therefore, the Gospels are in accord with these things, among which Christ Jesus is seated. For [the Gospel] according to John describes his original, effectual, and glorious generation from the Father, declaring, 'In the beginning was Word, and the Word was with God, and the Word was God.' . . . However, [the Gospel] according to Luke takes up His priestly character, beginning with Zachariah the priest offering sacrifice to God. . .. Now, Matthew describes His birth as a man, saying, 'The book of the generation of Jesus Christ, the son of David, the son of Abraham.' . . . This, then, is the Gospel of his humanity, . . . On the other hand, Mark begins with the prophetical Spirit coming down from on high to men, saying, 'The beginning of the Gospel of Jesus Christ, as it is written in Isaiah the prophet.' This points to the winged aspect of the Gospel. [41]

The difference between the two commentators is two hundred years. I believe Irenaeus had it closer to what John would have thought.

John, having learned humility, would not have attributed these images to Matthew, Mark, Luke, or himself. This book is about the revelation of Jesus Christ, not the apostles. Therefore, it must be a picture of Christ.

1. He was the Lion of Judah.

Hosea 5:14 For I will be unto Ephraim as a lion, and as a young lion to the house of Judah: I, even I, will tear and go away; I will take away, and none shall rescue him.

2. He was the sacrifice (calf).

Romans 3:25 Whom God hath set forth to be a propitiation through faith in his blood, to declare his righteousness for the remission of sins that are past, through the forbearance of God;

Hebrews 13:11-12 For the bodies of those beasts, whose blood is brought into the sanctuary by the high priest for sin, are burned without the camp. 12) Wherefore Jesus also, that he might sanctify the people with his own blood, suffered without the gate.

3. He came as a man.

---

[41] Ante-Nicene Fathers, Vol. 1, Pages 428, 429, as translated by David W. Bercot, Editor

Matthew 2:1 Now when Jesus was born in Bethlehem of Judaea in the days of Herod the king, behold, there came wise men from the East to Jerusalem,

Matthew 2:2 Saying, Where is he that is born King of the Jews? for we have seen his star in the east, and are come to worship him.

4. He is sovereign (eagle).

Jeremiah 49:22 Behold, he shall come up and fly as the eagle, and spread his wings over Bozrah: and at that day shall the heart of the mighty men of Edom be as the heart of a woman in her pangs.

In this verse, the eagle represents God's ability to cover a whole nation and cause them to be in tribulation and eventual destruction.

But these four beasts are more than that. These also represent the "link between Heaven and Earth," as the number 4. The Lion of Judah *was* the sacrifice. The ox represents worship, as when the children were brought out of Egypt and made the golden calf. It represented worship, but they worshipped the image instead of God. Man represents evAngelism and *is* man, whom Christ became and died for. The eagle represents the Holy Spirit, whose intercession for us flies easily to the ear of God the Father and the Son.

John would have recognized the living creatures from:

Ezekiel 1:5-11 Also out of the midst thereof came the likeness of four living creatures. And this was their appearance; they had the likeness of a man. 6) And every one had four faces, and every one had four wings. 7) And their feet were straight feet; and the sole of their feet was like the sole of a calf's foot: and they sparkled like the colour of burnished brass. 8) And they had the hands of a man under their wings on their four sides; and they four had their faces and their wings. 9) Their wings were joined one to another; they turned not when they went; they went every one straight forward. 10) As for the likeness of their faces, they four had the face of a man, and the face of a lion, on the right side: and they four had the face of an ox on the left side; they four also had the face of an eagle. 11) Thus were their faces: and their wings were stretched upward; two wings of every one were joined one to another, and two covered their bodies.

Revelation 4:8 And the four beasts had each of them six wings about him; and they were full of eyes within: and they rest not day and night, saying, Holy, holy, holy, Lord God Almighty, which was, and is, and is to come.

John not only would have recognized the Scriptures from Ezekiel, but he would also have known:

Isaiah 6:2 Above it stood the seraphims: each one had six wings; with twain he covered his face, and with twain he covered his feet, and with twain he did fly.

The fact that the beasts had eyes within and without shows the spiritual ability to see into the heart. The eyes are all-seeing. They had six wings, which is the number of man.

Revelation 4:9 And when those beasts give glory and honour and thanks to him that sat on the throne, who liveth for ever and ever,

The beasts give glory and honor and thanks to Him that sat on the throne. We should give glory and honor and thanks to Him, also. He made it possible for us to go to Heaven!

Revelation 4:10 The four and twenty elders fall down before him that sat on the throne, and worship him that liveth for ever and ever, and cast their crowns before the throne, saying,

They cast their crowns before the throne. They were given a crown of life. Since Christ gave His life for us, they represent that they then give their lives to Him—their spiritual lives. Furthermore, the word "cast" in Greek means to throw rather forcibly.

Some people believe that all people will cast their crowns before the throne, but the bible does not state that. The only ones mentioned as casting crowns are the twenty-four elders.

Revelation 4:11 Thou art worthy, O Lord, to receive glory and honour and power: for thou hast created all things, and for thy pleasure they are and were created.

Notice here that we were created for Christ's pleasure, not Him for our pleasure! We are not to take Him out of a "box from under our bed" and "play" with Him on one morning of the week, then put Him back in the box and shove Him under the bed again, not to have anything to do with Him until the following week. He wants a relationship with us. He wants to talk with us. The problem is that He talks, but we do not listen or talk with Him the way He wants us to.

The Seven Seals

Revelation Chapter 5 – 8:1

Revelation 5:1 And I saw in the right hand of him that sat on the throne a book written within and on the backside, sealed with seven seals.

In the Middle East, all power rests in the right side of the body. A child is not allowed to be left-handed. (It's nice to know Jesus was right-handed.) The right hand was the "clean" hand. The left hand was used to clean oneself after using the toilet, so it was considered the "unclean" hand.

Under the Mosaic Law, land could not be sold. So, if the land was lost, the land description was written down on a scroll and sealed. The conditions for getting the property back were written outside the scroll. Alternatively, a legal document would be written on the inside, rolled, and sealed. The description of the one who could open the scroll would be written on the outside, along with the conditions under which it could be opened. This scroll described in Revelation requires a sinless person to open it, and none will be found worthy except the Lamb who was slain for our sins.

Since the seals upon a scroll meant a legal document with a legal way to open the document, removing the seals meant the fulfillment of the law in order to remove the seals.

Matthew 5:17 Think not that I am come to destroy the law, or the prophets: I am not come to destroy, but to fulfil.

Revelation 5:2 And I saw a strong Angel proclaiming with a loud voice, Who is worthy to open the book, and to loose the seals thereof?

Revelation 5:3 And no man in Heaven, nor in Earth, neither under the Earth, was able to open the book, neither to look thereon.

Revelation 5:4 And I wept much, because no man was found worthy to open and to read the book, neither to look thereon.

John would have recognized this from the Holy Scriptures:

Isaiah 29:11 And the vision of all is become unto you as the words of a book that is sealed, which men deliver to one that is learned, saying, Read this, I pray thee: and he saith, I cannot; for it is sealed:

Esther 8:8 Write ye also for the Jews, as it liketh you, in the king's name, and seal it with the king's ring: for the writing which is written in the king's name, and sealed with the king's ring, may no man reverse.

No one can look at the sealed book except He who is worthy. Some religions claim we will use the thousand-year reign to look at this book, personally. That will not happen! Verse 3 plainly says no man was found worthy to open the book, nor to LOOK thereon!

Revelation 5:5 And one of the elders saith unto me, Weep not: behold, the Lion of the tribe of Juda, the Root of David, hath prevailed to open the book, and to loose the seven seals thereof.

The Lion of Judah, the Root of David, can open the book. He will fulfill the law written thereon.

Genesis 49:9 Judah is a lion's whelp: from the prey, my son, thou art gone up: he stooped down, he couched as a lion, and as an old lion; who shall rouse him up?

Romans 15:12 And again, Esaias saith, There shall be a root of Jesse, and he that shall rise to reign over the Gentiles; in him shall the Gentiles trust.

This reference to "Esaias" is Isaiah 11:1:

Isaiah 11:1 And there shall come forth a rod out of the stem of Jesse, and a Branch shall grow out of his roots:

And, in case you do not know:

Ruth 4:22 And Obed begat Jesse, and Jesse begat David.

So, David, the King of Israel, was the beginning of the root of Jesse. Christ was of the Root of David.

Revelation 5:6 And I beheld, and, lo, in the midst of the throne and of the four beasts, and in the midst of the elders, stood a Lamb as it had been slain, having seven horns and seven eyes, which are the seven Spirits of God sent forth into all the Earth.

The horns are kings, and kings have power, as we see in:

Revelation 17:12 And the ten horns which thou sawest are ten kings, which have received no kingdom as yet; but receive power as kings one hour with the beast.

Seven is the perfect number, and the Lamb is perfect. As Christ is the king of seven kingdoms, there are seven continents. John would not have known of the seven continents; however, John would have known that Jesus is King of kings and Lord of lords!

We are told that the eyes are the seven Spirits of God, which we saw in Revelation 5:6.

In the previous verse, Christ was described as a lion. Here, He is described as a Lamb.

Revelation 5:7 And he came and took the book out of the right hand of him that sat upon the throne.
Christ takes the book from His Father.
Daniel 7:9 I beheld till the thrones were cast down, and the Ancient of days did sit, whose garment was white as snow, and the hair of his head like the pure wool: his throne was like the fiery flame, and his wheels as burning fire.
Isaiah 66:1 Thus saith the LORD, The Heaven is my throne, and the Earth is my footstool: where is the house that ye build unto me? and where is the place of my rest?

Revelation 5:8 And when he had taken the book, the four beasts and four and twenty elders fell down before the Lamb, having every one of them harps, and golden vials full of odours, which are the prayers of Saints.
The twenty-four elders (patriarchs and disciples) worship the Lamb (Christ) because He IS worthy! They are praising God:
Psalm 33:2 Praise the LORD with harp: sing unto him with the psaltery and an instrument of ten strings.
The gold vials have been explained here in Revelation 5:8 as the prayers of Saints.
Genesis 8:20, 21a says Noah's offerings made the Lord smell a sweet savor.
Genesis 8:20-21 And Noah builded an altar unto the LORD; and took of every clean beast, and of every clean fowl, and offered burnt offerings on the altar. 21) And the LORD smelled a sweet savour;
Psalm 141:2 Let my prayer be set forth before thee as incense; and the lifting up of my hands as the evening sacrifice.

Revelation 5:9 And they sung a new song, saying, Thou art worthy to take the book, and to open the seals thereof: for thou wast slain, and hast redeemed us to God by thy blood out of every kindred, and tongue, and people, and nation;
Singing is praise, and we praise God.
2 Chronicles 29:30 Moreover Hezekiah the king and the princes commanded the Levites to sing praise unto the LORD with the words of David, and of Asaph the seer. And they sang praises with gladness, and they bowed their heads and worshipped.

48

Matthew 4:10 Then saith Jesus unto him, Get thee hence, Satan: for it is written, Thou shalt worship the Lord thy God, and him only shalt thou serve.

Revelation 22:8 And I John saw these things, and heard them. And when I had heard and seen, I fell down to worship before the feet of the Angel which shewed me these things.

Revelation 22:9 Then saith he unto me, See thou do it not: for I am thy fellowservant, and of thy brethren the prophets, and of them which keep the sayings of this book: worship God.

Jesus wants us to worship only the Father.

John 4:24 says to worship Him in spirit and in truth.

If we go back to the Greek, Romans 10:17 could be translated as, "So then conviction of the truth comes by preaching and preaching by an (rhema word) utterance from God, whether individually, collectively, or specifically spoken (to)."

Revelation 5:10 And hast made us unto our God kings and priests: and we shall reign on the Earth.

This refers to Revelation 1:6:

Revelation 1:6 And hath made us kings and priests unto God and his Father; to him be glory and dominion for ever and ever. Amen.

Revelation 5:11 And I beheld, and I heard the voice of many Angels round about the throne and the beasts and the elders: and the number of them was ten thousand times ten thousand, and thousands of thousands;

Daniel 7:10 mentions, *"thousand thousands and ten thousand times ten thousand ministered unto Him."* Daniel continues, *"and the judgment was set, and the books were opened."* We are about to see judgment take place.

Hebrews 12:22 But ye are come unto mount Sion, and unto the city of the living God, the Heavenly Jerusalem, and to an innumerable company of Angels,

Revelation 5:12 Saying with a loud voice, Worthy is the Lamb that was slain to receive power, and riches, and wisdom, and strength, and honour, and glory, and blessing.

Praise Jesus again for being the Lamb that was slain and paying our debt. Heaven is all about praise and worship.

2 Corinthians 8:9 For ye know the grace of our Lord Jesus Christ, that, though he was rich, yet for your sakes he became poor, that ye through his poverty might be rich.

Revelation 5:13 And every creature which is in Heaven, and on the Earth, and under the Earth, and such as are in the sea, and all that are in them, heard I saying, Blessing, and honour, and glory, and power, be unto him that sitteth upon the throne, and unto the Lamb for ever and ever.

1 Chronicles 16:31-33 Let the Heavens be glad, and let the Earth rejoice: and let men say among the nations, The LORD reigneth. Let the sea roar, and the fulness thereof: let the fields rejoice, and all that is therein. Then shall the trees of the wood sing out at the presence of the LORD, because he cometh to judge the Earth.

Can you imagine the noise on Earth when all animals start praising God and Jesus? Birds in trees (that are also singing), your dogs and cats, wild animals, every human being, and fish and mammals in the sea and other bodies of water—all saying the same thing. Will we understand them? Will it be in our language of whatever country we are in? Maybe we will hear with those spiritual ears! Everyone and everything will acknowledge Him.

Also, in Luke, when Jesus was about to enter Jerusalem on the donkey, as He came to the Mount of Olives, His disciples began to rejoice and praise God with a loud voice, saying, "Blessed be the King that comes in the name of the Lord; peace in Heaven and glory in the highest." Some of the Pharisees told Jesus to rebuke His disciples:

Luke 19:40 And he answered and said unto them, I tell you that, if these should hold their peace, the stones would immediately cry out.

And they will one day!

Revelation 5:14 And the four beasts said, Amen. And the four and twenty elders fell down and worshipped him that liveth for ever and ever.

In Revelation 4:8 and 10, the four beasts say, "Holy, Holy, Lord God Almighty, which was, and is, and is to come." And then, the 24 Elders fall before the throne to worship and cast their crowns. There is order in Heaven, for this follows the same order: the beasts speak, and then the twenty-four elders fall to worship God.

THE FIRST SEAL

Revelation 6:1 And I saw when the Lamb opened one of the seals, and I heard, as it were the noise of thunder, one of the four beasts saying, Come and see.

Revelation 6:2 And I saw, and behold a white horse: and he that sat on him had a bow; and a crown was given unto him: and he went forth conquering, and to conquer.

The Complete Jewish Bible says that the Angel says, "Go!"

By the time John finished writing this Book, he knew this was Christ. Christ was given a kingdom:

Luke 22:29 And I appoint unto you a kingdom, as my Father hath appointed unto me;

By the time the Book of Revelation is finished, Christ has gone forth to conquer and conquered:

Revelation 19:11 And I saw Heaven opened, and behold a white horse; and he that sat upon him was called Faithful and True, and in righteousness he doth judge and make war.

Revelation 19:12 His eyes were as a flame of fire, and on his head were many crowns; and he had a name written, that no man knew, but he himself.

So, we will see Christ go from one crown, which was given to Him, to many crowns, which He will win.

THE SECOND SEAL

Revelation 6:3 And when he had opened the second seal, I heard the second beast say, Come and see.

Revelation 6:4 And there went out another horse that was red: and power was given to him that sat thereon to take peace from the Earth, and that they should kill one another: and there was given unto him a great sword.

We know that this book is the revealing of Jesus Christ.

Matthew 10:34 Think not that I am come to send peace on Earth: I came not to send peace, but a sword.

Jesus SENT a sword. Here, we see the horseman with the sword being sent.

THE THIRD SEAL

Revelation 6:5 And when he had opened the third seal, I heard the third beast say, Come and see. And I beheld, and lo a black horse; and he that sat on him had a pair of balances in his hand.

Revelation 6:6 And I heard a voice in the midst of the four beasts say, A measure of wheat for a penny, and three measures of barley for a penny; and see thou hurt not the oil and the wine.

An easy answer is that famine always follows war. Food prices are inflated, and no one can afford much food. Oil and wine were particularly important to the people of the Middle East, but oil and wine were also used to represent types of prophets in Biblical prophecy.

Haggai 1:11 And I called for a drought upon the land, and upon the mountains, and upon the corn, and upon the new wine, and upon the oil, and upon that which the ground bringeth forth, and upon men, and upon cattle, and upon all the labour of the hands.

The oil and the wine (along with the corn) are the prophets. Matthew Henry wrote of this passage, "It was the complaint of the Jews in Babylon that they saw not their signs, and there was no more prophet (*Psalm 74:9 We see not our signs: there is no more any prophet: neither is there among us any that knoweth how long.*), which was a just judgment upon them for mocking and misusing the prophets. Though God uses prophets, he does not need them – He can do his work without them; but the lamp of Old Testament prophecy shall yet make some bright and glorious effort before it expires." [42]

This is also why literal oil is used to anoint the sick and afflicted, so that the elders may prophesy wellness over the sick person. (*James 5:14 Is any sick among you? let him call for the elders of the Church; and let them pray over him, anointing him with oil in the name of the Lord.*)

But what kind of prophets? In Matthew, Jesus tells the parable of the ten virgins – five of whom are wise and five of whom are foolish. The wise took oil, and the foolish took no oil. The bridegroom tarried, and then the cry went out that the bridegroom was coming. But they had no prophet to tell them exactly when He was coming, to give them the signs of the times, for no man knows the day nor the hour, but can know the time. (*Matthew 24:36 But of that day and hour knoweth no man, no, not the Angels of Heaven, but my Father only. Luke 12:56 Ye hypocrites, ye can discern the face of the sky and of the Earth; but how is it that ye do not discern this time?*) Therefore, the oil probably represents the prophet who tells them the time of Christ's coming. He does not want this prophet touched by what is represented as famine.

What about the wine?

Isaiah 16:10 And gladness is taken away, and joy out of the plentiful field; and in the vineyards there shall be no singing, neither shall there be shouting: the treaders shall tread out no wine in their presses; I have made their vintage shouting to cease.

Here, the wine is represented as singing and shouting—praising God. In Isaiah, God caused their praise to cease, but in Revelation, He does not want the praising to cease.

We also see in Jude where Moses' body hung in the balance:

---

[42] Matthew Henry's Commentary on the Whole Bible, Published 1708 – 1714; public domain

Jude v.9 Yet Michael the archAngel, when contending with the devil he disputed about the body of Moses, durst not bring against him a railing accusation, but said, The Lord rebuke thee.

In this instance, I will not going to speculate on exactly who or what John thought this horseman might be other than one of the spirits that God sent out. Zechariah 1:8 – 11 talks of horses being sent from the LORD to walk back and forth through the Earth.

Revelation is about the revealing of Jesus Christ. We, as Americans, recognize the balance scale as representing justice – the field of law. Who is more just than God and Jesus? They bring justice and judgment.

It could also be said that our lives "hang in the balance." We have a decision to make. God gave us the freedom of choice.

Deuteronomy 30:19 I call Heaven and Earth to record this day against you, that I have set before you life and death, blessing and cursing: therefore choose life, that both thou and thy seed may live:

THE FOURTH SEAL

Revelation 6:7 And when he had opened the fourth seal, I heard the voice of the fourth beast say, Come and see.

Revelation 6:8 And I looked, and behold a pale horse: and his name that sat on him was Death, and Hell followed with him. And power was given unto them over the fourth part of the Earth, to kill with sword, and with hunger, and with death, and with the beasts of the Earth.

Well, we have the name of the one on the horse! No speculation is needed! His name is Death, and Hell follows him. When "Earth" is mentioned in prophecy, it means men's hearts. This word translated here as "Earth" literally means "the whole terrene globe." So, Death and Hell were given power over one-fourth of men's hearts worldwide to cause their souls to die the second death – the lake of fire. The parable of the Sower shows that the ground, the soil, and the Earth are men's hearts.

THE FIFTH SEAL

Revelation 6:9 And when he had opened the fifth seal, I saw under the altar the souls of them that were slain for the word of God, and for the testimony which they held:

Revelation 6:10 And they cried with a loud voice, saying, How long, O Lord, holy and true, dost thou not judge and avenge our blood on them that dwell on the Earth?

John knew the answer to this question was in Isaiah:

Isaiah 26:21 For, behold, the LORD cometh out of his place to punish the inhabitants of the Earth for their iniquity: the Earth also shall disclose her blood, and shall no more cover her slain.

Revelation 6:11 And white robes were given unto every one of them; and it was said unto them, that they should rest yet for a little season, until their fellowservants also and their brethren, that should be killed as they were, should be fulfilled.

First, we see that the soul of man lives on after death.

Exodus talks about the two altars in the Temple. Exodus 30:1 - 10 explains the inner golden altar. Exodus 30:28 begins the explanation of the outer brass altar. The brass altar is where the animal sacrifices were made individually by and for the people. These were daily sacrifices.

The brass altar would have been where the souls were, for people were, and are, dying daily for our Lord and Savior. The high priest burned the incense several times daily on the inner golden altar. Once a year, the high priest made a meat sacrifice and started by sprinkling blood on the altar. This altar will be seen later in Revelation.

Victorinus wrote: "He relates that he saw under the altar of God, this is, under the Earth, the souls of them that were slain. For both Heaven and Earth are called God's altar, as saith the law, commanding in the symbolical form of the truth two altars to be made – a golden one within, and a brazen one without. But we perceive that the golden altar is thus called Heaven, by the testimony that our Lord bears to it; for He says, 'But because in the last time, moreover, the reward of the Saints will be perpetual, and the condemnation of the wicked shall come,' it was told them to wait. And for a solace to their body, there were given unto each of them white robes. White robes stand for righteousness. Christ knows how many martyrs there will be. When that number is reached, God will cause His wrath to come upon them the martyrs want avenged."

John would have recognized martyrs from 722 BC when the kingdom of Israel was overrun and fell to the Neo-Assyrian Empire. This was the first time the Jewish people died from actual persecution, and they would want to know when they were to be avenged.

The decreed exile was fulfilled, and the Israelites were allowed back to Jerusalem. King Josiah of Judah instituted significant reforms in 649 – 609 B.C., removing part of the law.

THE SIXTH SEAL

Revelation 6:12 And I beheld when he had opened the sixth seal, and, lo, there was a great Earthquake; and the sun became black as sackcloth of hair, and the moon became as blood;

The great Earthquake was the shaking of the very foundation of the Jewish nation, Israel. John would have known this from the story Joseph told his father about the sun, the moon, and the eleven stars bowing down to his star. Joseph's father knew he was the sun – the primary ruler; his wife was the moon – the lesser ruler of the house; the stars were their twelve children – eleven of whom were expected to bow down to Joseph. (Remember, this verse does not discuss the stars – just the sun and moon.)

John would have recognized that the sun was the high priest (the ruler), and the moon represented the other priests (the lesser rulers). He also would have recognized a reference from Isaiah:

Isaiah 13:10 For the stars of Heaven and the constellations thereof shall not give their light: the sun shall be darkened in his going forth, and the moon shall not cause her light to shine.

Revelation 6:13 And the stars of Heaven fell unto the Earth, even as a fig tree casteth her untimely figs, when she is shaken of a mighty wind.

The falling of the stars are the Angels – remember the reference in Revelation 1:20. They were called untimely figs because they fell before Satan did. Satan will be cast out later.

Revelation 6:14 And the Heaven departed as a scroll when it is rolled together; and every mountain and island were moved out of their places.

John knew that Heaven departing as a scroll when it is rolled together would mean the end of an ecclesiastical time – the end of the Jewish nation as it was known. Also, their time had ended due to their rejection of Christ.

Mountain in prophecy was a religion. An island is a sect. An island is nothing more than an undersea mountain.

Isaiah 2:2 And it shall come to pass in the last days, that the mountain of the LORD'S house shall be established in the top of the mountains, and shall be exalted above the hills; and all nations shall flow unto it.

Isaiah 11:9 They shall not hurt nor destroy in all my holy mountain: for the Earth shall be full of the knowledge of the LORD, as the waters cover the sea.

And:

Jeremiah 51:25 Behold, I am against thee, O destroying mountain, saith the LORD, which destroyest all the Earth: and I will stretch out mine hand upon thee, and roll thee down from the rocks, and will make thee a burnt mountain.

This prophecy in Jeremiah was against the religion of Baal, of whom God eventually destroyed every believer.

These verses show that every religion and sect would be moved out of their place. There will eventually only be one religion – the worship of the one, true God.

Revelation 6:15 And the kings of the Earth, and the great men, and the rich men, and the chief captains, and the mighty men, and every bondman, and every free man, hid themselves in the dens and in the rocks of the mountains;

John knew the verses from Isaiah:

Isaiah 2:19-21 And they shall go into the holes of the rocks, and into the caves of the Earth, for fear of the LORD, and for the glory of his majesty, when he ariseth to shake terribly the Earth. In that day a man shall cast his idols of silver, and his idols of gold, which they made each one for himself to worship, to the moles and to the bats; To go into the clefts of the rocks, and into the tops of the ragged rocks, for fear of the LORD, and for the glory of his majesty, when he ariseth to shake terribly the Earth.

During almost every battle in the Bible, you can read where the people hid themselves in the mountains, in the dens (caves) and rocks. This was a defensible position, for the people in the caves and rocks had missiles (rocks) to throw at their disposal. The soldiers coming up the mountainside would be vulnerable because throwing rocks down was easier than throwing weapons or rocks up. The prophetic case of this is the hiding of oneself in the nuances of a false religion, in the verses that deceive and tell them they are OK, they are going to Heaven and live forever.

Revelation 6:16 And said to the mountains and rocks, Fall on us, and hide us from the face of him that sitteth on the throne, and from the wrath of the Lamb:

Revelation 6:17 For the great day of his wrath is come; and who shall be able to stand?

This indicated that the Jews knew what this destruction was all about from the prophecies of Isaiah, Ezekiel, Hosea, and Jeremiah.

Four different prophets had warned them. They knew the wrath had come about and needed to repent! The Jews had allowed the pagan worshippers to influence how they felt about and dealt with God.

The "shaking of the Earth" occurred in 586 B.C. when Jerusalem fell to Nebuchadnezzar and Solomon's Temple was destroyed. God's people were being chastised again. They were sent into exile, but the Seal of the Law was removed in 539 B.C. when they were allowed to return to Jerusalem by permission of Cyrus.

THE TIME BETWEEN THE SIXTH AND SEVENTH SEALS

Revelation 7:1 And after these things I saw four Angels standing on the four corners of the Earth, holding the four winds of the Earth, that the wind should not blow on the Earth, nor on the sea, nor on any tree.

These are the winds that scatter the people of Israel. When the Angels hold the four winds of the Earth so the wind cannot blow on the Earth, nor the sea, nor any tree, that is the Angels holding back, at God's command, the scattering forces that would work on the nation of Israel.

Isaiah 17:13 The nations shall rush like the rushing of many waters: but God shall rebuke them, and they shall flee far off, and shall be chased as the chaff of the mountains before the wind, and like a rolling thing before the whirlwind.

It is also winds of doctrine that can lead them astray.

Eph 4:14 That we henceforth be no more children, tossed to and fro, and carried about with every wind of doctrine, by the sleight of men, and cunning craftiness, whereby they lie in wait to deceive;

The Earth or ground is men's hearts. (See Appendix A – Matthew 13:3-8, 19-23)

The sea is the sea of Christ's people, the Gentiles.

Isaiah 60:5 Then thou shalt see, and flow together, and thine heart shall fear, and be enlarged; because the abundance of the sea shall be converted unto thee, the forces of the Gentiles shall come unto thee.

Revelation 17:15 And he saith unto me, The waters which thou sawest, where the whore sitteth, are peoples, and multitudes, and nations, and tongues.

Trees are the Jewish people. Olive trees represent the priests and rulers of the Temple.

Judges 9:8 The trees went forth on a time to anoint a king over them; and they said unto the olive tree, Reign thou over us.

Judges 9:9 But the olive tree said unto them, Should I leave my fatness, wherewith by me they honour God and man, and go to be promoted over the trees?

The New Testament declares that we, as Christians, have been grafted into God's people. No scattering force nor wind of doctrine can act upon any of them until God releases these Angels.

THE SEALING OF THE 144,000

Revelation 7:2 And I saw another Angel ascending from the east, having the seal of the living God: and he cried with a loud voice to the four Angels, to whom it was given to hurt the Earth and the sea,

Revelation 7:3 Saying, Hurt not the Earth, neither the sea, nor the trees, till we have sealed the servants of our God in their foreheads.

Revelation 7:4 And I heard the number of them which were sealed: and there were sealed an hundred and forty and four thousand of all the tribes of the children of Israel.

Revelation 7:5 Of the tribe of Juda were sealed twelve thousand. Of the tribe of Reuben were sealed twelve thousand. Of the tribe of Gad were sealed twelve thousand.

Revelation 7:6 Of the tribe of Aser were sealed twelve thousand. Of the tribe of Nepthalim were sealed twelve thousand. Of the tribe of Manasses were sealed twelve thousand.

Revelation 7:7 Of the tribe of Simeon were sealed twelve thousand. Of the tribe of Levi were sealed twelve thousand. Of the tribe of Issachar were sealed twelve thousand.

Revelation 7:8 Of the tribe of Zabulon were sealed twelve thousand. Of the tribe of Joseph were sealed twelve thousand. Of the tribe of Benjamin were sealed twelve thousand.

There are Angels established to restrain Satan and his Angels. This was "another Angel," a fifth Angel, who came forth and cried to the four Angels who held the winds that could hurt men's hearts and Christ's people.

John would have recognized a verse from Isaiah:

Isaiah 1:9 Except the LORD of hosts had left unto us a very small remnant, we should have been as Sodom, and we should have been like unto Gomorrah.

This mark to be placed on the people's foreheads was a spiritual mark that God could see as plainly as if it were tattooed upon their foreheads. It is also the Word of God, which we know in our minds – which is "in" our foreheads. However, John may have thought this to be a literal mark, as it was in Ezekiel:

Ezekiel 9:4 And the LORD said unto him, Go through the midst of the city, through the midst of Jerusalem, and set a mark upon the foreheads of the men that sigh and that cry for all the abominations that be done in the midst thereof.

The original Patriarchs are:

Reuben, Simeon, Levi, Judah, Zebulun, Issachar, Dan, Gad, Asher, Naphtalli, Joseph and Benjamin.

In verses 4 through 8, there are to be 144,000 people sealed: 12,000 from each of the tribes of the children of Israel. The difference between this list and the standard list of Patriarchs from the Old Testament is that the tribe of Dan has been removed, and the tribe of Manasses has been added. Dan was removed from this list in Revelation because they fell into idolatry and a pagan religion. Judges chapter 18 tells how Dan went to Mount Ephraim, to the house of Micah, a priest. From there, they went to Laish and saw how the people lived without care, quiet, and secure. They schemed to overthrow them and take their land. The Bible tells how they had no business with any man there, meaning God had not told them to do this. Then, they returned to Micah, took all his idols, and set them up for themselves in their new place, Laish. Only the tribe of Dan burned the city and then built a new city called Dan. For this, they were removed from the list of apostles, like Judas would later be removed from the list of patriarchs.

There is a beautiful message in the meaning of the order of the names of the Patriarchs as presented in Revelation:

- Juda equals I will praise God (praise)
- Reuben equals God has seen my humiliation and given me a son (See, a Son!)
- Gad equals Good fortune has come (good fortune)
- Aser equals How happy I am (happy)
- Nepthalim equals I wrestled with my sister and won (my wrestling)
- Manasses equals God has caused me to forget all my troubles (causing to forget)
- Simeon equals God has heard I am unloved (unloved)
- Levi equals Now will my husband be joined to me (joining)
- Issachar equals God has given me my hire (hire/reward)
- Zabulon (Zebulon) equals Now my husband will live with me (living together)
- Joseph equals May God give me another son (may He add)

Benjamin equals Son of: the right hand/my strength/the South (originally Ben-Oni equals Son of my pain/grief/sorrow).

Here, we see what each name means. When each child was born, the mother made a statement and then named the child according to the meaning of what she had just uttered.

Except for the last one. Rachel only uttered the name of the child and then died. She named him Ben-Oni, which means son of my pain, grief, or sorrow. Lot, the child's father, called him Benjamin, which means son of my right hand or strength or the South. Put together, the sentence would read:

Praise God! See, a Son! Good fortune has come. How happy am I and blessed. I have wrestled and won. God has caused me to forget that I heard I was unloved. He joined to me, giving me my reward of living with Him. He gives the Son of His right hand (or He gives the Son of the South).

Son of the right hand or Son of the South both have spiritual meanings. For Christ stands at the right hand of His Father. And later, God causes the Kings of the North to come against Israel, making Christ the Son of the South, against the North.

Revelation 7:9 After this I beheld, and, lo, a great multitude, which no man could number, of all nations, and kindreds, and people, and tongues, stood before the throne, and before the Lamb, clothed with white robes, and palms in their hands;

Revelation 7:10 And cried with a loud voice, saying, Salvation to our God which sitteth upon the throne, and unto the Lamb.

John would have known the reference for this verse:

Isaiah 12:2 Behold, God is my salvation; I will trust, and not be afraid: for the LORD JEHOVAH is my strength and my song; he also is become my salvation.

This great multitude represents the people from other nations who would accept Christ as their Saviour. They now become Christ's people.

They wear white robes of righteousness and have palm branches in their hands. More Gentiles believe than Jewish people who believe.

Isaiah 54:1 Sing, O barren, thou that didst not bear; break forth into singing, and cry aloud, thou that didst not travail with child: for more are the children of the desolate than the children of the married wife, saith the LORD.

Here, we have the tribes of Israel and the multitudes praising God and the Lamb.

Revelation 7:11 And all the Angels stood round about the throne, and about the elders and the four beasts, and fell before the throne on their faces, and worshipped God,

Revelation 7:12 Saying, Amen: Blessing, and glory, and wisdom, and thanksgiving, and honour, and power, and might, be unto our God for ever and ever. Amen.

In Revelation 4, we are introduced to these elders and beasts. They consistently and constantly worship God.

Revelation 7:13 And one of the elders answered, saying unto me, What are these which are arrayed in white robes? and whence came they?

Revelation 7:14 And I said unto him, Sir, thou knowest. And he said to me, These are they which came out of great tribulation, and have washed their robes, and made them white in the blood of the Lamb.

Revelation 7:15 Therefore are they before the throne of God, and serve him day and night in his temple: and he that sitteth on the throne shall dwell among them.

Revelation 7:16 They shall hunger no more, neither thirst any more; neither shall the sun light on them, nor any heat.

Revelation 7:17 For the Lamb which is in the midst of the throne shall feed them, and shall lead them unto living fountains of waters: and God shall wipe away all tears from their eyes.

These questions are asked not for his own information, but for John's instruction. However, the question is not so much a question as it is praise for the ones who came out of the tribulation! The only place white robes are mentioned in the Bible is in Revelation.

Ecclesiastes 9:8 mentions keeping your garments white, which clothe us while on Earth. In Heaven, our "garments" are changed for "white robes".

Notice that it is only the blood of Jesus that washes white as snow. These are the ones who came out of great tribulation. We will all have tribulations in our lives. Tribulation does not separate us from the love of God, no matter how great that tribulation is. We must all be tried.

John 16:33 These things I have spoken unto you, that in me ye might have peace. In the world ye shall have tribulation: but be of good cheer; I have overcome the world.

Acts 14:22 Confirming the souls of the disciples, and exhorting them to continue in the faith, and that we must through much tribulation enter into the kingdom of God.

Serving God day and night was the job of the Levites. Now, we are made priests, and the faithful serve Him day and night. The holy of holies is open to all. We will have the right to come into God's presence.

We shall neither hunger nor thirst. Christ will feed us with the manna and give us living water.

There is also the tree of life, which bears twelve fruits, each in its season.

Revelation 22:2 In the midst of the street of it, and on either side of the river, was there the tree of life, which bare twelve manner of fruits, and yielded her fruit every month: and the leaves of the tree were for the healing of the nations.

But we must do His commandments to have the right to the tree of life.

Revelation 22:14 Blessed are they that do his commandments, that they may have right to the tree of life, and may enter in through the gates into the city.

This does not say there will be no tears in Heaven, but Christ will wipe the tears from our eyes. This may be from the sorrow we feel at not having our loved ones in Heaven. The reality of their lostness will set in, but our loving Father will wipe away our tears, comfort us, and turn our sorrow into rejoicing!

Isaiah 35:10 And the ransomed of the LORD shall return, and come to Zion with songs and everlasting joy upon their heads: they shall obtain joy and gladness, and sorrow and sighing shall flee away.

John also would have known from the Holy Scriptures that the tribes of Israel were scattered twice. God had sent them into captivity. Then, when Rome attacked Israel and destroyed the Temple in Jerusalem in 70 A.D., millions of Israelites were killed, and millions more fled to other countries.

Jeremiah had written that he wished his head were waters and his eyes a fountain of tears that he might cry day and night for the slain of the daughter of his people (Jeremiah 9:1).

The hundred and forty-four thousand were to be sealed before the scattering winds could take effect.

Jeremiah's prophecy also called for the mourners to come (Jeremiah 9:17). In Revelation 7:17, God will wipe away all tears. There will be no need for mourning. Death has been conquered.

THE SEVENTH SEAL

The message that there is a Son of God (from the names of the Tribes as presented in Chapter 7) was the prelude to the Seventh Seal. Jesus is born. Thirty years later, the Seventh Seal is opened.

Revelation 8:1 And when he had opened the seventh seal, there was silence in Heaven about the space of half an hour.

John knew prophetic time:

Ezekiel 4:6 And when thou hast accomplished them, lie again on thy right side, and thou shalt bear the iniquity of the house of Judah forty days: I have appointed thee each day for a year.

Three hundred sixty days in a year, divided by 24 hours a day equals 15 actual days divided by 2 (for only a half hour) equals 7 1/2 days.

John knew that Satan had access to Heaven:

Job 1:7 And the LORD said unto Satan, Whence comest thou? Then Satan answered the LORD, and said, From going to and fro in the Earth, and from walking up and down in it.

Job 2:2 And the LORD said unto Satan, From whence comest thou? And Satan answered the LORD, and said, From going to and fro in the Earth, and from walking up and down in it.

John also knew that God had a plan of Salvation.

John 3:16 For God so loved the world, that he gave his only begotten Son, that whosoever believeth in him should not perish, but have everlasting life.

John 3:17 For God sent not his Son into the world to condemn the world; but that the world through him might be saved.

Satan is the one who condemns us. God loves us. If God had a plan, He did not want Satan to know what that plan was. During the last week of Christ's life, death, and resurrection, there was silence in Heaven. This was "about" seven and one-half days. If you count Sunday as the day of His triumphal entry into Jerusalem, and then He arose on the next Sunday, that is eight days in total.

Jesus had a triumphant entrance into Jerusalem. He was examined, as was the Passover lamb. Although He was found to be without blemish, He was still sacrificed, as was the Passover lamb. When Christ hung on the cross, Satan thought he had won. When Christ died, Satan was sure he had won. Buried, Satan could rejoice. Satan just knew he would be the god of this world, no more problems from God.

Zechariah 2:13 Be silent, O all flesh, before the LORD: for he is raised up out of his holy habitation.

He was, indeed, raised up out of His holy habitation – He had come to Earth as a man, to be the ultimate sacrifice – to win the war against Satan.

But wait, you say – The Lamb who removed this seal was in Heaven. Jesus was on the Earth. It could not be the same person/God/Jesus. I invite you to read what Jesus said:

John 3:13 And no man hath ascended up to Heaven, but he that came down from Heaven, even the Son of man which is in Heaven.

63

For clarification, the word "even" has been added to this verse. However, what it may do is muddy the water. Let us look at it without that extra word:

John 3:13 And no man hath ascended up to Heaven, but he that came down from Heaven, the Son of man which is in Heaven.

This makes the verse a little clearer. Jesus is speaking here to Nicodemus. Notice that Jesus said He was in Heaven. However, He was on Earth, talking to Nicodemus. How can this be? What is the way He, The Lamb of God, could be in Heaven, removing the seals, and be here on Earth in His last week, having a triumphant entry into Jerusalem and then being crucified, buried, and then resurrected for our sins?

1 Corinthians 13:12 For now we see through a glass, darkly; but then face to face: now I know in part; but then shall I know even as also I am known.

Also, God showed me how this could be possible through much prayer. He showed me that He stands before the "tapestry of time." Everything is shown on that tapestry from the beginning of time until the end of time. He stands before it. He is there at each point in time, all the time. He is also omnipresent. He is everywhere at the same time. He can simultaneously be present with you and me at different points on Earth. So, He can be on Earth and in Heaven at the same time.

But why did He come to Earth?

2 Corinthians 8:9 For ye know the grace of our Lord Jesus Christ, that, though he was rich, yet for your sakes he became poor, that ye through his poverty might be rich.

In the Greek, this sentence structure is accusatory. "For YOUR sakes" is saying, "It is YOUR fault. YOU did this. YOU caused this tp happen. YOU messed up, and Jesus had to leave the riches of Heaven, become poor, and be the sacrifice for you. All so you can go to Heaven and share in His riches."

For your sake He was crucified. Animals cannot atone for our sins. Only the blood of a sinless man, Jesus, can atone for the sins of sinful man. The good news is, even if you were the only one who messed up, the only one who sinned, the only one who would believe on Him, He would still have done this just for you.

John 3:16-21 For God so loved the world, that he gave his only begotten Son, that whosoever believeth in him should not perish, but have everlasting life. For God sent not his Son into the world to condemn the world; but that the world through him might be saved. He that believeth on him is not condemned: but he that believeth not is condemned already, because he hath not believed in the name of the only

64

begotten Son of God. And this is the condemnation, that light is come into the world, and men loved darkness rather than light, because their deeds were evil. For every one that doeth evil hateth the light, neither cometh to the light, lest his deeds should be reproved. But he that doeth truth cometh to the light, that his deeds may be made manifest, that they are wrought in God.

If you have never accepted Jesus as your Savior and invited Him into your heart, now is the day of salvation. [43]

_____

[43] 2 Corinthians 6:2

The First Six Trumpets

Revelation 8:2 – Chapter 9

If John had recognized events from the past that led up to the Messiah's death, burial, and resurrection as the fulfillment of the law, he also would have recognized the events of the first trumpet. John was still alive during the Roman siege of what we know as Israel and the destruction of Jerusalem and the Temple.

Revelation 8:2 And I saw the seven Angels which stood before God; and to them were given seven trumpets.

The trumpets sound to announce God, His Word, and His Power. John recognized this vision from Exodus and Psalms:

Exodus 19:16 And it came to pass on the third day in the morning, that there were thunders and lightnings, and a thick cloud upon the mount, and the voice of the trumpet exceeding loud; so that all the people that was in the camp trembled.

Psalm 47:5 God is gone up with a shout, the LORD with the sound of a trumpet.

Revelation 8:3 And another Angel came and stood at the altar, having a golden censer; and there was given unto him much incense, that he should offer it with the prayers of all Saints upon the golden altar which was before the throne.

While the seven Angels prepare to sound the trumpets, another Angel (an eighth one—perhaps Jesus as the high priest) prepares for the "ceremony" with the censer. Notice that all the Saints are praying people. All God's children pray to Him.

1 Samuel 12:23 Moreover as for me, God forbid that I should sin against the LORD in ceasing to pray for you: but I will teach you the good and the right way:

Revelation 8:4 And the smoke of the incense, which came with the prayers of the Saints, ascended up before God out of the Angel's hand.

The smoke of the holy incense will increase the prayers of the Saints, and God will answer.

Psalm 141:2 Let my prayer be set forth before thee as incense; and the lifting up of my hands as the evening sacrifice.

Not only are our prayers put before God with holy incense, but our prayers are also filling vials and are full of odors:

Revelation 5:8 And when he had taken the book, the four beasts and four and twenty elders fell down before the Lamb, having every one of them harps, and golden vials full of odours, which are the prayers of Saints.

Revelation 8:5 And the Angel took the censer, and filled it with fire of the altar, and cast it into the Earth: and there were voices, and thunderings, and lightnings, and an Earthquake.

God's answer to these prayers was casting the altar's fire into the Earth. He was avenging the souls of the martyrs and avenging Himself with His enemies.

Deuteronomy 32:43 Rejoice, O ye nations, with his people: for he will avenge the blood of his servants, and will render vengeance to his adversaries, and will be merciful unto his land, and to his people.

Luke 18:7 And shall not God avenge his own elect, which cry day and night unto him, though he bear long with them?

Revelation 8:6 And the seven Angels which had the seven trumpets prepared themselves to sound.

We are not told how they prepared. They could have simply placed the trumpets—shofars—to their lips or went through some other preparation process.

1 Corinthians 14:8 For if the trumpet give an uncertain sound, who shall prepare himself to the battle?

This is spiritual warfare. We need to be prepared, hear God's warnings, and look around us for signs of the times. We cannot know the day or the hour, but we can know the season.

THE FIRST TRUMPET

Revelation 8:7 The first Angel sounded, and there followed hail and fire mingled with blood, and they were cast upon the Earth: and the third part of trees was burnt up, and all green grass was burnt up.

The first trumpet sounded for the people of Jerusalem in 70 A.D. Christ had come, and the Jewish people rejected Him. John knew what was about to happen.

Ezekiel 5:2-4 Thou shalt burn with fire a third part in the midst of the city, when the days of the siege are fulfilled: and thou shalt take a third part, and smite about it with a knife: and a third part thou shalt scatter in the wind; and I will draw out a sword after them. Thou shalt also take thereof a few in number, and bind them in thy skirts. Then take of them again, and cast them into the midst of the fire, and burn them in the fire; for thereof shall a fire come forth into all the house of Israel.

In Revelation 8:7, when it says, "and the third part of trees was burnt up, and all green grass was burnt up," Israel was often referred to as "trees" and the people as "grass".

Job 5:25 Thou shalt know also that thy seed shall be great, and thine offspring as the grass of the Earth.

We can also use this verse to show that the grass was the children of the people. Revelation 8:7 says that all green grass was burnt up. In the siege of Jerusalem, there were no children left.

Judges 9:8 The trees went forth on a time to anoint a king over them; and they said unto the olive tree, Reign thou over us.

Also, in Isaiah:

Isaiah 40:7 The grass withereth, the flower fadeth: because the spirit of the LORD bloweth upon it: surely the people is grass.

During the siege of Jerusalem, it was a terrible time. Josephus recorded that almost three million people had gone to Jerusalem for the Feast of the Tabernacle, and they had all, eventually, been slain by the Romans. [44] He also wrote of the "hail and fire mingled with blood. [45]

Matthew 24 and Josephus' account of the war are separate teachings from Revelation's. The majority of what Jesus taught in Matthew 24 dealt with the destruction of Jerusalem. He did get into the time when He would return, but the horrible things He was talking about were all about the destruction in 70 A.D. The siege started in 66 A.D. and lasted three and a half years. [46] This is the ONLY time when it could be said there would be a three-and-a-half-year tribulation!

Josephus recorded the story of the image of Caesar being set up on the top of the steps to the Temple. It was finally removed at the urging of the Jewish people, and then the slaughter started. Caesar had told his general, Petronius, that if the image were not set up, he would wage war against the people. "When the priests demanded the statue be removed, Petronius asked them, 'Will you then make war against Caesar?' The Jews said, 'We offer sacrifices twice every day for Caesar, and for the Roman people,' but that if he would place the images among them, he must first sacrifice the whole Jewish nation; and that they were ready to expose themselves, together with their children and wives, to be killed." [47]

[44] The New Complete Works of Josephus, Translated by William Whiston, © 1999 by Kregel Publications, The Jewish War, Book 1, Chapter 1.1, P670
[45] Ibid.
[46] Ibid.
[47] Ibid., Book 2, Chapter 10.4, P742.

Josephus also recorded how the "hail" was huge stones, weighing a talent, hurled by catapults, which he called "machines". Oil was also poured over the stones, and they were set on fire. The mingling with the blood came when they would hit a person and continue their journey to hit a building or the ground. Josephus recorded how one of these stones hit a pregnant woman's stomach and knocked the baby out of her, and it "was carried the distance of half a furlong, so great was the force of that engine."

When Jesus said in Matthew 24 to flee to the mountains, Josephus recorded how some of those who made it to the high places in the mountains were able to survive, while the rest died.

When Jesus told them, "Woe unto them that are with child, and to them that give suck in those days!" it was because the women ended up roasting their children so they could eat. Prior to that, Caesar would punish the women for having their children circumcised by killing the child and having it hung around the mother's neck.

Josephus writes about the fighting that occurred:

"To give a detailed account of their outrageous conduct is impossible, but we may sum it up by saying that no other city has ever endured such horrors, and no generation in history has fathered such wickedness. In the end they brought the whole Hebrew race into contempt to make their own impiety seem less outrageous in foreign eyes, and confessed the painful truth that they were slaves, the dregs of humanity, bastards, and outcasts of their nation . . . It is certain that when from the upper city they watched the Temple burning they did not turn a hair, though many Romans were moved to tears." [48]

The flight was in the summer, not the winter, and not on the Sabbath day. The siege, however, lasted three and a half years before the city and the temple were destroyed, and over two million people lay dead.

THE SECOND TRUMPET

Revelation 8:8 And the second Angel sounded, and as it were a great mountain burning with fire was cast into the sea: and the third part of the sea became blood;

Revelation 8:9 And the third part of the creatures which were in the sea, and had life, died; and the third part of the ships were destroyed.

John would not have known precisely what was to transpire for the future. To find out how the following visions fit into history and

---

[48] http://www.templemount.org/destruct2.html

to discover where we are now, please read the next book, "Revelation: Where Are We?" Due out by 2023. We are in that period that Jesus was showing John:

*Revelation 1:19 Write the things which thou hast seen, and the things which are, and **the things which shall be hereafter;*** (Author's emphasis)

Notice that the first Angel covers one-third of the trees, representing the Jews. Now, this Angel covers one-third of the sea, representing all people, but especially the Gentile nations.

John would have known that the ships being destroyed were the "ships of state." This reference was from Ezekiel:

Ezekiel 27:29 And all that handle the oar, the mariners, and all the pilots of the sea, shall come down from their ships, they shall stand upon the land;

Daniel 11:30 says:

For the ships of Chittim shall come against him: therefore he shall be grieved, and return, and have indignation against the holy covenant: so shall he do; he shall even return, and have intelligence with them that forsake the holy covenant.

THE THIRD TRUMPET

Revelation 8:10 And the third Angel sounded, and there fell a great star from Heaven, burning as it were a lamp, and it fell upon the third part of the rivers, and upon the fountains of waters;

Revelation 8:11 And the name of the star is called Wormwood: and the third part of the waters became wormwood; and many men died of the waters, because they were made bitter.

John would have recognized this star falling and burning as a lamp as an ecclesiastical "star," someone prominent among the clergy. Burning as a lamp is a shining light, meaning giving out knowledge (teaching).

The third part of the rivers would represent the going out of the Word, and the fountains of waters would represent the putting forth of the Word of God.

This "star" poisons the Word of God and causes men to die. John would have guessed that someone in a prominent position would twist the word of God, poisoning it, and thereby leading people to hell instead of Heaven.

THE FOURTH TRUMPET

Revelation 8:12 And the fourth Angel sounded, and the third part of the sun was smitten, and the third part of the moon, and the third part of the stars; so as the third part of them was darkened, and the day shone not for a third part of it, and the night likewise.

There is a reference in Isaiah which John would have known:

Isaiah 13:10 For the stars of Heaven and the constellations thereof shall not give their light: the sun shall be darkened in his going forth, and the moon shall not cause her light to shine.

John would have known the sun would be their ruler(s). The Jewish people would lose their Rabbis and other clergy, and they would be without the light of teaching.

If you go back to Genesis, when Joseph dreamed that the sun, moon, and eleven stars bowed before him, his father answered, "Shall I, your mother, and your brothers bow down to you on this Earth?" The sun, then, is the spiritual leader (the husband/father is to be the spiritual leader of the home), and the moon is an heir to the sun, according to 1 Peter 3:7: *Likewise, ye husbands, dwell with them* [your wives] *according to knowledge, giving honour unto the wife, as unto the weaker vessel, and as being heirs together of the grace of life; that your prayers be not hindered.*

Revelation 8:13 And I beheld, and heard an Angel flying through the midst of Heaven, saying with a loud voice, Woe, woe, woe, to the inhabiters of the Earth by reason of the other voices of the trumpet of the three Angels, which are yet to sound!

Josephus recorded that a precursor of this very thing happened in Jerusalem:

"But what is still more terrible, there was one Jesus, the son of Ananus, a plebeian and a husbandman, who, four years before the war began, and at a time when the city was in very great peace and prosperity, came to that feast whereon it is our custom for everyone to make Tabernacles to G od in the temple, and began on a sudden to cry aloud, 'A voice from the east, a voice from the west, a voice from the four winds, a voice against Jerusalem and the holy house, a voice against the bridegrooms and the brides, and a voice against this whole people!' This was his cry, as he went about by day and by night, in all the lanes of the city. However, certain of the most eminent among the populace had great indignation at this dire cry of his, and took up the man, and gave him a great number of severe stripes; yet did not he either say anything for himself, or anything peculiar to those that chastised him, but still went on with the same words which he cried before. But our rulers, supposing, as the case proved to be, that this was a sort of divine fury in the man, brought him to the Roman procurator, where he was whipped until his bones were laid bare; yet he did not make any supplication for himself, nor shed any tears, but turning his voice to the most lamentable tone possible, at every stroke of the while his answer was, 'Woe, woe to Jerusalem:' ... and he continued this ditty for seven years and five months, without growing hoarse, or being tired with it, until the very time that he saw his presage in earnest fulfilled in our siege, when it ceased; for as he was going round upon the wall, he cried out with his utmost force, 'Woe, woe to the city again, and to the people, and to the holy house!' And just as he added at the last, 'Woe, woe to myself also!' there came a stone out of one of the engines [catapults], and struck him, and killed him immediately; and as he was uttering the very same presages he gave up the ghost." [49]

For this reason, some theologians believe all the trumpets were for Jerusalem. John would have recognized this as what theologians now call "an interlude" in the Scriptures and a warning of what was to come.

Trumpets five, six, and seven would be the start of a terrible time on Earth.

THE FIFTH TRUMPET

Revelation 9:1 And the fifth Angel sounded, and I saw a star fall from Heaven unto the Earth: and to him was given the key of the bottomless pit.

John would have known that a key was an instrument for locking or unlocking. Another definition is how a mystery or a guide may be disclosed, or anything difficult explained. This key unlocks the bottomless pit—Sheol, Gehenna, Hell.

An Angel has the key to the pit and comes to Earth. This is not a good thing. Jesus had obtained the key to death, hell, and the grave. Now, it has been given to an Angel so he can unlock it and let it loose.

1–36 of 1 Enoch).

The Watchers were originally a group of Angels assigned to watch over humanity. However, led by Semjaza (or Shemihazah), they

---

[49] The New Complete Works of Josephus, Translated by William Whiston, © 1999 by Kregel Publications, The Jewish War, Book 1, Chapter 1.1, P670.

became enamored with human women and decided to descend to Earth to take them as wives. 1 Enoch 6:1-6 records their reasoning:

"And it came to pass, when the children of men had multiplied, that in those days were born unto them beautiful and comely daughters. And the Angels, the children of Heaven, saw and lusted after them, and said to one another: 'Come, let us choose us wives from among the children of men and beget us children.'" (1 Enoch 6:1-2)

Semjaza, fearing that he alone would bear the consequences if they went through with this rebellion, made the other 200 Watchers swear an oath to go through with it together:

"Then swore they all together and bound themselves by mutual imprecations upon it. And they were in all two hundred; who descended in the days of Jared on the summit of Mount Hermon, and they called it Mount Hermon, because they had sworn and bound themselves by mutual imprecations upon it." (1 Enoch 6:5-6)

Once on Earth, the fallen Angels took human wives and produced Nephilim, giant offspring who were violent and destructive. The Watchers also corrupted humanity by teaching them forbidden knowledge and skills, such as:

Metallurgy – crafting weapons for war

Cosmetics – beautifying women and leading to seduction

Divination and Sorcery – astrology, enchantments, and the interpretation of omens

This corruption led to significant violence and wickedness on Earth, which ultimately provoked God's judgment.

In response to the Watchers' rebellion, God sent the archAngels Michael, Gabriel, Raphael, and Uriel to deal with them. They were judged as follows:

The Nephilim were destroyed in a great flood (this parallels the story of Noah in Genesis).

The Watchers were imprisoned in the depths of the Earth (in Tartarus or a deep abyss) to await final judgment.

The leaders, Semjaza and Azazel, received harsher punishments. Azazel, in particular, was blamed for much of the corruption and was bound in chains in the desert until the final judgment. Now, an Angel of God (Raphael) comes to free him.

Revelation 9:2 And he opened the bottomless pit; and there arose a smoke out of the pit, as the smoke of a great furnace; and the sun and the air were darkened by reason of the smoke of the pit.

There is a reference from Isaiah which John would have known:

Isaiah 13:10 For the stars of Heaven and the constellations thereof shall not give their light: the sun shall be darkened in his going forth, and the moon shall not cause her light to shine.

John knew that smoke obscures. The sun was a ruler and Satan is the ruler of the air.

Eph 2:2 Wherein in time past ye walked according to the course of this world, according to the prince of the power of the air, the spirit that now worketh in the children of disobedience:

Have you ever heard the term "smoke and mirrors"? The smoke here darkens the light of knowledge.

Smoke is not substantial – it will not hold up to scrutiny. Nevertheless, it makes you believe what a magician tries to show you. John knew there would be false teachings that would lead people straight to hell.

Revelation 9:3 And there came out of the smoke locusts upon the Earth: and unto them was given power, as the scorpions of the Earth have power.

Historians refer to the Arabs as "locusts." Arabia is known for its locusts. John would have recognized the locusts as Arabs from:

Judges 6:3-5 And so it was, when Israel had sown, that the Midianites came up, and the Amalekites, and the children of the east, even they came up against them; And they encamped against them, and destroyed the increase of the Earth, till thou come unto Gaza, and left no sustenance for Israel, neither sheep, nor ox, nor ass. 5 For they came up with their cattle and their tents, and they came as grasshoppers for multitude; for both they and their camels were without number: and they entered into the land to destroy it.

Judges 7:12 And the Midianites and the Amalekites and all the children of the East lay along in the valley like grasshoppers for multitude; and their camels were without number, as the sand by the sea side for multitude.

The word grasshoppers is better translated as locusts. The Midianites and the Amalekites were Arabs.

Nahum 3:17 Thy crowned are as the locusts, and thy captains as the great grasshoppers, which camp in the hedges in the cold day, but when the sun ariseth they flee away, and their place is not known where they are.

It is interesting to note that when the sun arises, they flee, and their place is unknown. When the light of true teaching tries to reach them, they run from it.

Revelation 9:4 And it was commanded them that they should not hurt the grass of the Earth, neither any green thing, neither any tree; but only those men which have not the seal of God in their foreheads.

John knew the grass of the Earth was the progeny of the Jews, but he also knew that the Christians were "grafted into the olive tree." Therefore, the grass of the Earth would be the children of the Christians.

Locusts typically come to eat anything that is growing and green. These locusts come to hurt men.

Revelation 9:5 And to them it was given that they should not kill them, but that they should be tormented five months: and their torment was as the torment of a scorpion, when he striketh a man.

John knew that five months times 30 days equals 150 (years in prophecy).

In prophecy, a day is a year according to

Ezekiel 4:6 And when thou hast accomplished them, lie again on thy right side, and thou shalt bear the iniquity of the house of Judah forty days: I have appointed thee each day for a year.

When verse five says that men should be tormented for five months, this is 150 years.

Revelation 9:6 And in those days shall men seek death, and shall not find it; and shall desire to die, and death shall flee from them.

The torment will be such that men will want to die but cannot commit suicide. People would rather die outright than be tortured to death, or worse, tortured and then left to die a slow, painful death. But they cannot kill each other or commit suicide.

Job 7:15 So that my soul chooseth strangling, and death rather than my life.

Jeremiah 8:3 And death shall be chosen rather than life by all the residue of them that remain of this evil family, which remain in all the places whither I have driven them, saith the LORD of hosts.

Revelation 9:7 And the shapes of the locusts were like unto horses prepared unto battle; and on their heads were as it were crowns like gold, and their faces were as the faces of men.

The crowns, which are turbans, are described in:

Ezekiel 23:42 And a voice of a multitude being at ease was with her:

75

and with the men of the common sort were brought Sabeans from the wilderness, which put bracelets upon their hands, and beautiful crowns upon their heads.

Nahum 3:17 Thy crowned are as the locusts, and thy captains as the great grasshoppers, which camp in the hedges in the cold day, but when the sun ariseth they flee away, and their place is not known where they are.

Their faces, as the faces of men, mean they have beards.

Revelation 9:8 And they had hair as the hair of women, and their teeth were as the teeth of lions.

These people will have long, uncut hair—the hair of women.

Their message will spread with the teeth of lions—one either obeys that message, or one dies by the sword. Their mantra becomes, "Convert or die."

Joel 1:5-7 Awake, ye drunkards, and weep; and howl, all ye drinkers of wine, because of the new wine; for it is cut off from your mouth. For a nation is come up upon my land, strong, and without number, whose teeth are the teeth of a lion, and he hath the cheek teeth of a great lion. He hath laid my vine waste, and barked my fig tree: he hath made it clean bare, and cast it away; the branches thereof are made white.

John would have recognized the symbol of Babylon—a lion.

Revelation 9:9 And they had breastplates, as it were breastplates of iron; and the sound of their wings was as the sound of chariots of many horses running to battle.

We would recognize breastplates, "as it were breastplates of iron," as being chain mail. John would not have known about chain mail in his day. Wings is a Biblical symbol for speed.

Ezekiel 3:13 I heard also the noise of the wings of the living creatures that touched one another, and the noise of the wheels over against them, and a noise of a great rushing.

This is also foretold in Joel 2:1 – 11, and then what to do about it in Joel 2:12 – 32.

Joel 2:1-32 Blow ye the trumpet in Zion, and sound an alarm in my holy mountain: let all the inhabitants of the land tremble: for the day of the LORD cometh, for it is nigh at hand; 2) A day of darkness and of gloominess, a day of clouds and of thick darkness, as the morning spread upon the mountains: a great people and a strong; there hath not been ever the like, neither shall be any more after it, even to the years of many generations. 3) A fire devoureth before them; and behind them a flame burneth: the land is as the garden of Eden before them, and behind them a desolate wilderness; yea, and nothing shall escape them. 4) The appearance of them is as the appearance of horses; and as horsemen, so shall they run. 5)Like the noise of chariots on the tops of mountains shall they leap, like the noise of a flame of fire that devoureth the stubble, as a strong people set in battle array. 6) Before their face the people shall be much pained: all faces shall gather blackness. 7) They shall run like mighty men; they shall climb the wall like men of war; and they shall march every one on his ways, and they shall not break their ranks: 8) Neither shall one thrust another; they shall walk every one in his path: and when they fall upon the sword, they shall not be wounded. 9) They shall run to and fro in the city; they shall run upon the wall, they shall climb up upon the houses; they shall enter in at the windows like a thief. 10) The Earth shall quake before them; the Heavens shall tremble: the sun and the moon shall be dark, and the stars shall withdraw their shining: 11) And the LORD shall utter his voice before his army: for his camp is very great: for he is strong that executeth his word: for the day of the LORD is great and very terrible; and who can abide it? What to do: 12) therefore also now, saith the LORD, turn ye even to me with all your heart, and with fasting, and with weeping, and with mourning: 13) And rend your heart, and not your garments, and turn unto the LORD your God: for he is gracious and merciful, slow to anger, and of great kindness, and repenteth him of the evil. 14) Who knoweth if he will return and repent, and leave a blessing behind him; even a meat offering and a drink offering unto the LORD your God? 15) Blow the trumpet in Zion, sanctify a fast, call a solemn assembly: 16) Gather the people, sanctify the congregation, assemble the elders, gather the children, and those that suck the breasts: let the bridegroom go forth of his chamber, and the bride out of her closet. 17) Let the priests, the ministers of the LORD, weep between the porch and the altar, and let them say, Spare thy people, O LORD, and give not thine heritage to reproach, that the heathen should rule over them: wherefore should they say among the people, Where is their God? 18) Then will the LORD be jealous for his land, and pity his people. 19) Yea, the LORD will answer and say unto his people, Behold, I will send you corn, and wine, and oil, and ye shall be satisfied therewith: and I will no more make you a reproach among the heathen: 20) But I will remove far off from you the northern army, and will drive him into a land barren and desolate, with his face toward the East sea, and his hinder part toward the utmost sea, and his stink shall come up, and his ill savour shall come up, because he hath done great things. 21) Fear not, O land; be glad and rejoice: for the LORD will do great things. 22) Be not afraid, ye beasts of the field: for the pastures of the wilderness do spring, for the tree beareth her fruit, the fig tree and the vine do yield their strength. 23) Be glad then, ye children of Zion, and rejoice in the LORD your God: for he hath given you the former rain moderately, and he will cause to come down for you the rain, the former rain, and the latter rain in the first month. 24) And the floors shall be full of wheat, and the fats shall overflow with wine and oil. 25) And I will restore to you the years that the locust hath eaten, the cankerworm, and the caterpiller, and the palmerworm, my great army which I sent among you. 26) And ye shall eat in plenty, and be satisfied, and praise the name of the LORD your God, that hath dealt wondrously with you: and my people shall never be ashamed. 27) And ye shall know that I am in the midst of Israel, and that I am the LORD your God, and none else: and my people shall never be ashamed. 28) And it shall come to pass afterward, that I will pour out my spirit upon all flesh; and your sons and your daughters shall prophesy, your old men shall dream dreams, your young men shall see visions: 29) And also upon the servants and upon the handmaids in those days will I pour out my spirit. 30) And I will shew wonders in the Heavens and in the Earth, blood, and fire, and pillars of smoke. 31) The sun shall be turned into darkness, and the moon into blood, before the great and the terrible day of the LORD come. 32) And it shall come to pass, that whosoever shall call on the name of the LORD shall be delivered: for in mount Zion and in Jerusalem shall be deliverance, as the LORD hath said, and in the remnant whom the LORD shall call.

Revelation 9:10 And they had tails like unto scorpions, and there were stings in their tails: and their power was to hurt men five months.
According to Isaiah, the prophet that teaches lies is the tail
Isaiah 9:15 The ancient and honourable, he is the head; and the prophet that teacheth lies, he is the tail.
2 Chronicles 10:14 And answered them after the advice of the young men, saying, My father made your yoke heavy, but I will add thereto: my father chastised you with whips, but I will chastise you with scorpions.
God uses these "scorpions" to chastise His people. Is He getting ready to chastise us?
In this verse, we see, again, that 150 years. The opening of the abyss was the release of deceptions. Scorpions inject their venom

through their tail. John would have known that these people were teaching lies that would lead straight to hell.

Revelation 9:11 And they had a king over them, which is the Angel of the bottomless pit, whose name in the Hebrew tongue is Abaddon, but in the Greek tongue hath his name Apollyon.

Some people say the last part of this—the Angel to whom the key to the bottomless pit was given—is Christ. However, this Angel "falls from Heaven." He lost his position in Heaven and was banished, so he came to Earth. Christ had to give him the keys to the pit since he won them when he arose from the grave. So, he is free to be on Earth.

Abaddon – let us look at

Job 28:22 Destruction and death say, We have heard the fame thereof with our ears.

The word Destruction is from the Hebrew word Abaddon, meaning Hades or destruction, that is from another Hebrew word, abad (aw-bad'), meaning to wander away, that is, lose oneself. [50]

Christ came to seek and save that which was lost. However, He also recognizes that we have choices. No man can pluck us out of the Father's hand, but we can "abad" or wander away and lose ourselves.

Jews recognize Abaddon in Hebrew as a destroying Angel and the Greek's Apollyon as the Destroyer. Of course, we recognize the Destroyer as Satan. It should be noted that the Greek god of war was Apollo, and war destroys.

Revelation 9:12 One woe is past; and, behold, there come two woes more hereafter.

One woe—and there are two more. They will be even worse!

THE SIXTH TRUMPET

Revelation 9:13 And the sixth Angel sounded, and I heard a voice from the four horns of the golden altar which is before God,

Revelation 9:14 Saying to the sixth Angel which had the trumpet, Loose the four Angels which are bound in the great river Euphrates.

Revelation 9:15 And the four Angels were loosed, which were prepared for an hour, and a day, and a month, and a year, for to slay the third part of men.

Revelation 9:16 And the number of the army of the horsemen were two hundred thousand thousand: and I heard the number of them.

---

[50] Strong's Hebrew and Greek Dictionaries, Published 1890, public domain

John knew the four horns of the golden altar were in the Holy of Holies, and they were, indeed, "before God."

John would also have recognized that preparing for an hour, a day, and a month, and a year, meant 391 years and 15 days.

360 days in a year divided by 24 hours in a day equals 15 Days
A Day in prophecy is a year in our time
A month is 30 days or 30 years in prophecy
And a year is 360 days, or 360 years in prophecy
So,

$$\begin{array}{r} 360 \text{ years} \\ +\quad 30 \text{ years} \\ +\quad \underline{1 \text{ year}} \end{array}$$

391 years PLUS the 15 days.

The four Angels we see here are ministers of judgment.

The number of the horsemen: Two hundred thousand thousand has come to be interpreted as two million. However, that is not how the ancient Jewish people wrote their numbers. Two hundred thousand thousand would be written: 200,000,000. You write the first number, two hundred, put zeroes behind it to indicate "thousand," and then add more zeroes to indicate another "thousand." It becomes two hundred million. THAT is a LOT of horsemen!

Revelation 9:17 And thus I saw the horses in the vision, and them that sat on them, having breastplates of fire, and of jacinth, and brimstone: and the heads of the horses were as the heads of lions; and out of their mouths issued fire and smoke and brimstone.

Revelation 9:18 By these three was the third part of men killed, by the fire, and by the smoke, and by the brimstone, which issued out of their mouths.

Revelation 9:19 For their power is in their mouth, and in their tails: for their tails were like unto serpents, and had heads, and with them they do hurt.

This vision would have fascinated John. He probably had no idea what was going on.

Three three things killed one third of men—a third of the population. The three things were fire, smoke, and brimstone—all of which came from the horses' mouths.

Revelation 9:20 And the rest of the men which were not killed by these plagues yet repented not of the works of their hands, that they should not worship devils, and idols of gold, and silver, and brass, and stone, and of wood: which neither can see, nor hear, nor walk:

Revelation 9:21 Neither repented they of their murders, nor of their sorceries, nor of their fornication, nor of their thefts.

John knew they would be a false religion from the statement "that they should not worship devils, and idols of gold, and silver, and brass, and stone, and wood:"

How many things do we have today that are made of these materials? We do not think of them as idols. After all, they do not represent some little god we pray to or expect to run our lives. However – think about it – some things DO run our lives. They come between us and God. Will we repent?

Notice that these men in Revelation did not repent. They were still involved in idolatry.

John knew the way out of these kinds of tribulation:

Exodus 15:26 And said, If thou wilt diligently hearken to the voice of the LORD thy God, and wilt do that which is right in his sight, and wilt give ear to his commandments, and keep all his statutes, I will put none of these diseases upon thee, which I have brought upon the Egyptians: for I am the LORD that healeth thee.

John also knew the results of non-repentance from the Holy Scriptures:

Jeremiah 1:16 And I will utter my judgments against them touching all their wickedness, who have forsaken me, and have burned incense unto other gods, and worshipped the works of their own hands.

Isaiah 47:9 But these two things shall come to thee in a moment in one day, the loss of children, and widowhood: they shall come upon thee in their perfection for the multitude of thy sorceries, and for the great abundance of thine enchantments.

God will utter His judgments against those who have forsaken Him and turned to other gods and those who think they are responsible for their eternal destiny. The false religions will lose their "children" (those who worship under that religion), and they will have widowhood – they will be without their "husband." They will not be the "bride" to their god.

Interlude Between
the Sixth and Seventh Trumpets

Revelation Chapter 10

As we saw an interlude between the sixth and seventh seals, we now see an interlude between the sixth and seventh trumpets. As we saw preparation for the first advent of Christ, will we now see the preparation for the second advent of Christ? Keep reading to find out!

Revelation 10:1 And I saw another mighty Angel come down from Heaven, clothed with a cloud: and a rainbow was upon his head, and his face was as it were the sun, and his feet as pillars of fire:
There are several clues as to who this Angel is:
- "mighty Angel." He is the mightiest of Angels
- "clothed with a cloud." We cannot look upon His glory
- "rainbow upon His head." The rainbow was the covenant between God and man during the time of Noah and forever after.
- "face as it were the sun." There will be no sun nor moon in Heaven—
Revelation 21:23 And the city had no need of the sun, neither of the moon, to shine in it: for the glory of God did lighten it, and the Lamb is the light thereof.
Revelation 22:5 And there shall be no night there; and they need no candle, neither light of the sun; for the Lord God giveth them light: and they shall reign for ever and ever.
- "feet as pillars of fire."
This is Christ, God the Son. Revealed in His glory!

Revelation 10:2 And he had in his hand a little book open: and he set his right foot upon the sea, and his left foot on the Earth,
John would have recognized the little book from Ezekiel.
Ezekiel 2:9 And when I looked, behold, an hand was sent unto me; and, lo, a roll of a book was therein;
This little open book is the Book of Prophecy. Revelation is an open book—it was not sealed, as opposed to Daniel's prophecy, which was sealed until the end.

He set his right foot upon the sea and his left foot on the Earth. John would have known the sea was the Gentile nation and the Earth was men's hearts, as discussed previously. He has dominion over the land, the sea, and all creatures on it and in it. Further, He has dominion over people (the sea) and over men's hearts (the Earth). To understand that this Earth, as stated here, is men's hearts, we look to the parable of the Sower, particularly as drawn from Matthew chapter 13. The word of the Gospel is sown, and men receive it – the word "ground" in Matthew is the same Greek word as the word "Earth" in this verse in Revelation.

So, men's hearts receive the word. Some do not understand, some have hardened hearts, some are unfruitful, but some hear, understand, and bear fruit. For further explanation, please see Appendix A – Men's Hearts.

Isaiah 60:5 Then thou shalt see, and flow together, and thine heart shall fear, and be enlarged; because the abundance of the sea shall be converted unto thee, the forces of the Gentiles shall come unto thee.

So, Christ has dominion over the sea and the Earth – the Gentiles and our hearts!

Revelation 10:3 And cried with a loud voice, as when a lion roareth: and when he had cried, seven thunders uttered their voices.

John knew the lion of Judah roars:

Hosea 11:10 They shall walk after the LORD: he shall roar like a lion: when he shall roar, then the children shall tremble from the west.

I wonder if John also related this to a prophecy from 2 Esdras:

2 Esdras 11:37 And I beheld, and lo, as it were a roaring lion chased out of the wood:

2 Esdras 12:31-34 And the lion, whom thou sawest rising up out of the wood, and roaring, and speaking to the eagle, and rebuking her for her unrighteousness with all the words which thou hast heard; This is the anointed, which the Highest hath kept for them and for their wickedness unto the end: he shall reprove them, and shall upbraid them with their cruelty. For he shall set them before him alive in judgment, and shall rebuke them, and correct them. For the rest of my people shall he deliver with mercy, those that have been pressed upon my borders, and he shall make them joyful until the coming of the day of judgment, whereof I have spoken unto thee from the beginning.

This was the fourth beast of Daniel. [51]

More on this subject will be in my next book, Revelation: Where Are We?

---

[51] 2 Esdras 11:39-40,12:11

Revelation 10:4 And when the seven thunders had uttered their voices, I was about to write: and I heard a voice from Heaven saying unto me, Seal up those things which the seven thunders uttered, and write them not.

John would have understood the thunders to be judgments.

Psalm 18:13 The LORD also thundered in the Heavens, and the Highest gave his voice; hail stones and coals of fire.

John knew that Daniel's prophecies were sealed until the end of time and that this book was not sealed; however, here we see the Angel tell John to seal up the things the seven thunders uttered. These seven thunders' utterances are not to be unsealed – ever. At least not in the current time. One day, we may know—when time will be no longer. People who speculate (and even write pamphlets or books) on the seven thunders do not know what they are writing. If God sealed it, He certainly will not reveal it until He says it may be unsealed—and He did not give us a time.

Revelation 10:5 And the Angel which I saw stand upon the sea and upon the Earth lifted up his hand to Heaven,

Revelation 10:6 And sware by him that liveth for ever and ever, who created Heaven, and the things that therein are, and the Earth, and the things that therein are, and the sea, and the things which are therein, that there should be time no longer:

John recognized the raising of hands for two reasons: to worship God and praise Him and to swear an oath. Here, we read that Christ lifts His hand to the Father to make an oath, a statement of truth – and that truth is that time shall be no longer. John's thoughts would have been on Christ's return to take His children home to Heaven.

We are at the end of the 6th Trumpet, just before the 7th Trumpet sounds. This is the only place in the Bible where it states that time shall be no more. However:

Revelation 16:17 And the seventh Angel poured out his vial into the air; and there came a great voice out of the temple of Heaven, from the throne, saying, It is done.

If time is to be no more, how can we go on to the seven vials and the voice saying, "It is done"? There are two possibilities:

1. It is because time is no more for the Christians. The lost will continue to reap God's wrath.
2. The visions may overlap. The vials and trumpets may come together near the last trumpet—in that "interlude" that takes place.

John would have the answer to this. Only he knows how he saw those visions. Seeing several scenes at one time and trying to write about them logically are two different things. One of the ways John did this was to say "and" in his writings. That could indicate both going on at the same time, as opposed to saying "then" something happened, which would indicate it happened afterward.

Revelation 10:7 But in the days of the voice of the seventh Angel, when he shall begin to sound, the mystery of God should be finished, as he hath declared to his servants the prophets.

What is this mystery of God?

Romans 11:25-27 For I would not, brethren, that ye should be ignorant of this mystery, lest ye should be wise in your own conceits; that blindness in part is happened to Israel, until the fulness of the Gentiles be come in. And so all Israel shall be saved: as it is written, There shall come out of Sion the Deliverer, and shall turn away ungodliness from Jacob: For this is my covenant unto them, when I shall take away their sins.

Romans 11:31-33 Even so have these also now not believed, that through your mercy they also may obtain mercy. For God hath concluded them all in unbelief, that he might have mercy upon all. O the depth of the riches both of the wisdom and knowledge of God! how unsearchable are his judgments, and his ways past finding out!

This mystery is Jesus Saves! Why He did it, and how the shedding of His blood accomplished this is a mystery. Our blood cannot save anyone. A few units given in an emergency can help preserve a mortal body, but we cannot redeem a soul. We cannot keep someone for all eternity.

No, this mystery of God is finished. The Church's mission is to teach all nations that the Gospel of Christ is what matters.

Revelation 10:8 And the voice which I heard from Heaven spake unto me again, and said, Go and take the little book which is open in the hand of the Angel which standeth upon the sea and upon the Earth.

Revelation 10:9 And I went unto the Angel, and said unto him, Give me the little book. And he said unto me, Take it, and eat it up; and it shall make thy belly bitter, but it shall be in thy mouth sweet as honey.

Revelation 10:10 And I took the little book out of the Angel's hand, and ate it up; and it was in my mouth sweet as honey: and as soon as I had eaten it, my belly was bitter.

John would have recognized the command and the eating of the little book from Ezekiel:

Ezekiel 3:1-3, 14 Moreover he said unto me, Son of man, eat that thou findest; eat this roll, and go speak unto the house of Israel. So I opened my mouth, and he caused me to eat that roll. And he said unto me, Son of man, cause thy belly to eat, and fill thy bowels with this roll that I give thee. Then did I eat it; and it was in my mouth as honey for sweetness. . . So the spirit lifted me up, and took me away, and I went in bitterness, in the heat of my spirit; but the hand of the LORD was strong upon me.

Revelation 10:11 And he said unto me, Thou must prophesy again before many peoples, and nations, and tongues, and kings.

John was commanded to take the Book of Prophecy.

Moreover, he was warned of its effect. To be sweet in the mouth is the anticipation of speaking prophecy, but it becomes bitter when the speaker realizes what that prophecy holds. God usually had prophets go out when He needed the people to repent. The prophecy was to repent, or they would feel God's justice. No one wants to be the bearer of unwelcome news.

When God called me to teach the Book of Revelation, it all began with a question: "Father, what does the year 2012 hold for us?" (This was in 2008.)

After a few minutes of my explanation to God, He simply answered, "Study Revelation." After a few more minutes of my further explanation to God, He simply answered, "Study Revelation."

So, after agreeing, God then told me to teach it. I was all excited. I would get to teach God's word! How sweet! Then, as I studied and began to realize the importance of some of the passages and their predictions, it became bitter.

Victorinus wrote that to eat it up was to commit it to memory. [52] It at least means to study avidly and devour God's words.

So, John ate the book, and it immediately had the effect the Angel warned him of.

And John DID prophesy again before many peoples, nations, tongues, and kings. God knew that Domitian was going to die before John did and that John would be released from the Isle of Patmos so he could continue God's work. Furthermore, God knew this book of Revelation would be the prophesying again, and again, and again,

---

[52] CHURCH FATHERS: Commentary on the Apocalypse (Victorinus) - New Advent, https://www.newadvent.org/fathers/0712.htm.

throughout all the world, before many people, nations, tongues, and kings. John hoped he would be alive to read this prophecy before many people. He knew Jeremiah had been told about his book:

Jeremiah 36:6 Therefore go thou, and read in the roll, which thou hast written from my mouth, the words of the LORD in the ears of the people in the LORD'S house upon the fasting day: and also thou shalt read them in the ears of all Judah that come out of their cities.

Measuring the Temple

Revelation 11:1 - 2

Revelation 11:1 And there was given me a reed like unto a rod: and the Angel stood, saying, Rise, and measure the temple of God, and the altar, and them that worship therein.

Revelation 11:2 But the court which is without the temple leave out, and measure it not; for it is given unto the Gentiles: and the holy city shall they tread under foot forty and two months.

John knew the rod from Jeremiah:

Jeremiah 1:11-12 Moreover the word of the LORD came unto me, saying, Jeremiah, what seest thou? And I said, I see a rod of an almond tree. Then said the LORD unto me, Thou hast well seen: for I will hasten my word to perform it.

John knew from these words that the almond tree, because it was the first to bud in the Spring, was nicknamed "the hasty tree;" therefore, God told Jeremiah, "I will hasten my word." The rod represented action—God would perform what He said He would do.

The measuring rod is like the one used when Noah built the ark and Solomon built the Temple. It is used here to determine whether we have performed God's call.

Here, we (God's Temple) are to be measured to see if we are built correctly upon the Gospel.

The Church's altar is to be measured—to see if the Church took Christ as its altar and laid all upon Him.

Those who worship will be measured to see if they have a suitable relationship with God.

The court was to be left out of the measurements.

"For it is given to the Gentiles: and the holy city shall they tread under foot forty and two months." (Verse 2)

There is a lot of meat in this verse. There are over 1,260 years of history in this verse.

First, we MUST understand that a day in prophecy equals a physical year. This comes from Ezekiel 4:6: *And when thou hast accomplished them, lie again on thy right side, and thou shalt bear the iniquity of the house of Judah forty days: I have appointed thee each day for a year.*

These verses show that a year on Earth can be a day by God's reckoning. It can also be that a day on Earth can be an actual year by God's reckoning.

Now, we can look at the Court of the Gentiles.

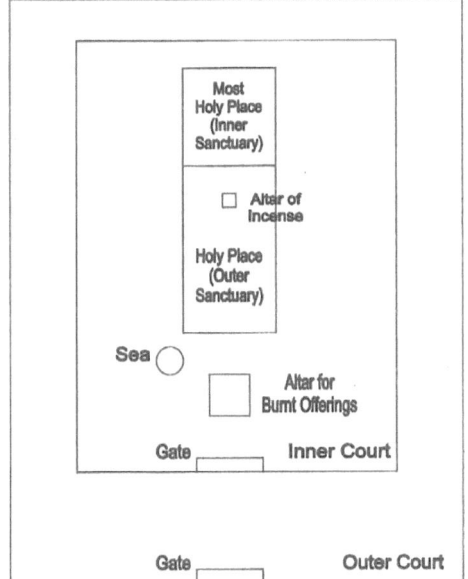

Inner Sanctuary
In His Presence—Worshippers receive anointing from God and/or hear God's voice. He gives us power from on high, we get answers to our prayers, and we receive instructions to depart as vessels for His use. Worshippers then make requests of God to receive all that we will need to carry out the instructions He has given.

Outer Sanctuary
Thanksgiving and Adoration—Worshippers review the past, reflect on the present and receive encouragement about the future. We are then moved to thank God for what He has done and adore God for who He is. We worship through prayer and praise, our incense offerings.

Inner Court
Covenant—The Word of God is read as a review of our covenant with Him. We are then convicted of breaking our covenant through sin and compelled to recommit ourselves to the covenant.
Confession and Repentance—Worshippers confess sins to God and cry out to Him for forgiveness. To repent, we lay our flesh on the altar, thus denying our sinful nature and believing that God can fill us with His Spirit. Sin is atoned for by the Blood of the sacrificed Lamb and worshippers are cleansed to bring pure incense offerings to God.

Outer Court
Preparation for Worship—The hearts and minds of worshippers are prepared for the experience God desires to have with us. He must draw our focus to Him, thereby preparing us for meaningful worship.

Here is the floor plan for the Tabernacle, drawn from the instructions in the Bible. According to the Word of God, Solomon's Temple was fashioned after this. You can read the entire description of the Temple's outside and inside in 1 Kings, Chapters 5 and 6.

The Eastern Gate in the drawing here would be on the bottom. One could walk through the Eastern Gate and into the Temple—that is how Jesus rode on Palm Sunday. Now, there is NO Court of the Gentiles on this plan. It was NOT part of the plan for Solomon's Temple.

Nevertheless, the Court of the Gentiles was built all around the outside of the Temple. Warning signs were placed everywhere on the outside balustrade, the stairway that led to the Temple, telling non-Jews not to enter the balustrades or any part of the Temple. Gentiles could ONLY be in the Court of the Gentiles.

The Two Witnesses

Revelation 11:3 - 14

Revelation 11:3 And I will give power unto my two witnesses, and they shall prophesy a thousand two hundred and threescore days, clothed in sackcloth.

The two witnesses are to prophesy for 1,260 years. A score is twenty and three of those makes sixty, a thousand, two hundred and sixty days equals 1,260 years. There is something that needs to be addressed here. The 1,260 days of the testimony of the two witnesses and the forty-two months of the trampling of the Holy City are said to have happened simultaneously. This cannot be. The reason is that John's prophecy says, "When they have finished their testimony" (not before), the beast from the Abyss will declare war, conquer and kill the witnesses." The forty-two months happen after the 1,260 days. If that is the case, when do these 1,260 years begin?

Daniel 9:27 And he shall confirm the covenant with many for one week: and in the midst of the week he shall cause the sacrifice and the oblation to cease, and for the overspreading of abominations he shall make it desolate, even until the consummation, and that determined shall be poured upon the desolate.

Here, we see that there is one set of seven, or one week, and halfway into the week, this ruler will end the sacrifices and then set up the Abomination of Desolation, which we know is ... you will have to read the book, Revelation: Where Are We? in order to find out because all this happened after John's lifetime.

Revelation 11:9 And they of the people and kindreds and tongues and nations shall see their dead bodies three days and an half, and shall not suffer their dead bodies to be put in graves.

Revelation 11:4 These are the two olive trees, and the two candlesticks standing before the God of the Earth.

Who are the two olive trees and the two candlesticks?

Romans 11:24 For if thou wert cut out of the olive tree which is wild by nature, and wert graffed contrary to nature into a good olive tree: how much more shall these, which be the natural branches, be graffed into their own olive tree?

Paul is talking about the Jews being the olive tree and the Christians being grafted into it. So, the olive trees are the Jews.

Revelation 1:20 The mystery of the seven stars which thou sawest in my right hand, and the seven golden candlesticks. The seven stars are the Angels of the seven Churches: and the seven candlesticks which thou sawest are the seven Churches.

Jesus told us that candlesticks are Churches.

Why two of each?

2 Corinthians 13:1 This is the third time I am coming to you. In the mouth of two or three witnesses shall every word be established.

It should also be noted that there are two "houses" of Judaism: the House of Judah and the House of Efraim, formerly the House of Israel. There are two major branches of Christianity: Catholics and Protestants. Two of the Jews and two of the Christians! John also knew the olive trees represented the Jewish nation:

Judges 9:8 The trees went forth on a time to anoint a king over them; and they said unto the olive tree, Reign thou over us.

Paul wrote to the Romans about the Jews being "cast away" because of their unbelief, and the Gentiles being a wild olive tree and grafted in among them:

Romans 11:15-18 For if the casting away of them be the reconciling of the world, what shall the receiving of them be, but life from the dead? For if the firstfruit be holy, the lump is also holy: and if the root be holy, so are the branches. And if some of the branches be broken off, and thou, being a wild olive tree, wert graffed in among them, and with them partakest of the root and fatness of the olive tree; Boast not against the branches. But if thou boast, thou bearest not the root, but the root thee.

So, we see that the two olive trees represent Jews. There are two houses of Judaism: the House of Judah and the House of Ephraim (formerly the House of Israel).

We also confirm that the candlesticks represent the Church—the Christians. John would not have recognized the two branches of the Church. There was only one Christian Church (The Way) in John's time.

Revelation 11:5 And if any man will hurt them, fire proceedeth out of their mouth, and devoureth their enemies: and if any man hurts them, he must be killed in this manner.

Verse 5 says that if any man hurts them, fire proceeds out of their mouths and devours their enemies, and if any man hurts them, he must be killed in this manner, that is, by the fire from their mouths.

Jeremiah 5:14 Wherefore thus saith the LORD God of hosts, Because ye speak this word, behold, I will make my words in thy mouth fire, and this people wood, and it shall devour them.

Matthew Henry wrote in his commentary on this verse: "Because you speak this word of contempt concerning the prophets, and the word in their mouths, therefore God will honor them and their words. God owns them for his words, though men denied them, and will as surely make them take effect as the fire consumes combustible material that is in its way. The Word shall be fire and the people wood. Sinners by sin make themselves fuel to that wrath of God which is revealed from Heaven against all ungodliness and unrighteousness of men in the scripture."

John would also recognize this from:

2 Samuel 22:7-21 In my distress I called upon the LORD, and cried to my God: and he did hear my voice out of his temple, and my cry did enter into his ears. 8) Then the earth shook and trembled; the foundations of heaven moved and shook, because he was wroth. 9) There went up a smoke out of his nostrils, and fire out of his mouth devoured: coals were kindled by it. 10) He bowed the heavens also, and came down; and darkness was under his feet. 11) And he rode upon a cherub, and did fly: and he was seen upon the wings of the wind. 12) And he made darkness pavilions round about him, dark waters, and thick clouds of the skies. 13) Through the brightness before him were coals of fire kindled. 14) The LORD thundered from heaven, and the most High uttered his voice. 15) And he sent out arrows, and scattered them; lightning, and discomfited them. 16) And the channels of the sea appeared, the foundations of the world were discovered, at the rebuking of the LORD, at the blast of the breath of his nostrils. 17) He sent from above, he took me; he drew me out of many waters; 18) He delivered me from my strong enemy, and from them that hated me: for they were too strong for me. 19) They prevented me in the day of my calamity: but the LORD was my stay. 20) He brought me forth also into a large place: he delivered me, because he delighted in me. 21) The LORD rewarded me according to my righteousness: according to the cleanness of my hands hath he recompensed me.

Revelation 11:6 These have power to shut Heaven, that it rain not in the days of their prophecy: and have power over waters to turn them to blood, and to smite the Earth with all plagues, as often as they will.

We have power through Christ only, not of ourselves. However, we must be holy to receive that power. We must keep the things that are written in His Book! We must bear fruit. We must stay connected in prayer. Without that, we have no power.

Here, it talks of the plagues God brought upon Pharaoh during the time of Moses.

John knew that Jesus had given power to those who follow Him:

Act 1:8 But ye shall receive power, after that the Holy Ghost is come upon you: and ye shall be witnesses unto me both in Jerusalem, and in all Judaea, and in Samaria, and unto the uttermost part of the Earth.

John 14:12 Verily, verily, I say unto you, He that believeth on me, the works that I do shall he do also; and greater works than these shall he do; because I go unto my Father.

Revelation 11:7 And when they shall have finished their testimony, the beast that ascendeth out of the bottomless pit shall make war against them, and shall overcome them, and kill them.

The time of the testimony in Jerusalem is over. The two witnesses lay dead in the streets of Jerusalem.

John 15:13 Greater love hath no man than this, that a man lay down his life for his friends.

Revelation 11:8 And their dead bodies shall lie in the street of the great city, which spiritually is called Sodom and Egypt, where also our Lord was crucified.

Revelation 11:9 And they of the people and kindreds and tongues and nations shall see their dead bodies three days and an half, and shall not suffer their dead bodies to be put in graves.

John knew Jeremiah had prophesied:

Jeremiah 9:22 Speak, Thus saith the LORD, Even the carcasses of men shall fall as dung upon the open field, and as the handful after the harvestman, and none shall gather them.

John knew the previous portions of his writing involved teaching and twisting God's Word so that it deceived people. Here, he had hope that God's word was still being taught correctly—although the false teachers would eventually overcome the true Christians. The great city, which is called Sodom and Egypt, is Jerusalem. God had destroyed Sodom (and Gomorrah), and Jesus' family was called out of Egypt. [53]

John would have recognized verse 9 as a reference to the Valley of Dry Bones in Ezekiel 37:

Ezekiel 37:1-14 The hand of the LORD was upon me, and carried me out in the spirit of the LORD, and set me down in the midst of the valley which was full of bones, 2) And caused me to pass by them round about: and, behold, there were very many in the open valley; and, lo, they were very dry. 3) And he said unto me, Son of man, can these bones live? And I answered, O Lord GOD, thou knowest. 4) Again he said unto me, Prophesy upon these bones, and say unto them, O ye dry bones, hear the

---

[53] Matthew 2:15, Hosea 11:1, Exodus 4:22

word of the LORD. 5) Thus saith the Lord GOD unto these bones; Behold, I will cause breath to enter into you, and ye shall live: 6) And I will lay sinews upon you, and will bring up flesh upon you, and cover you with skin, and put breath in you, and ye shall live; and ye shall know that I am the LORD. 7) So I prophesied as I was commanded: and as I prophesied, there was a noise, and behold a shaking, and the bones came together, bone to his bone. 8) And when I beheld, lo, the sinews and the flesh came up upon them, and the skin covered them above: but there was no breath in them. 9) Then said he unto me, Prophesy unto the wind, prophesy, son of man, and say to the wind, Thus saith the Lord GOD; Come from the four winds, O breath, and breathe upon these slain, that they may live. 10) So I prophesied as he commanded me, and the breath came into them, and they lived, and stood up upon their feet, an exceeding great army. 11) Then he said unto me, Son of man, these bones are the whole house of Israel: behold, they say, Our bones are dried, and our hope is lost: we are cut off for our parts. 12) Therefore prophesy and say unto them, Thus saith the Lord GOD; Behold, O my people, I will open your graves, and cause you to come up out of your graves, and bring you into the land of Israel. 13) And ye shall know that I am the LORD, when I have opened your graves, O my people, and brought you up out of your graves, 14) And shall put my spirit in you, and ye shall live, and I shall place you in your own land: then shall ye know that I the LORD have spoken it, and performed it, saith the LORD.

Revelation 11:10 And they that dwell upon the Earth shall rejoice over them, and make merry, and shall send gifts one to another; because these two prophets tormented them that dwelt on the Earth.

Revelation 11:11 And after three days and an half the Spirit of life from God entered into them, and they stood upon their feet; and great fear fell upon them which saw them.

Revelation 11:12 And they heard a great voice from Heaven saying unto them, Come up hither. And they ascended up to Heaven in a cloud; and their enemies beheld them.

Revelation 11:13 And the same hour was there a great Earthquake, and the tenth part of the city fell, and in the Earthquake were slain of men seven thousand: and the remnant were affrighted, and gave glory to the God of Heaven.

The Greek word translated as "Earthquake" in verse 13 is "seismos. [54] Unbelievably, the first definition listed is not Earthquake but commotion, followed by gale and then Earthquake. Since

---

[54] Strong's Hebrew and Greek Dictionaries, Published 1890, public domain

commotion is first, let us put it in the passage, and we will get a better understanding.

"At the same hour was there a great commotion, and the tenth part of the city fell, and in the commotion were slain of men seven thousand: and the remnant were affrighted, and gave glory to the God of Heaven."

This puts a whole new spin on this.

Revelation 11:14 The second woe is past; and, behold, the third woe cometh quickly.

The Seventh Trumpet

Revelation 11:15 - 19

Revelation 11:15 And the seventh Angel sounded; and there were great voices in Heaven, saying, The kingdoms of this world are become the kingdoms of our Lord, and of his Christ; and he shall reign for ever and ever.

The word translated world is the Greek word kosmos, which means an orderly arrangement and, by implication, means the entire world (globe) and the people living on it. [55]

The literal translation of this verse is: And the seventh Angel sounded; and there were great voices in Heaven, saying, The kingdom of this world has become of our Lord, and of his Christ; and he shall reign for ever and ever.

Notice the difference? Singular kingdom – not plural kingdoms. There is only one, and the kingdom of this *world* has become Christ's kingdom. They announce it from Heaven. The wrath of God is about to pour out on the seat of the beast to convert them to God. The witnesses will rise from their state of being dead.

Revelation 11:16 And the four and twenty elders, which sat before God on their seats, fell upon their faces, and worshipped God,

Revelation 11:17 Saying, We give thee thanks, O Lord God Almighty, which art, and wast, and art to come; because thou hast taken to thee thy great power, and hast reigned.

Revelation 11:18 And the nations were angry, and thy wrath is come, and the time of the dead, that they should be judged, and that thou shouldest give reward unto thy servants the prophets, and to the Saints, and them that fear thy name, small and great; and shouldest destroy them which destroy the Earth.

Revelation 11:19 And the temple of God was opened in Heaven, and there was seen in his temple the ark of his testament: and there were lightnings, and voices, and thunderings, and an Earthquake, and great hail.

The elders fall on their faces and worship God. They praise God and thank Him because He has taken all power and now reigns alone.

---

[55] Ibid.

However, those who are surrounding Israel are angry. Now, the judgment has come. God and Christ will judge the dead and reward the prophets, the Saints, and those who fear His name, both small and great men. God destroys those who are left because they destroyed the Earth—both literally, meaning this world as we know it, and because they destroyed men's hearts. They turned men away from the one true, living God to worship a false god and caused them to hate God's people.

The temple in Heaven – God and Christ are the temple. The temple was opened, and the ark of His testament was seen. This was known as the Ark of the Covenant and was kept in the Holy of Holies on Earth.

The final judgments upon the Earth and those who reject Christ and worship the beast are the lightning, voices, thundering, Earthquake, and hail.

The Woman and The Dragon

Revelation Chapter 12

Revelation 12:1 And there appeared a great wonder in Heaven; a woman clothed with the sun, and the moon under her feet, and upon her head a crown of twelve stars:

John would have recognized this woman in several ways. The first is Israel, who tried to be birthed as a nation. The crown with twelve stars would represent the Patriarchs. He might have recognized her as Mary, the mother of Jesus, who tried to bring her child, the Son of God, into this world—clothed by God and the Holy Spirit, with the twelve Patriarchs in her ancestry. He might have recognized her as The Church – called The Way in John's day. The Church clothed (covered) by God, standing upon the Word of Jesus, crowned by the twelve apostles.

There is speculation as to who the woman is. Some say she is Mary, the mother of Jesus. Moreover, they may be correct.

Some say it is Israel and goes on to try to birth the nation. They may be correct.

Some say it is Israel trying to come back as a nation. They may be correct.

Some say it is the Church trying to be birthed. They may be correct.

The problem is, there is Scripture that can be quoted to back up all of this. Jesus rules with an iron rod and is caught up to God's throne. He was born of Mary, in Israel. We could argue all day, and nothing I can say will change anyone's mind about who this woman is. Everyone is convinced they are right and everyone else is wrong.

For the few of you who do not know, I can only offer that history repeats itself. The prophecy about the virgin in the pagan temple having a child called Emmanuel is repeated about the virgin Mary having a child called Jesus.

We do not know what John thought of this image. He does not interject his own thoughts, but is faithful to God and Jesus, as we all should be.

Revelation 12:2 And she being with child cried, travailing in birth, and pained to be delivered.

Three times the woman travails in John's time:

1. Trying to birth Israel to start with. In Genesis 11:31, God had sent Abram's father, Terah, along with Abram, and Lot, the son of Haran, and Sarai, Abram's wife (from Ur of the Chaldees) to Canaan to live. [56] But, they stopped short in Haran and lived there. God had to wait and tell Abram to go to Canaan. He changed his name to Abraham, Sarai's name to Sarah, etc. Satan had dispersed the Jewish people several times from Israel. Satan thought he had won in 722 B.C. when Israel fell to the Neo-Assyrian Empire, again in 586 B.C. when Nebuchadnezzar destroyed Solomon's Temple; again in 70 A.D. when the Roman army destroyed Israel, Jerusalem, and Herod's temple, and killed over two million people in Jerusalem alone.

2. The birth of Christ. Christ, who rules with a rod of iron. Christ, whom Satan chased into Egypt. Christ, whom Satan thought he had defeated at the cross.

3. The Church – Can you imagine starting a Church with twelve members? By the time Acts 2:41 rolls around, three thousand souls were baptized.

One of those explanations ought to satisfy some – and they can say the other two are wrong. As I said, we each have an opinion. We will find out one day:

1 Corinthians 13:12 For now we see through a glass, darkly; but then face to face: now I know in part; but then shall I know even as also I am known.

A couple of interesting verses in Isaiah, which John would have known:

Isaiah 13:8 And they shall be afraid: pangs and sorrows shall take hold of them; they shall be in pain as a woman that travaileth: they shall be amazed one at another; their faces shall be as flames.

Isaiah 13:9 Behold, the day of the LORD cometh, cruel both with wrath and fierce anger, to lay the land desolate: and he shall destroy the sinners thereof out of it.

These verses are fascinating because Revelation is about revealing Jesus Christ and how he will destroy the sinners of this world. John most likely recognized her as the Church. Perhaps he recognized her as all those images. Personally, I believe that this is the Church. I think

---

[56] Genesis 11:26, 31

that Revelation chapters 12 through 14 overlay at least the seven trumpets.

The clues I base this on are:

*Revelation 12:1 **And** there appeared*... (emphasis mine)

1. Usually, John wrote, "After this . . . "(Revelation 4:1), "And after these things . . ." (Revelation 7:1), and, "After this . . ." (Revelation 7:9). Here, John simply says, "And there appeared . . ." John did this, indicating more than one image appeared at the same time

2. The seventh trumpet sounds in Revelation 11:15: And the seventh Angel sounded; and there were great voices in Heaven, saying, *The kingdoms of this world are become the kingdoms of our Lord, and of his Christ; and he shall reign for ever and ever.*

Also, Chapter 14 ends with the reaping of the Earth. The rapture, or reaping of the Christians, takes place at the sound of the seventh trumpet. This is gleaned from 1 Corinthians 15:52: *In a moment, in the twinkling of an eye, at the last trump: for the trumpet shall sound, and the dead shall be raised incorruptible, and we shall be changed.*

It is also taken from 1 Thessalonians 4:16-17: *For the Lord himself shall descend from Heaven with a shout, with the voice of the archAngel, and with the trump of God: and the dead in Christ shall rise first: Then we which are alive and remain shall be caught up together with them in the clouds, to meet the Lord in the air: and so shall we ever be with the Lord.*

Revelation 12:3 And there appeared another wonder in Heaven; and behold a great red dragon, having seven heads and ten horns, and seven crowns upon his heads.

Notice this verse starts with "And...." John apparently is seeing this vision along with another.

John would have known the seven heads were seven hills; the ten horns were ten kingdoms, and only seven crowns – seven kings in those ten kingdoms. Cities of importance were built upon seven hills. Rome was the most famous of all. To begin with, John must have recognized the dragon as Rome. Rome had persecuted the Church, and John probably thought what he was being shown was to prepare the Christians for persecution. Only that did not happen. The persecution let up for John. He was released from Patmos. He went back and preached all that he was shown. Moreover, he died of old age.

Revelation 12:4 And his tail drew the third part of the stars of Heaven, and did cast them to the Earth: and the dragon stood before the woman which was ready to be delivered, for to devour her child as soon as it was born.

John recognized the stars as Angels.

Revelation 1:20 The mystery of the seven stars which thou sawest in my right hand, and the seven golden candlesticks. The seven stars are the Angels of the seven Churches: and the seven candlesticks which thou sawest are the seven Churches.

Many Angels have fallen from Heaven:

Revelation 6:13 And the stars of Heaven fell unto the Earth, even as a fig tree casteth her untimely figs, when she is shaken of a mighty wind.

Revelation 8:12 And the fourth Angel sounded, and the third part of the sun was smitten, and the third part of the moon, and the third part of the stars; so as the third part of them was darkened, and the day shone not for a third part of it, and the night likewise.

Satan was ready to devour Jesus as soon as He was born. Joseph had to flee to Egypt. Satan tempted Jesus when He was ready to start His ministry. Satan thought he won when Jesus was crucified and died.

Revelation 12:5 And she brought forth a man child, who was to rule all nations with a rod of iron: and her child was caught up unto God, and to his throne.

John would have recognized this man-child as Jesus—The Messiah—John's beloved Lord who died and is risen and ascended to Heaven.

Revelation 12:6 And the woman fled into the wilderness, where she hath a place prepared of God, that they should feed her there a thousand two hundred and threescore days.

John knew Mary did not have to flee Jerusalem until the Roman siege. It all started with an image of Caesar at the Temple steps. [57] John probably thought the Christians would be dispersed into the wilderness (away from Jerusalem) for 1,260 years before they could come back.

On the other hand, John knew they would be spreading the Gospel while they were not in Jerusalem:

Revelation 11:3 And I will give power unto my two witnesses, and they shall prophesy a thousand two hundred and threescore days, clothed in sackcloth.

Revelation 12:7 And there was war in Heaven: Michael and his Angels fought against the dragon; and the dragon fought and his Angels,

---

[57] The New Complete Works of Josephus, Translated by William Whiston, © 1999 by Kregel Publications, Jewish War, Book 2, Chapter 10.3 (194) and Chapter 10.4 (195), P742

Revelation 12:8 And prevailed not; neither was their place found any more in Heaven.

John knew this was Satan being thrown out of Heaven—at last! Satan would not have access to Heaven anymore. He and his Angels were cast out—onto the Earth:

Revelation 12:9 And the great dragon was cast out, that old serpent, called the Devil, and Satan, which deceiveth the whole world: he was cast out into the Earth, and his Angels were cast out with him.

John knew the word world was indicative of the land under control of the Roman Empire. That is where Christianity got its start. That is where the Satan would start.

Ephesians 6:12 For we wrestle not against flesh and blood, but against principalities, against powers, against the rulers of the darkness of this world, against spiritual wickedness in high places.

We do not fight a physical war but a spiritual war

Although Satan and his Angels are a great power, they do not prevail. Satan had been going back and forth to Heaven and accusing the Saints before God.

Job 1:6-7 Now there was a day when the sons of God came to present themselves before the LORD, and Satan came also among them. And the LORD said unto Satan, Whence comest thou? Then Satan answered the LORD, and said, From going to and fro in the Earth, and from walking up and down in it.

Now, Satan has been cast out of Heaven. He cannot go before God to accuse the Saints. He can only have the Saints accuse each other. That plan is working well!

Revelation 12:10 And I heard a loud voice saying in Heaven, Now is come salvation, and strength, and the kingdom of our God, and the power of his Christ: for the accuser of our brethren is cast down, which accused them before our God day and night.

Christ has won, and He is responsible for the salvation of the Church. His blood has cleansed us, and Satan cannot accuse us of our forgiven sins.

Revelation 12:11 And they overcame him by the blood of the Lamb, and by the word of their testimony; and they loved not their lives unto the death.

Even John knew that we are saved only by the blood of the Lamb. We are to give this constant testimony and be willing to lay down our lives for the One who laid down His life for us.

Revelation 12:12 Therefore rejoice, ye Heavens, and ye that dwell in them. Woe to the inhabiters of the Earth and of the sea! for the devil is come down unto you, having great wrath, because he knoweth that he hath but a short time.

Since Satan was kicked out of Heaven, he now dwells among us. He is furious, and he knows he has only a short time to persecute and torment us and bring the nations to war.

Revelation 13:7 And it was given unto him to make war with the Saints, and to overcome them: and power was given him over all kindreds, and tongues, and nations.

Revelation 12:13 And when the dragon saw that he was cast unto the Earth, he persecuted the woman which brought forth the man child.

John knew the Christians would be persecuted. That is why he was on the Isle of Patmos. John thought the persecution was going to get worse in his lifetime. He wanted to prepare the Christians for what was coming. When Domitian died, things started to get better for the Christians. The persecution John expected did not happen.

Revelation 12:14 And to the woman were given two wings of a great eagle, that she might fly into the wilderness, into her place, where she is nourished for a time, and times, and half a time, from the face of the serpent.

Job 33:14, Job 40:5, and Psalm 62:11 make this "time" once and" times" twice, only twice! Add half a time, and you get two and a half "times." Most interpret this as three and a half, but Hebrew scholars, plus the Jewish Tanach, do not support three and a half as correct. The interpretation of time and times is not in the Old Testament but in

2 Peter 3:8 But, beloved, be not ignorant of this one thing, that one day is with the Lord as a thousand years, and a thousand years as one day.

This does not look like much, but we already have the definition of a day. If we go back to the original Greek, the actual word here is Hemera, which translates as period, moment, season, year, and "time." [58]

Translators went with the most common usage, but God always gives us a translation for prophecy, we just must have ears to hear and eyes to see! Hemera is translated as time in four verses in the KJV and twelve verses in the NAS, with time being 1,000 days/years.

John recognized the prophecy from Daniel. All the Apostles had thought Jesus was coming back soon. It took them twenty to forty

---

[58] Strong's Hebrew and Greek Dictionaries, Published 1890, public domain

years to begin to think that He was not coming back "quickly", and they needed to write down all they remembered.

God gave Daniel the vision of four beasts coming out of the sea (the people of the Earth),

Daniel 7:25 And he shall speak great words against the most High, and shall wear out the Saints of the most High, and think to change times and laws: and they shall be given into his hand until a time and times and the dividing of time.

God tells Daniel about "time" and "times". Satan speaks out against God, and the Jewish people were the Saints in that day. God was telling Daniel that Satanically controlled Gentiles would rule the Jews for 2500 years! Daniel is given a second vision of "time, times, and a half" in:

Daniel 12:7 And I heard the man clothed in linen, which was upon the waters of the river, when he held up his right hand and his left hand unto Heaven, and sware by him that liveth for ever that it shall be for a time, times, and an half; and when he shall have accomplished to scatter the power of the holy people, all these things shall be finished.

Revelation 12:15 And the serpent cast out of his mouth water as a flood after the woman, that he might cause her to be carried away of the flood.

John knew the water would represent people. Satan sent people after the woman – the Jews and Christians.

Revelation 12:16 And the Earth helped the woman, and the Earth opened her mouth, and swallowed up the flood which the dragon cast out of his mouth.

John knew the Earth was men's hearts. Men's hearts were opened and helped the woman—the Church. The Earth's people listened to the Gospel and took the message to heart.

Revelation 12:17 And the dragon was wroth with the woman, and went to make war with the remnant of her seed, which keep the commandments of God, and have the testimony of Jesus Christ.

Here, John knew the Church would be at war with the dragon—Satan. John fully expected persecution to get worse in what remained of his life. It did not happen, but that does not mean it is not going to happen! God's word is true! We see it today.

The Two Beasts

Revelation Chapter 13

THE FIRST BEAST

Revelation 13:1 And I stood upon the sand of the sea, and saw a beast rise up out of the sea, having seven heads and ten horns, and upon his horns ten crowns, and upon his heads the name of blasphemy.

John knew a "beast" would arise from the sea of Gentiles. The word that is translated into "beast" in Revelation 4:6 (for the winged beasts that are before the throne of God) are more at "living creatures." The word translated into "beast" here is more at "dangerous animal." [59] So, John knew that whatever happened, this danger would arise from the sea of Gentiles.

Isaiah 60:5 Then thou shalt see, and flow together, and thine heart shall fear, and be enlarged; because the abundance of the sea shall be converted unto thee, the forces of the Gentiles shall come unto thee.

The heads represent mountains.

Revelation 17:9 And here is the mind which hath wisdom. The seven heads are seven mountains, on which the woman sitteth.

John knew that Rome sat on seven hills, and he also knew Jerusalem sat on seven hills: Scopus, Nob, the highest point of Olivet called Mount Corruption, Mount Zion between Kedron and Tyropoeon Valleys, Ophel Mount, the rock on which Fort Antonia was built, and the New Mount Zion.

Furthermore, he very well might have known that when people sought their country's capital, they looked for a place with seven hills. Many cities in John's time were built on seven hills. Just from this description, John would not have known which city it was.

The horns represent kings without power, so we would call their "kingdoms" as "provinces."

Revelation 17:12 And the ten horns which thou sawest are ten kings, which have received no kingdom as yet; but receive power as kings one hour with the beast.

The crowns represent kings and, therefore, "kingdoms." Whenever a king conquered another country, he took that country's crown for his own.

---

[59] Strong's Hebrew and Greek Dictionaries, Published 1890, public domain

2 Samuel. 12:29 And David gathered all the people together, and went to Rabbah, and fought against it, and took it.

2 Samuel 12:30 And he took their king's crown from off his head, the weight whereof was a talent of gold with the precious stones: and it was set on David's head. And he brought forth the spoil of the city in great abundance.

Blasphemy is opposition to God, and this beast is in direct opposition to God. Some think this is the pope, who is an image (pretense) of idolatry and is worshipped like a god. The city that sits on seven hills is Rome. The Catholic Church began its rise here. We can compare the beast here with the four beasts that rose out of the sea in the Book of Daniel.

HOWEVER – when we get to the next verse, Revelation 13:2, it has nothing to do with Rome.

Revelation 13:2 And the beast which I saw was like unto a leopard, and his feet were as the feet of a bear, and his mouth as the mouth of a lion: and the dragon gave him his power, and his seat, and great authority.

John knew this beast was not from Rome or the Catholic Church. He knew the lion represented Babylon, the bear represented Medo-Persia, and the Leopard represented Greece. These countries today are called Iraq, Iran, Syria, and Lebanon. As we saw in Chapter 12, the dragon is Satan, who gives him his power, seat, and great authority.

Revelation 13:3 And I saw one of his heads as it were wounded to death; and his deadly wound was healed: and all the world wondered after the beast.

John knew this beast would be watched by the entire world, for that is the meaning of this word. The whole globe's inhabitants would wonder (marvel) after the beast. So, we have seen Satan start in the Roman Empire and come to be watched by the whole world. We will see him spread his false religion into all the world, too.

"Ten horns, ten diadems, seven heads; all sported by a beast from the sea." [60] One of the heads is fatally wounded. Yet, "he" recovers! [61] Talk about disguise!

John would not have known what events would occur to bring this vision to fruition.

---

[60] www.alamongordo.com/jack-smith-prophecies Accessed 5/23/22
[61] WhenthePiecesFit.org

Revelation 13:4 And they worshipped the dragon which gave power unto the beast: and they worshipped the beast, saying, Who is like unto the beast? who is able to make war with him?

Exodus 15:11 Who is like unto thee, O LORD, among the gods? who is like thee, glorious in holiness, fearful in praises, doing wonders?

Isaiah 46:5 To whom will ye liken me, and make me equal, and compare me, that we may be like?

Notice that the beast tries to compare itself with God—who is like him (the beast) as opposed to who is like Him (God).

The prophet answered this question:

Jeremiah 10:6 Forasmuch as there is none like unto thee, O LORD; thou art great, and thy name is great in might.

John might have thought that a group of people might arise who would be engaged in Satan worship.

Revelation 13:5 And there was given unto him a mouth speaking great things and blasphemies; and power was given unto him to continue forty and two months.

Forty-two months of days, on today's calendar, equals 1,279 day/ years.

2 Thessalonians 2:3 Let no man deceive you by any means: for that day shall not come, except there come a falling away first, and that man of sin be revealed, the son of perdition;

We have yet to find out who the man of sin is – although a lot of political figures have been named, especially leaders of different countries – including our own President in different eras. There has definitely been a falling away from the Christian religion.

1 John 2:18 Little children, it is the last time: and as ye have heard that antichrist shall come, even now are there many antichrists; whereby we know that it is the last time.

Revelation 13:6 And he opened his mouth in blasphemy against God, to blaspheme his name, and his Tabernacle, and them that dwell in Heaven.

This "beast" will blaspheme God. It does not say that they will blaspheme the Holy Spirit (or Holy Ghost). They have a chance of being forgiven:

Matthew 12:31 Wherefore I say unto you, All manner of sin and blasphemy shall be forgiven unto men: but the blasphemy against the Holy Ghost shall not be forgiven unto men.

Revelation 13:7 And it was given unto him to make war with the Saints, and to overcome them: and power was given him over all kindreds, and tongues, and nations.

The beast persecutes the Jews and the Christians and declared war against the "infidels". They have a simple plan for conversion. John knew that Satan would overcome the Saints. That is scary! That is why John thought the persecution would worsen in his lifetime and wanted to prepare the Saints for what was coming.

Revelation 13:8 And all that dwell upon the Earth shall worship him, whose names are not written in the book of life of the Lamb slain from the foundation of the world.

This word translated into world is the Greek word kosmos. It is from the Greek komizo and indicates an orderly arrangement or decoration; by implication, it is the world in either a wide or a narrow sense, including the inhabitants. [62]

All non-Christians will accept the teaching of the beast. If you are not worshipping God, you are worshipping a false god (Satan).

Revelation 13:9 If any man have an ear, let him hear.

This is a consistent phrase used throughout this book. We must have ears to hear the Holy Spirit and God. We must have ears to hear what is coming.

Colossians 1:9-10 For this cause we also, since the day we heard it, do not cease to pray for you, and to desire that ye might be filled with the knowledge of his will in all wisdom and spiritual understanding; That ye might walk worthy of the Lord unto all pleasing, being fruitful in every good work, and increasing in the knowledge of God;

Revelation 13:10 He that leadeth into captivity shall go into captivity: he that killeth with the sword must be killed with the sword. Here is the patience and the faith of the Saints.

John knew Jeremiah and the prophecy concerning Babylon and Egypt:

Jeremiah 43:11 And when he cometh, he shall smite the land of Egypt, and deliver such as are for death to death; and such as are for captivity to captivity; and such as are for the sword to the sword.

This is in answer to the martyrs who are beneath the altar:

Revelation 6:9 And when he had opened the fifth seal, I saw under the altar the souls of them that were slain for the word of God, and for the testimony which they held:

---

[62] Strong's Hebrew and Greek Dictionaries, Published 1890, public domain

Revelation 6:10 And they cried with a loud voice, saying, How long, O Lord, holy and true, dost thou not judge and avenge our blood on them that dwell on the Earth?

Revelation 18:6 Reward her even as she rewarded you, and double unto her double according to her works: in the cup which she hath filled fill to her double.

This is what the final judgment will be about. The Saints must have faith it will happen and have patience. Everything happens in God's timing, not in ours.

THE SECOND BEAST

Revelation 13:11 And I beheld another beast coming up out of the Earth; and he had two horns like a lamb, and he spake as a dragon.

John knew this was another dangerous animal and it was coming out of men's hearts, because of the reference in Matthew and the parable of the Sower.

Look at how this new beast is described: It is "like a lamb". The Greek word used here for lamb is arnion, defined as "a little lambkin." [63] Arnion appears twenty-six times in Revelation, and every time except this one, arnion referred to the "lamb of God, which taketh away the sins of the world" (John 1:29); so, why did the Lord use a lamb to describe this new beast? Because of its character. This beast will appear Christ-like – it will appear to be Christian, but the two-horned beast speaks like the dragon. In other words, this beast would sound just like a Christian empire, but it, too, would be militant and strongly influenced by Satan.

This beast has two horns, meaning this empire would have two major kings or kingdoms. These kingdoms might exist at the same time – or from examples like:

Daniel 8:3 Then I lifted up mine eyes, and saw, and, behold, there stood before the river a ram which had two horns: and the two horns were high; but one was higher than the other, and the higher came up last.

and

Daniel 8:8 Therefore the he goat waxed very great: and when he was strong, the great horn was broken; and for it came up four notable ones toward the four winds of Heaven.

They could appear one after the other. How can we know who these kingdoms are? The Bible does not explicitly state who but tells when they will rule.

---

[63] Ibid.

Revelation 13:12 And he exerciseth all the power of the first beast before him, and causeth the Earth and them which dwell therein to worship the first beast, whose deadly wound was healed.

The Old English of the King James Version of the Bible is a little confusing here, but "before him" in Greek is enopion, or "in the sight of." [64] The two-horned beast will rule in the sight of, or in the presence of, the Leopard-Bear-Lion beast. [65] The Leopard, Bear, and Lion are the three major symbols of countries in the Middle East. That is the key to the identity of the Two-Horned Beast.

"In his presence" also means something else. The two-horned beast and the Leopard-Bear-Lion beast will coexist. The two-horned beast will not destroy the Leopard-Bear-Lion beast but will be given authority while the Leopard-Bear-Lion beast remains in the Holy Land. [66]

Revelation 13:13 And he doeth great wonders, so that he maketh fire come down from Heaven on the Earth in the sight of men,

I do not know what John thought of this verse. "Fire come down from Heaven" might have meant lightning – or literal fire – to John. At times, I wish John were an artist!

Revelation 13:14 And deceiveth them that dwell on the Earth by the means of those miracles which he had power to do in the sight of the beast; saying to them that dwell on the Earth, that they should make an image to the beast, which had the wound by a sword, and did live.

This second beast, this "little lambkin," will cause the people to worship the first beast, which had a head wound and lived. However, they do not just worship the beast; they make an idol (likeness) of him.

Revelation 13:15 And he had power to give life unto the image of the beast, that the image of the beast should both speak, and cause that as many as would not worship the image of the beast should be killed.

John knew this was going to be a terrible thing. This second beast makes an image of the first beast and makes people worship even the image of the first beast, by "giving life" to the image. With our electronic age, it would be so easy to have microphones to hear what people are saying in the presence of the image, then have someone respond directly to them. It would seem the image was alive. This vision would have amazed John!

---

[64] Ibid.
[65] The False Prophet, Ellis H. Skolfield, © 2001, Pages 125-126
[66] Ibid. Page 126

John knew this would be the worst of the anti-Christs.

1 John 2:18 Little children, it is the last time: and as ye have heard that antichrist shall come, even now are there many antichrists; whereby we know that it is the last time.

The second beast also causes those who will not worship the image of the first beast to die. Convert or be killed!

Revelation 13:16 And he causeth all, both small and great, rich and poor, free and bond, to receive a mark in their right hand, or in their foreheads:

John knew this would be a spiritual mark, just as the mark God put on the 144,000.

Revelation 7:3 Saying, Hurt not the Earth, neither the sea, nor the trees, till we have sealed the servants of our God in their foreheads.

The mark in their forehead may be "brain-washing" into the religion; Or memorize things for the sake of religion.

Revelation 13:17 And that no man might buy or sell, save he that had the mark, or the name of the beast, or the number of his name.

Even with all the persecution the Christians had gone through in John's lifetime, I do not believe he ever found it so that Christians could not buy or sell. Christians would never think of persecuting others to this extent. At least not true Christians. Although there was the Inquisition . . .

Revelation 13:18 Here is wisdom. Let him that hath understanding count the number of the beast: for it is the number of a man; and his number is Six hundred threescore and six.

Notice that this verse does not say that the beast IS a man; it is only the number of a man, and that number is the number 666. Numerology is still a part of life in the Middle East, and there is speculation about who this number represents. Even today, theologians speculate about WHO fits the "666" numerology equation. They try every way to spell a person's name, using the full name, the first and last name, the nickname, and anything to try to make it fit.

The Harvest

Revelation Chapter 14

Revelation 14:1 And I looked, and, lo, a Lamb stood on the mount Sion, and with him an hundred forty and four thousand, having his Father's name written in their foreheads.

John knew this Lamb was Jesus. The 144,000 who had been sealed back in Chapter 7, are with Him. God's name – YHWH – is written in their foreheads. "In" could very well mean that they **knew** God. They had a very personal relationship with Him. He was on their minds.

Revelation 14:2 And I heard a voice from Heaven, as the voice of many waters, and as the voice of a great thunder: and I heard the voice of harpers harping with their harps:

Revelation 14:3 And they sung as it were a new song before the throne, and before the four beasts, and the elders: and no man could learn that song but the hundred and forty and four thousand, which were redeemed from the Earth.

This is a singular voice. It is as loud as many waters, as loud as a great thunder, but as melodious as harps. They sing the song only the redeemed Jews can sing. No one else can truly empathize with them, and therefore, no one else can truly learn the song and the meaning and feeling that goes with it. The world's best songwriters will tell you that you must "feel" the music. You write songs from your heart. These 144,000 sing from their hearts – they sing the music and words felt in their souls.

Revelation 14:4 These are they which were not defiled with women; for they are virgins. These are they which follow the Lamb whithersoever he goeth. These were redeemed from among men, being the firstfruits unto God and to the Lamb.

This is a spiritual virginity. They were Jews who worshipped only God, and then found their Messiah, and came to know the fullness of His love and to really know the meaning of salvation and grace!

Revelation 14:5 And in their mouth was found no guile: for they are without fault before the throne of God.

The blood of Jesus covered all their sins. No deceit was found in them. Because they had their sins covered, there were no "excuses" to be given.

Revelation 14:6 And I saw another Angel fly in the midst of Heaven, having the everlasting gospel to preach unto them that dwell on the Earth, and to every nation, and kindred, and tongue, and people,

Revelation 14:7 Saying with a loud voice, Fear God, and give glory to him; for the hour of his judgment is come: and worship him that made Heaven, and Earth, and the sea, and the fountains of waters.

It is the Gospel, the good news, which saves man. Furthermore, today, this Gospel is preached in every nation and every tongue. Just as Jesus had told John and the other disciples, ". . . you will be my witnesses in Jerusalem and in all Judea and Samaria, and to the end of the Earth." [67]

God is a loving God, for He so loved the world that He gave His only begotten Son. He is an awesome God, a fearful God. He has the power to smite, to kill, and to judge. The time of that judgment has come.

Revelation 14:8 And there followed another Angel, saying, Babylon is fallen, is fallen, that great city, because she made all nations drink of the wine of the wrath of her fornication.

John knew that fornication was spiritual adultery. He also would have recognized this from Isaiah:

Isaiah 21:9 And, behold, here cometh a chariot of men, with a couple of horsemen. And he answered and said, Babylon is fallen, is fallen; and all the graven images of her gods he hath broken unto the ground.

Hippolytus wrote, c. 200 A.D., "John sees, when on the Isle of Patmos, a revelation of awe-inspiring mysteries, which he freely recounts and makes known to others. Tell me, blessed John—apostle and disciple of the Lord—what did you see and hear concerning Babylon?" [68]

This is the first time we see the Angel saying Babylon has fallen.

Revelation 14:9 And the third Angel followed them, saying with a loud voice, If any man worship the beast and his image, and receive his mark in his forehead, or in his hand,

Revelation 14:10 The same shall drink of the wine of the wrath of God, which is poured out without mixture into the cup of his indignation;

---

[67] Acts 1:8
[68] Ante-Nicene Fathers, as translated by David W. Bercot, Editor, Vol. 5, Page 211,

and he shall be tormented with fire and brimstone in the presence of the holy Angels, and in the presence of the Lamb:

Revelation 14:11 And the smoke of their torment ascendeth up for ever and ever: and they have no rest day nor night, who worship the beast and his image, and whosoever receiveth the mark of his name.

John would have recognized the cup of God's wrath from Jeremiah:

Jeremiah 51:7 Babylon hath been a golden cup in the LORD'S hand, that made all the Earth drunken: the nations have drunken of her wine; therefore the nations are mad.

Babylon was the previous seat of Baal worship. John knew this mystery Babylon would twist God's word and poison the hearts of men. This was not Babylon (the ruins of which lie in Iraq). This was not the city the Christians called "Babylon," which was the code-word for Rome. This city John would not have recognized. It is a mystery as to which one it is.

The third Angel begins his speech about what will happen to those who believe in the false religion – if they worship the beast and his image and receive his mark in their forehead or in their hand, then they drank the wine of Babylon's fornication, and now they will have to drink of the wine of the wrath of God. Fire and brimstone (hell) is their final sentence of judgment.

They will be tormented forever in hell.

They will burn without being consumed.

Revelation 14:12 Here is the patience of the Saints: here are they that keep the commandments of God, and the faith of Jesus.

If the Saints keep their faith in Jesus and the commandments, their patience will pay off. They will see justice.

Revelation 14:13 And I heard a voice from Heaven saying unto me, Write, Blessed are the dead which die in the Lord from henceforth: Yea, saith the Spirit, that they may rest from their labours; and their works do follow them.

John was instructed to write, "Blessed are the dead which die in the Lord . . ." The true Christians are blessed. They will have rest from their labors. Notice that our works will follow us to Heaven and be tried by fire.

1 Corinthians 3:13 Every man's work shall be made manifest: for the day shall declare it, because it shall be revealed by fire; and the fire shall try every man's work of what sort it is.

114

1 Corinthians 3:14 If any man's work abide which he hath built thereupon, he shall receive a reward.

1 Corinthians 3:15 If any man's work shall be burned, he shall suffer loss: but he himself shall be saved; yet so as by fire.

Revelation 14:14 And I looked, and behold a white cloud, and upon the cloud one sat like unto the Son of man, having on his head a golden crown, and in his hand a sharp sickle.

Revelation 14:15 And another Angel came out of the temple, crying with a loud voice to him that sat on the cloud, Thrust in thy sickle, and reap: for the time is come for thee to reap; for the harvest of the Earth is ripe.

Revelation 14:16 And he that sat on the cloud thrust in his sickle on the Earth; and the Earth was reaped.

This is the rapture. The Earth is reaped.

John has completed the vision through the time of the seventh trumpet, which we saw in Revelation 11:15:

Revelation 11:15 And the seventh Angel sounded; and there were great voices in Heaven, saying, The kingdoms of this world are become the kingdoms of our Lord, and of his Christ; and he shall reign for ever and ever.

Revelation 14:17 And another Angel came out of the temple which is in Heaven, he also having a sharp sickle.

Revelation 14:18 And another Angel came out from the altar, which had power over fire; and cried with a loud cry to him that had the sharp sickle, saying, Thrust in thy sharp sickle, and gather the clusters of the vine of the Earth; for her grapes are fully ripe.

Revelation 14:19 And the Angel thrust in his sickle into the Earth, and gathered the vine of the Earth, and cast it into the great winepress of the wrath of God.

Revelation 14:20 And the winepress was trodden without the city, and blood came out of the winepress, even unto the horse bridles, by the space of a thousand and six hundred furlongs.

The non-believers are then taken. While we are of the vine of Jesus, these are of the vine of the Earth. But they are not taken to Heaven. The great winepress of the wrath of God will be the battle of Armageddon. It will be outside the city of Jerusalem. Mount Zion is outside the walls of Jerusalem. In verse twenty, we see that 1,600 furlongs would equal two hundred miles. This is a lot of blood and much carnage. Theologians agree the two hundred miles represent the whole of the original Holy Land.

As the removal of the Seven Seals was the fulfillment and, therefore, the removal of the Law, the Seven Trumpets are the removal of God's Grace. He will no longer bear with man.

Romans 5:20-21 Moreover the law entered, that the offence might abound. But where sin abounded, grace did much more abound: That as sin hath reigned unto death, even so might grace reign through righteousness unto eternal life by Jesus Christ our Lord

John 16:26 At that day ye shall ask in my name: and I say not unto you, that I will pray the Father for you:

The Wrath

Revelation Chapters 15 – 16

God is the same yesterday, today, and forever—He will save His people from the wrath. We must go through the Tribulation—as seen in this Book. From this point forward, the saved Christians (born again) are about to be harvested. God will call for the ones who are left to repent.

Revelation 15:1 And I saw another sign in Heaven, great and marvellous, seven Angels having the seven last plagues; for in them is filled up the wrath of God.

Seven, of course, is God's number, the perfect number. Moreover, Jesus was perfect. The Angels are going to finish pouring out God's wrath on Babylon and the anti-Christ. BUT ... there is that word "And" again. Was John seeing the wrath vials (or bowls) poured out simultaneously as the trumpets sounded? It is highly possible.

Revelation 15:2 And I saw as it were a sea of glass mingled with fire: and them that had gotten the victory over the beast, and over his image, and over his mark, and over the number of his name, stand on the sea of glass, having the harps of God.

Contrast this with:

Revelation 14:1-5: 1) And I looked, and, lo, a Lamb stood on the mount Sion, and with him an hundred forty and four thousand, having his Father's name written in their foreheads. 2) And I heard a voice from Heaven, as the voice of many waters, and as the voice of a great thunder: and I heard the voice of harpers harping with their harps: 3) And they sung as it were a new song before the throne, and before the four beasts, and the elders: and no man could learn that song but the hundred and forty and four thousand, which were redeemed from the Earth. 4) These are they which were not defiled with women; for they are virgins. These are they which follow the Lamb whithersoever he goeth. These were redeemed from among men, being the firstfruits unto God and to the Lamb. 5) And in their mouth was found no guile: for they are without fault before the throne of God.

117

John would have recognized the verses from Chapter 14 as the Jews who converted to Christianity. In contrast, the people mentioned here in Chapter 15 are the ones who believed in the beast and then converted to Christianity.

The "Sea of Glass" John would have seen the "sea" that was outside the temple, as described in 1 Kings 7:23-39.

Revelation 15:3 And they sing the song of Moses the servant of God, and the song of the Lamb, saying, Great and marvellous are thy works, Lord God Almighty; just and true are thy ways, thou King of Saints.

Revelation 15:4 Who shall not fear thee, O Lord, and glorify thy name? for thou only art holy: for all nations shall come and worship before thee; for thy judgments are made manifest.

Revelation 4:6 mentions the sea of glass being before the throne of God. Fire illuminates. Those who had obtained victory over the beast, being converted from this false religion to Christianity, were illuminated with the truth. They now stand on the glassy sea before the throne of God.

Two songs of Moses are mentioned in the Holy Scriptures or Old Testament.

One in Exodus 15:1-9, and then in Deuteronomy 31:19- 32:44, which God gave him to write. You can read both in Appendix B.

Revelation 15:5 And after that I looked, and, behold, the temple of the Tabernacle of the testimony in Heaven was opened:

In Exodus 30:36, God tells Moses to put perfume before the testimony in the Tabernacle of the congregation, where He would meet with Moses. The tablets of the law are called the testimony. In that Tabernacle was the ark of the testimony, placed in the Holy of Holies. In Heaven is seen the ark of His Testament. This is the Holy of Holies. This is where the High Priest (Jesus) intercedes for the people, and God communes with His people.

Revelation 15:6 And the seven Angels came out of the temple, having the seven plagues, clothed in pure and white linen, and having their breasts girded with golden girdles.

In Revelation 1:13, we saw the Son of Man in a garment down to his feet and having a golden girdle. So, these Angels are similarly clothed. This was the high priest's clothing when he entered the Holy of Holies. This shows the Angels were acting in accordance with God's direction. They are acting as the High Priests.

118

Revelation 15:7 And one of the four beasts gave unto the seven Angels seven golden vials full of the wrath of God, who liveth for ever and ever.

Revelation 15:8 And the temple was filled with smoke from the glory of God, and from his power; and no man was able to enter into the temple, till the seven plagues of the seven Angels were fulfilled.

The Angels received from one of the four beasts that we saw before the throne, the wrath of God, divided into seven parts, which is the perfect number, to be poured out upon the anti-Christian people in answer to the martyrs' prayers. Seven, the perfect number, reveals Jesus, who was, is, and will always be perfect.

During the exodus, when God descended upon Mount Sinai, the smoke descended with Him, and no one could enter the Tabernacle. No one can enter the temple until after the seven plagues are over.

Revelation 16:1 And I heard a great voice out of the temple saying to the seven Angels, Go your ways, and pour out the vials of the wrath of God upon the Earth.

The seven vials in this chapter have often been compared to the seven seals and to the seven trumpets, especially the trumpets. One form of interpretation has been to view the vials as merely an enlargement on the trumpet judgments corresponding to them. [69] There is undoubtedly a similarity between the trumpet judgments and the judgments of the pouring out of the vials of the wrath of God.

In both the trumpets and the vials, the first deals with the Earth, [70] the second with the sea, [71] the third with rivers and fountains of water, [72] the fourth with the sun, [73] the fifth with darkness, [74] the sixth with the Euphrates River, [75] and the seventh with lightning, thunder, and a great Earthquake. [76] A careful study of the seven vials as compared to the seven trumpets will reveal differences. The first four trumpet judgments deal only with one-third of the Earth, while the vial judgments are global. [77]

---

[69] https://bible.org/seriespage/16-vials-wrath-god#:~:text=One%20form%20of%20 interpretation%20has%20been%20to%20view,of%20the%20vials%20of%20the%20wrath%20 of%20God.

[70] Revelation 8:7, 16:2

[71] Revelation 8:8, 16:3

[72] Revelation 8:10, 16:4

[73] Revelation 8:12, 16:8

[74] Revelation 9:1-2, 16:10

[75] Revelation 9:14, 16:12

[76] Revelation 11:19, 16:18

[77] bible.org/seriespage/16-vials-wrath-god

THE FIRST VIAL OF WRATH

Revelation 16:2 And the first went, and poured out his vial upon the Earth; and there fell a noisome and grievous sore upon the men which had the mark of the beast, and upon them which worshipped his image.

With the pouring [78] out of the first vial, a terrible judgment falls upon men with the mark of the beast. This is the Leopard-Bear-Lion beast. There is a notable contrast between the first vial and the first trumpet: the first trumpet (Revelation 8:7) burns up a third part of the trees and all the green grass.

Here, the judgment is specifically upon men and is directed to a particular group of men (humans), namely, the beast worshipers who have received the beast's mark. The judgment is described as a sore or ulcer (Gr., *helkos*), [79] which is terrible (Gr., *kakos*), [80] and evil or malignant (Gr., *poneros*). [81] It is a "noisome" sore. This Greek word, *kakos*, which here has been translated as *noisome*, [82] which means worthless, injurious, bad, evil, wicked. Almost everyone seems to comply with the demand that all men worship the beast and receive his mark. The vial judgment, therefore, follows this edict.

The warning in Revelation 14:9-11 is now reinforced in a preliminary judgment that anticipates the ultimate doom of the beast worshipers. [83] Everything that can be used by the anti-Christ is set for destruction. The people had marked themselves by their sins; now, God marked them by His judgment.

John knew this could be avoided:

Exodus 15:26 And said, If thou wilt diligently hearken to the voice of the LORD thy God, and wilt do that which is right in his sight, and wilt give ear to his commandments, and keep all his statutes, I will put none of these diseases upon thee, which I have brought upon the Egyptians: for I am the LORD that healeth thee.

THE SECOND VIAL OF WRATH

Revelation 16:3 And the second Angel poured out his vial upon the sea; and it became as the blood of a dead man: and every living soul died in the sea.

God knew the deadly poison that was given to the sea of people by the false religion—it was setting men's souls for judgment in the lake

---

[78] Ibid.
[79] Strong's Hebrew and Greek Dictionaries, Published in 1890; public domain
[80] Ibid.
[81] Ibid.
[82] Ibid.
[83] bible.org/seriespage/16-vials-wrath-god

of fire and brimstone because of the pretense of salvation it offered. John knew God's judgment would "congeal" (as the blood of a dead man does) and that every soul of the nation of Gentiles would end up with the second death.

If only they would listen:

Exodus 15:26 And said, If thou wilt diligently hearken to the voice of the LORD thy God, and wilt do that which is right in his sight, and wilt give ear to his commandments, and keep all his statutes, I will put none of these diseases upon thee, which I have brought upon the Egyptians: for I am the LORD that healeth thee.

THE THIRD VIAL OF WRATH

Revelation 16:4 And the third Angel poured out his vial upon the rivers and fountains of waters; and they became blood.

Revelation 16:5 And I heard the Angel of the waters say, Thou art righteous, O Lord, which art, and wast, and shalt be, because thou hast judged thus.

Revelation 16:6 For they have shed the blood of Saints and prophets, and thou hast given them blood to drink; for they are worthy.

Revelation 16:7 And I heard another out of the altar say, Even so, Lord God Almighty, true and righteous are thy judgments.

John knew that God and Jesus are the Lord which art, and wast, and shalt be:

Revelation 11:17 Saying, We give thee thanks, O Lord God Almighty, which art, and wast, and art to come; because thou hast taken to thee thy great power, and hast reigned.

As we saw in the judgments by the Trumpets upon the Christian people, the people who worship the beast also have their poisoned water, which is the giving of the twisted Word. Just as the waters of the Nile became blood, here we see the same thing happening worldwide. The physical affliction stems from spiritual apostasy.[84]

John then hears "the Angel of the waters" deliver a justification of God for this judgment. The Angel may be a holy being who has some authority over water. There seems to be a variety of ministries assigned to Angels. The Angel declares that because men have shed the blood of Saints and prophets, God is righteous in giving them blood to drink. Blood is red, and there is a red wine that would have been common in Jesus' day. A cup of blood-red wine is served as God's wrath.

Revelation 14:8 And there followed another Angel, saying, Babylon is fallen, is fallen, that great city, because she made all nations drink of the wine of the wrath of her fornication.

---

[84] bible.org/seriespage/16-vials-wrath-god

Revelation 14:10 The same shall drink of the wine of the wrath of God, which is poured out without mixture into the cup of his indignation; and he shall be tormented with fire and brimstone in the presence of the holy Angels, and in the presence of the Lamb:

Just as the Saints are worthy of rest and reward, so the wicked are worthy of divine judgment.

THE FOURTH VIAL OF WRATH

Revelation 16:8 And the fourth Angel poured out his vial upon the sun; and power was given unto him to scorch men with fire.

Revelation 16:9 And men were scorched with great heat, and blasphemed the name of God, which hath power over these plagues: and they repented not to give him glory.

John would have known the sun was a ruler. Fire is another form of the judgment of God. Fire also illuminates. This ruler scorches men with fire—he teaches them in a way that leads them to hell and burns them for eternity. In reality, the time and place where we live, I have noticed the sun getting hotter. I cannot spend as much time in the sun without feeling that heat, and it burns! There is a spiritual connotation to God's word and a reality to God's word.

Genesis 19:24 Then the LORD rained upon Sodom and upon Gomorrah brimstone and fire from the LORD out of Heaven;

THE FIFTH VIAL OF WRATH

Revelation 16:10 And the fifth Angel poured out his vial upon the seat of the beast; and his kingdom was full of darkness; and they gnawed their tongues for pain,

Revelation 16:11 And blasphemed the God of Heaven because of their pains and their sores, and repented not of their deeds.

The fifth vial is directed to the throne of the beast. The result of the judgment is darkness and pain. "The seat of the beast" is more accurately "the throne of the beast" [85] (Gr., *thronos*). [86] Some theologians say the beast is probably the first beast of Revelation 13. Satan had handed off his power to the Leopard-Bear-Lion. As in the fifth trumpet and in the ninth plague of Egypt (Exodus 10:21-23), there is darkness over the Earth, meaning there is no preaching or teaching of God's word—Spiritual darkness. Then, this is only part of the divine judgment.

---

[85] Ibid.
[86] Strong's Hebrew and Greek Dictionaries; Published in 1890; public domain

Now, the teaching of the beast is stopped. His kingdom is dark.

As in both trumpet and vial judgments, there is also pain and torment. The wicked, in their suffering, are declared to gnaw their tongues for pain, a description of severe agony. [87]

John would have known the verse from Isaiah:

Isaiah 1:6 From the sole of the foot even unto the head there is no soundness in it; but wounds, and bruises, and putrifying sores: they have not been closed, neither bound up, neither mollified with ointment.

"Again, we have the sad note that they blasphemed God as the author of these judgments and did not repent of their deeds." [88]

Though they are declared once more in verse twenty-one to have blasphemed God, this is the last opportunity to repent. [89] The Scriptures plainly refute the notion that evil people will repent when faced with judgment. In fact, they seem to "double down" on their intentions.

THE SIXTH VIAL OF WRATH

Revelation 16:12 And the sixth Angel poured out his vial upon the great river Euphrates; and the water thereof was dried up, that the way of the kings of the East might be prepared.

Revelation 16:13 And I saw three unclean spirits like frogs come out of the mouth of the dragon, and out of the mouth of the beast, and out of the mouth of the false prophet.

Revelation 16:14 For they are the spirits of devils, working miracles, which go forth unto the kings of the Earth and of the whole world, to gather them to the battle of that great day of God Almighty.

Revelation 16:15 Behold, I come as a thief. Blessed is he that watcheth, and keepeth his garments, lest he walk naked, and they see his shame.

Revelation 16:16 And he gathered them together into a place called in the Hebrew tongue Armageddon.

In verse fourteen, the word translated *world* means specifically the land of the Roman Empire. So, this battle takes place in the Middle East.

John knew the Euphrates River had been dried up once in the Holy Scriptures (Old Testament). The city of Babylon was built over part of the river. The king's enemies, while the king was secure in the city and celebrating by drinking, diverted the river, walked in under the wall of the city, and conquered it.

---

[87] bible.org/seriespage/16-vials-wrath-god
[88] Ibid.
[89] Ibid.

In verse thirteen, the three unclean spirits are "like frogs." The word translated *like* is the Greek word *homoios*, [90] which means similar in character. In researching the *character* of a frog, I found some interesting things:

1. A frog likes to be near water—and in prophecy, water is people.
2. They do not have to chase their food. They sit in one place and, with their long tongue, reach out and snatch their food out of the air around them, devouring any insect which gets too close. This would relate to this religion, which has a long tongue with which to talk and deceive people. They tell people what they want to hear. This religion preys on people's greed and self-centeredness. It will begin to incite them to violence.

These spirits, with the characteristics of frogs, are to *gather the world to the battle of that great day of God Almighty.* This is Satan:

Revelation 20:7 And when the thousand years are expired, Satan shall be loosed out of his prison,

Revelation 20:8 And shall go out to deceive the nations which are in the four quarters of the Earth, Gog and Magog, to gather them together to battle: the number of whom is as the sand of the sea.

The sixth vial has caused more commentary than any of the preceding vials, and numerous interpretations have been offered. As the sixth vial is poured out, its objective is the great Euphrates River. [91] As the result of judgment, the water of the river is dried up, and the way of the kings of the East is prepared. The most natural explanation is the best, namely, that this is the judgment that dries up the great Euphrates River, thereby preparing for an invasion from the East. [92]

The river Euphrates here called "the great" is one of the prominent rivers of the world and forms the eastern boundary of the ancient Roman Empire as well as the prophesied eastern boundary of the land which God promised to the seed of Abraham. In Genesis 15:18, Deuteronomy 1:7, and Joshua 1:4, it is called "the great river Euphrates" as it is here. These references unmistakably establish the geographic usage in this passage. In Isaiah 11:15 and Zechariah 10:11, there is a similar prediction concerning the drying up of the Euphrates River, though the name of the river is not mentioned.

From what follows with this same vial, we learn that the kings of the entire Earth—not just the area of the Roman Empire—are about

---

[90] Strong's Hebrew and Greek Dictionaries, Published 1890, public domain
[91] Bible.org/seriespage/16-vials-wrath-god
[92] Ibid.

to be gathered for the great battle against God, in which He shall be victorious, and they shall utterly perish. The time has now come for this gathering, and by the drying up of the Euphrates, the way of those kings coming to it from the East is ready. [93]

We also see that these verses indicate the coming of Christ:

Revelation 16:15 Behold, I come as a thief. Blessed is he that watcheth, and keepeth his garments, lest he walk naked, and they see his shame.

John knew that Christ came at the end of the Seven Seals. That first time, He came as a baby in a manger, grew to manhood, and died for our sins, to be resurrected to sit at the Father's right hand.

John knew Christ would have His second appearance – and it will take place at the sound of the Last Trumpet, in our time. At this point in Revelation, that event has already taken place.

Now, here we see Christ coming for the Seventh Vial. This statement by Christ is at the end of the Sixth Vial, just before Armageddon. Just before the pouring out of the Seventh Vial. Christ has given people a final chance to come to Him through the judgments He has poured out upon humanity. If there are any at that point in time, He returns for them. Then, Armageddon occurs.

THE SEVENTH VIAL OF WRATH

Revelation 16:17 And the seventh Angel poured out his vial into the air; and there came a great voice out of the temple of Heaven, from the throne, saying, It is done.

The vial of the seventh Angel is poured out into the air, and the resulting action is catastrophic. [94] It is done, and then a great voice from the Temple in Heaven and the throne states in emphatic terms, "It is done!" In Greek, the statement is one word, *gegonen*, in the perfect tense, indicating action accomplished. [95]

Satan, as the prince of the power of the air, has been cast down from Heaven. The fact that Satan has been cast out of the third Heaven, however, does not mean that he still does not have great power in the atmospheric Heavens that we see here. It is also apparent in our modern day that the control of the air and space has become increasingly important in military matters. Undoubtedly, air and space travel will increase rather than decrease as the end of the age comes upon the world. The seventh vial poured out in the air,

---

[93] Ibid.
[94] Ibid.
[95] Strong's Hebrew and Greek Dictionaries, Published 1890, public domain

has its principal resulting action on the Earth, as the following verses indicate. The solemn accompaniment of the affirmation "It is done" by the great voice from the Temple in Heaven and from the throne is a most ominous introduction to this final judgment. [96] Another thought that occurred to me is that "electro-magnetic bursts (or pulses)" (EMBs / EMPs) are possible. The burst of energy kills engines. If planes are flying, the engines can die and cause the planes to crash, killing everyone on board. I have had my vehicle and my cell phone affected by EMBs. Luckily, I was not driving when the EMB affected my car.

THE CITY DIVIDED INTO THREE PARTS

Revelation 16:18 And there were voices, and thunders, and lightnings; and there was a great Earthquake, such as was not since men were upon the Earth, so mighty an Earthquake, and so great.

Revelation 16:19 And the great city was divided into three parts, and the cities of the nations fell: and great Babylon came in remembrance before God, to give unto her the cup of the wine of the fierceness of his wrath.

Verse 19 declares that "the great city" is split into "three parts" and that the other cities of the Gentile world fall. The question about the great city has been raised since Babylon is mentioned later in the verse. [97] Some have used both references to indicate Babylon, and others have identified Jerusalem as the first great city in the verse. In Verse 11:8, Jerusalem is referred to as "the great city, which spiritually is called Sodom and Egypt, where also our Lord was crucified."

More than that, if we go back to Jeremiah 25, we find that God gave Jeremiah a wine cup of fury to give to the nations to whom God sent Jeremiah, to make them a desolation, an astonishment, a hissing, and a curse, and one of the places God sent him was to Jerusalem.

Revelation 16:20 And every island fled away, and the mountains were not found.

John knew that the mountains would have been religions, and the islands would have been different sects of those religions. Not only is God not worshipped in the Jewish or Christian religions, but neither is Allah worshipped by Muslims. (John would not have known about Muslims.) Furthermore, Satan is not worshipped in covens. No god of any kind is worshipped. There is no faith on Earth.

---

[96] bible.org/seriespage/16-vials-wrath-god
[97] Ibid.

Luke 18:8 I tell you that he will avenge them speedily. Nevertheless when the Son of man cometh, shall he find faith on the Earth?

The construction of this sentence in Greek requires a negative answer. There will be no faith on the Earth. No religions. No religious persons.

Revelation 16:21 And there fell upon men a great hail out of Heaven, every stone about the weight of a talent: and men blasphemed God because of the plague of the hail; for the plague thereof was exceeding great.

Though the talent in different periods of history varied in weight, the reference here is to the talent weighing about a thousand pounds. [98] In the destruction of Jerusalem in 70 A.D., Josephus wrote of stones being hurled by the Roman "machines"—catapults—weighing a talent, which, at that point in time, was about 1,000 pounds—a half of a ton. [99] The Scriptural reference was also to hail the size of a talent. It should also be noted that the smallest tactical nuclear weapons are several kilos-sized bombs with the capacity to destroy a city block. [100]

Such a hail from Heaven falling upon men would have a devastating effect and destroy much still left standing by the Earthquake. It is a judgment compared to the destruction of Sodom and Gomorrah but extends over the entire Earth.

There is no repentance. But more than that, the people that are left go in the opposite direction—they blaspheme God.

Though, from the contemporary point of view, all the details of these dramatic judgments are not immediately understood, the unmistakable impression of the Scriptures is that the entire world is being brought to judgment before Christ as King of kings and Lord of lords. The nature of humans is such that they will reject the sovereignty of God in the face of such overwhelming evidence and confirms that even the lake of fire will not produce repentance on the part of those who have hardened their hearts against the grace of God.

There will be many souls in hell. More than in Heaven. How will hell hold all those souls?

Isaiah 5:14 Therefore hell hath enlarged herself, and opened her mouth without measure: and their glory, and their multitude, and their pomp, and he that rejoiceth, shall descend into it.

---

[98] Ibid.

[99] The New Complete Works of Josephus Translated by William Whiston, © 1999 by Kregel Publications, The Jewish War, Book 3, Chapter 7.9, P785. Also See Revelation 8:7

[100] https://www.rottenibrary.net/library/crime/terrorism/terror-tactics/suitcase-nukes/

The Judgement Of The Whore

Revelation Chapters 17 – 19:10

Revelation 17:1 And there came one of the seven Angels which had the seven vials, and talked with me, saying unto me, Come hither; I will shew unto thee the judgment of the great whore that sitteth upon many waters:

As we go through these verses, it is necessary to keep in mind that they are about the *judgment* of the whore. And who is this great whore? Verse 18 says:

Revelation 17:18 And the woman which thou sawest is that great city, which reigneth over the kings of the Earth.

That she sits upon many waters is, in the prophetic, people.

Revelation 17:15 And he saith unto me, The waters which thou sawest, where the whore sitteth, are peoples, and multitudes, and nations, and tongues.

John would also have recognized this as a reference to:

Jeremiah 51:12-13 Set up the standard upon the walls of Babylon, make the watch strong, set up the watchmen, prepare the ambushes: for the LORD hath both devised and done that which he spake against the inhabitants of Babylon. O thou that dwellest upon many waters, abundant in treasures, thine end is come, and the measure of thy covetousness.

The many waters (the rivers of Babylon, including the mighty Euphrates, and a significant system of irrigation canals) were proverbial. [101]

Revelation 17:2 With whom the kings of the Earth have committed fornication, and the inhabitants of the Earth have been made drunk with the wine of her fornication.

John knew this is spiritual fornication. The word translated "Earth" means the whole globe. [102] This religion has spread throughout the world. And it worships a false god.

---

[101] Archaeological Study Bible, ©1973, '78, '84, by International Bible Society, Zondervan, Pg. 1287

[102] Strong's Hebrew and Greek Dictionaries, Published 1890, Public Domain

Revelation 17:3 So he carried me away in the spirit into the wilderness: and I saw a woman sit upon a scarlet coloured beast, full of names of blasphemy, having seven heads and ten horns.

The seven heads of the beast are seven mountains on which the woman sits, according to Verse 9:

Revelation 17:9 And here is the mind which hath wisdom. The seven heads are seven mountains, on which the woman sitteth.

There are sixty-one cities which were built upon seven hills each. Out of those sixty-one cities, there are only six which are in the Middle East or controlled the Middle East:

Amman, Jordan, which has now expanded to cover nineteen hills

Istanbul, Turkey

Jerusalem, Israel

Mecca, Saudi Arabia

Tehran, Iran

Rome, Italy, which is not in the Middle East, but which ruled that area, including Turkey, Israel, Jordan, and the Tigris and Euphrates river basins in Iraq and Iran, but not the entire countries, in John's time. John would have thought this was Rome.

Revelation 17:10 And there are seven kings: five are fallen, and one is, and the other is not yet come; and when he cometh, he must continue a short space.

Revelation 17:11 And the beast that was, and is not, even he is the eighth, and is of the seven, and goeth into perdition.

In John's time, and shortly thereafter, there had been the following rulers/dynasties over Israel:

1. Assyria (722 - 586 B.C.)
2. Babylon (586 - 536 B.C.)
3. Medo-Persian empire (536 - 332 B.C.)
4. Greeks (332 - 166 B.C.)
5. Seleucids (142 - 129 B.C.) aka the Hasmonean Dynasty

Jewish rule again

Roman Empire (63 B.C. – past John's time)

Now, after John's lifetime:

John must have wondered at this. You will just have the read my next book, Revelation: Where Are We?

Revelation 17:4 And the woman was arrayed in purple and scarlet colour, and decked with gold and precious stones and pearls, having a golden cup in her hand full of abominations and filthiness of her fornication:

John knew this woman from Jeremiah, which also describes what happens to her:

Jeremiah 4:30 And when thou art spoiled, what wilt thou do? Though thou clothest thyself with crimson, though thou deckest thee with ornaments of gold, though thou rentest thy face with painting, in vain shalt thou make thyself fair; thy lovers will despise thee, they will seek thy life.

This "woman" represents a kingdom – purple was the color of kings. She is rich, represented by the gold and precious stones and pearls. But she has a cup of abominations and filthiness of her fornication – spiritual idolatry. She does not worship God. John's belief that was Rome would have been strengthened by this description. Purple is the color for royalty. Rome was the seat of Caesar. The Roman government had oppressed the Christians. Romans worshipped pagan gods, so they were committing "fornication" since they had not believed in the true God. If you are not married, then it is fornicating instead of committing adultery.

Revelation 17:5 And upon her forehead was a name written, MYSTERY, BABYLON THE GREAT, THE MOTHER OF HARLOTS AND ABOMINATIONS OF THE EARTH.

This verse says, "upon her forehead." This was not written "in her forehead," as other verses were written. This is a title. This is Mystery Babylon. It is neither Babylon itself nor Jerusalem, which was called Babylon—the mother of those who commit fornication—spiritual idolatry and abominations of the Earth.

Matthew 24:15 When ye therefore shall see the abomination of desolation, spoken of by Daniel the prophet, stand in the holy place, (whoso readeth, let him understand:)

And to clarify:

Mark 13:14 But when ye shall see the abomination of desolation, spoken of by Daniel the prophet, standing where it ought not, (let him that readeth understand,) then let them that be in Judaea flee to the mountains:

These passages from Matthew and Mark were speaking of the coming destruction of Jerusalem by the Roman army. Prophecy, like history, has a habit of repeating itself. This prophecy can also be related to a future time. When we see this abomination that causes the desolation of the soul (desolate meaning deserted, alone – without God), we are to flee from it.

130

Revelation 17:6 And I saw the woman drunken with the blood of the Saints, and with the blood of the martyrs of Jesus: and when I saw her, I wondered with great admiration.

This word, translated into admiration, means wonder. [103] That is much more appropriate than admiration. To rephrase the last part of this verse: "I wondered with great wonder." John was thinking hard about what this could mean. He had already gathered that this was about some country in the Middle East, not Jerusalem nor the original Babylon, which was the headquarters of some false religion that controlled the whole Earth. He had thought the Romans were going to persecute the Jews and Christians, and there was some "upstart" coming along and being worse than any previous persecutor had ever thought about being.

Revelation 17:7 And the Angel said unto me, Wherefore didst thou marvel? I will tell thee the mystery of the woman, and of the beast that carrieth her, which hath the seven heads and ten horns.

John will get some answers, but he still will not understand the full implications of what he sees and hears.

Revelation 17:8 The beast that thou sawest was, and is not; and shall ascend out of the bottomless pit, and go into perdition: and they that dwell on the Earth shall wonder, whose names were not written in the book of life from the foundation of the world, when they behold the beast that was, and is not, and yet is.

From the foundation of the world – the making of the whole globe and the inhabitants. *They that dwell on the Earth* – everybody around the world, in every nation, the whole globe.

Verse 11 says the beast that was, and is not, even he is the eighth, and is of the seven, and goeth into perdition. John would not have known who or what this false religion was all about. There has been a lot written about these verses; however, this being in the time of the judgment of the whore, which is after the whole of the seven trumpets and the whole of the seven vials, these kings could not have been alive in John's time.

Revelation 17:9 And here is the mind which hath wisdom. The seven heads are seven mountains, on which the woman sitteth.

We covered the seven mountains.

---

[103] Strong's Hebrew and Greek Dictionaries, Published 1890, Public Domain

Revelation 17:10 And there are seven kings: five are fallen, and one is, and the other is not yet come; and when he cometh, he must continue a short space.

Victorinus wrote, c. 280 A.D., "The date that the Apocalypse was written must be remembered. For at that time, Caesar Domitian reigned. But before him there had been Titus (his brother), Vespasian, Otho, Vitellius, and Galba. These are the five who have fallen. One remains – Domitian – under whom the Apocalypse was written. 'The other has not yet come.' This refers to Nerva. 'And when he is come, he will be for a short time.'" Nerva did not even reign two full years. 'And the beast that you saw is of the seven.' Nero reigned before those kings. . . Now [in saying] that one of the heads was, as it were, slain to death . . . he speaks of Nero." [104]

But keep in mind that prophecy, like history, repeats itself. There is nothing new under the sun. We have seen the whole of the seven trumpets and the seven vials. These verses deal with the judgment of the whore. If we maintain that Revelation is a symbolic timeline, then these verses do not deal with anything that happened in John's or our past. All this is future for us and neither John nor we have any real idea who these people are.

Revelation 17:11 And the beast that was, and is not, even he is the eighth, and is of the seven, and goeth into perdition.

Revelation 17:12 And the ten horns which thou sawest are ten kings, which have received no kingdom as yet; but receive power as kings one hour with the beast.

Irenaeus wrote, c. 180 A.D., "In a still clearer light has John, in the Apocalypse, indicated to the Lord's disciples what will happen in the last times, and concerning the ten kings who will then arise." [105]

These ten kings, represented by the Christians, war with the Lamb. One hour is fifteen days.

Revelation 17:13 These have one mind, and shall give their power and strength unto the beast.

These kings give their power and strength to the false religion.

Revelation 17:14 These shall make war with the Lamb, and the Lamb shall overcome them: for he is Lord of lords, and King of kings: and they that are with him are called, and chosen, and faithful.

---

[104] Ante-Nicene Fathers, as translated by David W. Bercot, Editor, Vol. 7, Page 358,
[105] Ante-Nicene Fathers, as translated by David W. Bercot, Editor, Vol. 1, Page 554,

They make war with the Lamb, who overcomes them because Christ is Lord of lords and King of kings. The Lamb overcomes them, and those with Him are called, chosen, and faithful. This describes God's people – God calls us because he chose us, and we are faithful because we love Him. This speaks of spiritual warfare.

Ephesians 6:12 For we wrestle not against flesh and blood, but against principalities, against powers, against the rulers of the darkness of this world, against spiritual wickedness in high places.

Revelation 17:15 And he saith unto me, The waters which thou sawest, where the whore sitteth, are peoples, and multitudes, and nations, and tongues.

Revelation 17:16 And the ten horns which thou sawest upon the beast, these shall hate the whore, and shall make her desolate and naked, and shall eat her flesh, and burn her with fire.

Do not forget that the woman is a city. The ten kings will destroy the city. The city will be burned and made desolate one last time because God will ensure His will is done.

Obadiah 1:18 And the house of Jacob shall be a fire, and the house of Joseph a flame, and the house of Esau for stubble, and they shall kindle in them, and devour them; and there shall not be any remaining of the house of Esau; for the LORD hath spoken it.

Jeremiah had written in Lamentations:

Lamentations 1:2 She weepeth sore in the night, and her tears are on her cheeks: among all her lovers she hath none to comfort her: all her friends have dealt treacherously with her, they are become her enemies.

The passage in Lamentations referred to Jerusalem in Judah. Or, it could relate to the Great Whore–a whore has many lovers. These ten kingdoms will hate the whore and make her desolate. They will deal treacherously with her and burn her with fire. They are, indeed, her enemies.

Revelation 17:17 For God hath put in their hearts to fulfil his will, and to agree, and give their kingdom unto the beast, until the words of God shall be fulfilled.

Notice that God has been in control all the time—they fulfilled His will and agreed to give their kingdom to the false religion until the words of God are fulfilled. Just as God used Pharoah, He will use the people who worship the beast.

Revelation 17:18 And the woman which thou sawest is that great city, which reigneth over the kings of the Earth.

It appears that all the kings of the Earth are of the false religion, with the seat of that religion in this great city.

Revelation 18:1 And after these things I saw another Angel come down from Heaven, having great power; and the Earth was lightened with his glory.

Revelation 18:2 And he cried mightily with a strong voice, saying, Babylon the great is fallen, is fallen, and is become the habitation of devils, and the hold of every foul spirit, and a cage of every unclean and hateful bird.

John recognized this, not only from the first time he wrote it (Revelation 14:8), but from Isaiah:

Isaiah 21:9 And, behold, here cometh a chariot of men, with a couple of horsemen. And he answered and said, Babylon is fallen, is fallen; and all the graven images of her gods he hath broken unto the ground.

Babylon has fallen again! The unclean and hateful birds are related to the fowls in Matthew:

Matthew 13:4 And when he sowed, some seeds fell by the way side, and the fowls came and devoured them up:

This is explained:

Matthew 13:19 When any one heareth the word of the kingdom, and understandeth it not, then cometh the wicked one, and catcheth away that which was sown in his heart. This is he which received seed by the way side.

These fowls are the wicked one – Satan and/or his demons.

Revelation 18:3 For all nations have drunk of the wine of the wrath of her fornication, and the kings of the Earth have committed fornication with her, and the merchants of the Earth are waxed rich through the abundance of her delicacies.

This false religion will make the merchants of the Earth rich. It makes moving wealth around easy. The world has been defrauded. The nations, that is, the kings of the Earth, have been in bed with this religion, which has become a way of life. They welcomed it because of how it was presented to them, and they, in their greed, saw it as beneficial. They have the location of the source of wealth. They worship this as their god instead of God.

Revelation 18:4 And I heard another voice from Heaven, saying, Come out of her, my people, that ye be not partakers of her sins, and that ye receive not of her plagues.

God makes one last plea to His people to come out of "Babylon" as he did in Jeremiah when God was going to destroy Babylon and make her desolate forever:

Jeremiah 51:45 My people, go ye out of the midst of her, and deliver ye every man his soul from the fierce anger of the LORD.

We see God calling His people out of her – out of the battle. This is the last call to come to Him through His Son, Jesus. God is getting ready to destroy everything, and these people have one last chance to repent. Here is the final call to come to Jesus.

God has some of His people in this city. Amazingly, there are believers after all that has happened, and there is no more teaching. Some may manage to pick up a Bible, and these people will come to know the true God.

Revelation 18:5 For her sins have reached unto Heaven, and God hath remembered her iniquities.

One sin, to God, is no worse than any other sin. Sin is sin. End of story. Nevertheless, this harlot has been unrepentant. She thinks she is doing right but is not following God's word. God will give her double for her trouble. She thinks she is untouchable and so rich that no trouble can harm her.

Revelation 18:6 Reward her even as she rewarded you, and double unto her double according to her works: in the cup which she hath filled fill to her double.

She is going to get double what she gave the Saints.

Revelation 18:7 How much she hath glorified herself, and lived deliciously, so much torment and sorrow give her: for she saith in her heart, I sit a queen, and am no widow, and shall see no sorrow.

John recognized this from the prophecy of Isaiah:

Isaiah 47:8-15 Therefore hear now this, thou that art given to pleasures, that dwellest carelessly, that sayest in thine heart, I am, and none else beside me; I shall not sit as a widow, neither shall I know the loss of children: 9) But these two things shall come to thee in a moment in one day, the loss of children, and widowhood: they shall come upon thee in their perfection for the multitude of thy sorceries, and for the great abundance of thine enchantments. 10) For thou hast trusted in thy wickedness: thou hast said, None seeth me. Thy wisdom and thy knowledge, it hath perverted thee; and thou hast said in thine heart, I am, and none else beside me. 11) Therefore shall evil come upon thee; thou shalt not know from whence it riseth: and mischief shall fall upon thee; thou shalt not be able to put it off: and desolation shall come upon thee suddenly, which thou shalt not know. 12) Stand now with thine enchantments, and with the multitude of thy sorceries, wherein thou hast laboured from thy youth; if so be thou shalt be able to profit, if so be thou mayest prevail. 13) Thou art wearied in the multitude of thy counsels. Let now the astrologers, the stargazers, the monthly prognosticators, stand up, and save thee from these things that shall come upon thee. 14) Behold, they shall be as stubble; the fire shall burn them; they shall not deliver themselves from the power of the flame: there shall not be a coal to warm at, nor fire to sit before it. 15) Thus shall they be unto thee with whom thou hast laboured, even thy merchants, from thy youth: they shall wander every one to his quarter; none shall save thee.

Christ said she is a widow, regardless of how she felt about herself. God will also see to it that she loses all her "children." You are probably thinking that there is a difference between being a "widow" and "losing all your children." In Biblical times, if a woman at least had a son, she could go out in public with that son. A woman could not appear in public without a man. If she had a daughter, her son-in-law could take over the son's/husband's duties as far as appearing in public. Also, if her deceased husband had brothers and she had no children by her late husband, the late husband's brothers were honor-bound to have one of them marry her and have a son to continue the family name. We sometimes refer to this as a "widow indeed." Yes, she would become a widow regardless of how she felt about herself.

To reinforce this, let us look at Lamentations:

Lamentations 1:1 How doth the city sit solitary, that was full of people! how is she become as a widow! she that was great among the nations, and princess among the provinces, how is she become tributary!

Revelation 18:8 Therefore shall her plagues come in one day, death, and mourning, and famine; and she shall be utterly burned with fire: for strong is the Lord God who judgeth her.

As we saw previously, one day in prophecy is an actual year. So, in one year, she shall be destroyed. Fire is judgment. Moreover, as we saw in Obadiah, that, too, said the house of Esau would be burned, and none of the house of Esau would remain – it would be destroyed. Who are the other nations around Israel but of the house of Esau?

Revelation 18:9 And the kings of the Earth, who have committed fornication and lived deliciously with her, shall bewail her, and lament for her, when they shall see the smoke of her burning,

Revelation 18:10 Standing afar off for the fear of her torment, saying, Alas, alas, that great city Babylon, that mighty city! for in one hour is thy judgment come.

In one hour—that is equivalent to fifteen days. It would be a fleeting time for her judgment to be completed.

Revelation 18:11 And the merchants of the Earth shall weep and mourn over her; for no man buyeth their merchandise any more:

John knew God's wrath on the merchant city:

Isaiah 23:11 He stretched out his hand over the sea, he shook the kingdoms: the LORD hath given a commandment against the merchant city, to destroy the strong holds thereof.

The kings of the Earth (even in far countries) and merchants bemoan her death. They mourn because, without the system, they can no longer buy or sell outside their area—no more imports and exports. You must produce your own goods. There would be no way to "outsource" goods.

Revelation 18:12 The merchandise of gold, and silver, and precious stones, and of pearls, and fine linen, and purple, and silk, and scarlet, and all thyine wood, and all manner vessels of ivory, and all manner vessels of most precious wood, and of brass, and iron, and marble,

Revelation 18:13 And cinnamon, and odours, and ointments, and frankincense, and wine, and oil, and fine flour, and wheat, and beasts, and sheep, and horses, and chariots, and slaves, and souls of men.

Revelation 18:14 And the fruits that thy soul lusted after are departed from thee, and all things which were dainty and goodly are departed from thee, and thou shalt find them no more at all.

These three verses list all the goods traded through this city—including the souls of men. This harlot leads men astray, away from God's teachings, and they begin to have other idols—like money. Nevertheless, everything she had before is gone. She has nothing now.

Revelation 18:15 The merchants of these things, which were made rich by her, shall stand afar off for the fear of her torment, weeping and wailing,

Revelation 18:16 And saying, Alas, alas, that great city, that was clothed in fine linen, and purple, and scarlet, and decked with gold, and precious stones, and pearls!

Revelation 18:17 For in one hour so great riches is come to nought. And every shipmaster, and all the company in ships, and sailors, and as many as trade by sea, stood afar off,

The merchants stand afar off for the fear of her torment and are seen weeping and wailing. Everyone distances themselves from her now. She had been prosperous before – clothed in fine linen, purple, scarlet, and decked with gold, precious stones, and pearls.

In Verse 8, it said in one "day", which equals a year, she was brought to death.

Verse 17 says that in one hour, equal to 15 days, all her riches have come to naught or nothing.

The shipmasters and company in ships, sailors, and as many as trade by sea are the people of other governments: the ambassadors and liaisons to her.

They stay away, too.

Revelation 18:18 And cried when they saw the smoke of her burning, saying, What city is like unto this great city!

She burns, in Verse 18. Now, we do not know if this is a literal burning or a spiritual burning. Then, reading further into Revelation, it may be a literal burning at the war of Armageddon.

Revelation 18:19 And they cast dust on their heads, and cried, weeping and wailing, saying, Alas, alas, that great city, wherein were made rich all that had ships in the sea by reason of her costliness! for in one hour is she made desolate.

In verse nineteen, these ambassadors and others from the governments of other nations are mourning because this harlot had made them rich, and now they are poor. Again, one hour is equal to 15 days. It happens quickly, and they want to distance themselves from her.

Revelation 18:20 Rejoice over her, thou Heaven, and ye holy apostles and prophets; for God hath avenged you on her.

While there is lamenting on Earth, there is rejoicing in Heaven! God has avenged those souls under the altar!

Revelation 18:21 And a mighty Angel took up a stone like a great millstone, and cast it into the sea, saying, Thus with violence shall that great city Babylon be thrown down, and shall be found no more at all.

The great millstone being cast into the sea means the people and the city will be destroyed. A millstone was used to grind and pulverize the grain. Meaning God will pulverize these people and their city.

Revelation 18:22 And the voice of harpers, and musicians, and of pipers, and trumpeters, shall be heard no more at all in thee; and no craftsman, of whatsoever craft he be, shall be found any more in thee; and the sound of a millstone shall be heard no more at all in thee;

There will be silence. No joy. No work.

Isaiah 24:8 The mirth of tabrets ceaseth, the noise of them that rejoice endeth, the joy of the harp ceaseth.

Revelation 18:23 And the light of a candle shall shine no more at all in thee; and the voice of the bridegroom and of the bride shall be heard no more at all in thee: for thy merchants were the great men of the Earth; for by thy sorceries were all nations deceived.

Before, we saw where the sun was darkened, there was not much light teaching God's word. Here, there is not so much light as a candle.

Isaiah 8:20 To the law and to the testimony: if they speak not according to this word, it is because there is no light in them.

Christ is the bridegroom, and neither He nor His bride will be heard any more. These people deceived the entire world.

Revelation 18:24 And in her was found the blood of prophets, and of Saints, and of all that were slain upon the Earth.

She had the blood of prophets, Saints, and all that were slain upon the Earth. The false religion's policy of convert-or-die killed these people physically, and their way of twisting God's word killed them spiritually.

GREAT REJOICING IN HEAVEN

Revelation 19:1 And after these things I heard a great voice of much people in Heaven, saying, Alleluia; Salvation, and glory, and honour, and power, unto the Lord our God:

Revelation 19:2 For true and righteous are his judgments: for he hath judged the great whore, which did corrupt the Earth with her fornication, and hath avenged the blood of his servants at her hand.

Revelation 19:3 And again they said, Alleluia. And her smoke rose up for ever and ever.

Revelation 19:4 And the four and twenty elders and the four beasts fell down and worshipped God that sat on the throne, saying, Amen; Alleluia.

Revelation 19:5 And a voice came out of the throne, saying, Praise our God, all ye his servants, and ye that fear him, both small and great.

Revelation 19:6 And I heard as it were the voice of a great multitude, and as the voice of many waters, and as the voice of mighty thunderings, saying, Alleluia: for the Lord God omnipotent reigneth.

Revelation 19:7 Let us be glad and rejoice, and give honour to him: for the marriage of the Lamb is come, and his wife hath made herself ready.

Revelation 19:8 And to her was granted that she should be arrayed in fine linen, clean and white: for the fine linen is the righteousness of Saints.

Revelation 19:9 And he saith unto me, Write, Blessed are they which are called unto the marriage supper of the Lamb. And he saith unto me, These are the true sayings of God.

Revelation 19:10 And I fell at his feet to worship him. And he said unto me, See thou do it not: I am thy fellowservant, and of thy brethren that have the testimony of Jesus: worship God: for the testimony of Jesus is the spirit of prophecy.

We see great rejoicing in Heaven, and we will see the Bride of Christ. She has been granted the privilege of being arrayed in fine white linen. Only through the Grace of God and the blood of the Lamb, which washes white as snow, are her garments white. The white linen is the righteousness of the Saints. God's people finally "got it right". All the time, God's people, the Jews, were wrong and doing wrong, not caring about their fellow man and being selfish and greedy. Are we there? Do we care, genuinely care about others? And then there was that horrible false religion that taught "convert or die." Their teachings led people straight to hell when the people thought they were going to Heaven for their reward.

We are blessed because we will be called to the marriage supper of the Lamb.

We see that the testimony of Jesus is the spirit of prophecy.

We also see that God is omnipotent—all-powerful. We knew that—but we must be reminded of the obvious sometimes.

The Triumphant Christ

Revelation Chapters 19:11 – 20:10

Revelation 19:11 And I saw Heaven opened, and behold a white horse; and he that sat upon him was called Faithful and True, and in righteousness he doth judge and make war.

What John knew:

*Deuteronomy 7:9 Know therefore that the LORD thy God, he is God, the **faithful** God, which keepeth covenant and mercy with them that love him and keep his commandments to a thousand generations;*

Jeremiah 10:10 But the LORD is the true God, he is the living God, and an everlasting king: at his wrath the Earth shall tremble, and the nations shall not be able to abide his indignation.

2 Timothy 4:8 Henceforth there is laid up for me a crown of righteousness, which the Lord, the righteous judge, shall give me at that day: and not to me only, but unto all them also that love his appearing.

John also knew that Jesus said:

John 10:30 I and my Father are one.

Revelation 19:12 His eyes were as a flame of fire, and on his head were many crowns; and he had a name written, that no man knew, but he himself.

When Christ was sent out and given a crown (kingdom), He went conquering and to conquer. [106] Here, He appears victorious, having won many crowns.

In most languages, a name has meaning. My name is Barbara, and it comes from the word "Barbarian." That word really means a stranger from a foreign country. There is an old hymn that goes, "This world is not my home, I'm just a passin' through. My treasures are laid up somewhere beyond the blue." That is me. I am Christ's. A child of the King! Heaven is my home, not this world—I am "just a passin' through"! The Biblical names had meaning, as we saw during the sealing of the 144,000.

This name, written for Christ, only He knows the fullness of its meaning. Only He knows the name He had written. Only He knew

---

[106] Revelation 6:2

141

what it took to get and live that name. In Verse 16, we see that the name written is King of kings and Lord of lords. However, only Christ knows the FULL meaning of those names.

Revelation 19:13 And he was clothed with a vesture dipped in blood: and his name is called The Word of God.

His vesture (His robe) was dipped in blood. His blood He shed for us. The blood that cleanses from all unrighteousness.

His name is called The Word of God.

John 1:1 In the beginning was the Word, and the Word was with God, and the Word was God.

Revelation 19:14 And the armies which were in Heaven followed him upon white horses, clothed in fine linen, white and clean.

God's armies—notice it is plural—go out with Him to do battle. They have no sin. Some say these are God's people fighting the battle in Heaven because of the reference to the fine, white linen. The white means righteousness, and we will wear white linen because Christ cleansed us from all unrighteousness. Others say these are God's Angels, and that makes perfect sense – for it was the Angels we saw previously in Heaven fighting the war with Satan. And there are plenty of Angels to have armies, plural, as we see in:

Revelation 5:11 And I beheld, and I heard the voice of many Angels round about the throne and the beasts and the elders: and the number of them was ten thousand times ten thousand, and thousands of thousands;

However, Revelation gives us the answer to this argument:

Revelation 17:14 These shall make war with the Lamb, and the Lamb shall overcome them: for he is Lord of lords, and King of kings: and they that are with him are called, and chosen, and faithful.

This verse says those with him are called, chosen, and faithful. We have a call from Christ. We must be faithful to that call, and we will win the battle!

Revelation 19:15 And out of his mouth goeth a sharp sword, that with it he should smite the nations: and he shall rule them with a rod of iron: and he treadeth the winepress of the fierceness and wrath of Almighty God.

In Verse 15, we see this two-edged sword again, and ruling with a rod of iron.

We also see that He treads the winepress of the wrath of God.

Revelation 1:16 said He had the sharp two-edged sword that goes out of His mouth.

As for the rod of iron,

Revelation 12:5 says the child was brought forth that would rule all nations with a rod of iron

Isaiah 63:3 I have trodden the winepress alone; and of the people there was none with me: for I will tread them in mine anger, and trample them in my fury; and their blood shall be sprinkled upon my garments, and I will stain all my raiment.

Revelation 19:16 And he hath on his vesture and on his thigh a name written, KING OF KINGS, AND LORD OF LORDS.

This is the name that we do not truly know.

THE SUPPER OF THE GREAT GOD

Revelation 19:17 And I saw an Angel standing in the sun; and he cried with a loud voice, saying to all the fowls that fly in the midst of Heaven, Come and gather yourselves together unto the supper of the great God;

John knew that this could either be the literal fowls, or it could mean the demons—the wicked one, from Matthew 13:9, as an explanation of Matthew 13:4.

The reference from the Old Testament prophecy is from Jeremiah:

Jeremiah 34:20 I will even give them into the hand of their enemies, and into the hand of them that seek their life: and their dead bodies shall be for meat unto the fowls of the Heaven, and to the beasts of the Earth.

This is the wedding feast—and it is for the fowls, not for us!

Revelation 19:18 That ye may eat the flesh of kings, and the flesh of captains, and the flesh of mighty men, and the flesh of horses, and of them that sit on them, and the flesh of all men, both free and bond, both small and great.

To eat the flesh is to consume utterly. This could, spiritually, mean that they were given over to Satan. Of course, the War to end all Wars was coming, and the carrion birds were being prepared.

Revelation 19:19 And I saw the beast, and the kings of the Earth, and their armies, gathered together to make war against him that sat on the horse, and against his army.

The kings of the Earth have united with Satan and the false religion. They fight against God and Christ.

We saw back in Revelation 17:14 that this war was coming and that The Lamb wins the war.

THE BEAST AND THE FALSE PROPHET AND THE LAKE OF FIRE

Revelation 19:20 And the beast was taken, and with him the false prophet that wrought miracles before him, with which he deceived them that had received the mark of the beast, and them that worshipped his image. These both were cast alive into a lake of fire burning with brimstone.

The beast and the false prophet are cast alive into the lake of fire. This was not the Hebrew sheol, which is the grave. This was a lake of fire. This is the image we Christians think of when we think of hell.

1 Enoch, Chapter 10, verses 4-7 tells a story of an Angel being buried in the "cauldron of God ("Dudael"):

1 Enoch, Chapter X, verses 4-7, describe the Angel Raphael burying Azazel:

4) And again the Lord said to Raphael: 'Bind Azâzêl hand and foot, and cast him into the darkness: and make an opening in the desert, which is in Dûdâêl, and cast him therein. 5) And place upon him rough and jagged rocks, and cover him with darkness, and let him abide there for ever, and cover his face that he may not see light. 6) And on the day of the great judgement he shall be cast into the fire. And heal the Earth which the Angels have corrupted, 7) and proclaim the healing of the Earth, that they may heal the plague, and that all the children of men may not perish through all the secret things that the Watchers have disclosed and have taught their sons.

In Hebrew, Azazel means "scapegoat." [107] Azazel is the name of a fallen Angel blamed for all the sins of mankind; thus, the scapegoat is known as the "Azazel goat."

Revelation 19:21 And the remnant were slain with the sword of him that sat upon the horse, which sword proceeded out of his mouth: and all the fowls were filled with their flesh.

And the remnant – those left on Earth – are slain by the Word of God, and the birds have the supper.

Revelation 20:1 And I saw an Angel come down from Heaven, having the key of the bottomless pit and a great chain in his hand.

Revelation 20:2 And he laid hold on the dragon, that old serpent, which is the Devil, and Satan, and bound him a thousand years,

In Verse 1, it only takes one Angel with a chain and the key to the bottomless pit. Not an army! Just One!! It took only one righteous man, the Son of God, to bind Satan and defeat him.

---

[107] Strong's Hebrew and Greek Dictionaries, Published in 1890; public domain.

In Verse 2, we see that Satan is bound for a thousand years. But is the thousand years a literal thousand years, or is it like so much in prophecy that is NOT what it says but has a different meaning – like days meaning years? If a day in prophecy is a year, that is that a thousand years? Or, like Numbers 14:34, is it reversed, and the years are only days? Or, is it a year of years? While Ezekiel had to lie on his side one day for each year, Moses and the Hebrew children got to wander in the desert one year for each day they searched out the land of Canaan:

Numbers 14:34 After the number of the days in which ye searched the land, even forty days, each day for a year, shall ye bear your iniquities, even forty years, and ye shall know my breach of promise.

Victorinus wrote, "...the years where Satan is bound are in the first Advent (coming or birth) of Christ, even to the end of the age; and they are called a thousand, according to that mode of speaking, wherein a part is signified by the whole, just as that passage,

"Psalm 105:8 He hath remembered his covenant for ever, the word which he commanded to a thousand generations although they are not a thousand." [108]

John would not have agreed with Victorinus, however. In Jewish numerology, a thousand is an indeterminate number. John thought of all this as a timeline of events. John saw Satan being locked up after the marriage feast. God and Christ would rule in peace—no more accusations of God's people. No more having silence in Heaven for fear Satan would learn of God's plans.

Revelation 20:3 And cast him into the bottomless pit, and shut him up, and set a seal upon him, that he should deceive the nations no more, till the thousand years should be fulfilled: and after that he must be loosed a little season.

Revelation 20:4 And I saw thrones, and they sat upon them, and judgment was given unto them: and I saw the souls of them that were beheaded for the witness of Jesus, and for the word of God, and which had not worshipped the beast, neither his image, neither had received his mark upon their foreheads, or in their hands; and they lived and reigned with Christ a thousand years.

Here, we see those who had lived during the wrath of God, found Christ as their Messiah, and did not take the mark of the beast will live and reign with Christ for a thousand years or as long as God deems necessary.

---

[108] CHURCH FATHERS: Commentary on the Apocalypse (Victorinus) - New Advent, https://www.newadvent.org/fathers/0712.htm.

Revelation 20:5 But the rest of the dead lived not again until the thousand years were finished. This is the first resurrection.

It is said that the first resurrection was the resurrection of Christ from the tomb.

Victorinus wrote that there are two resurrections. However, the first resurrection is of the souls by the faith, which does not permit men to pass to the second death.

The rest of the dead did not live again until the thousand years were finished.

2 Corinthians 5:8 We are confident, I say, and willing rather to be absent from the body, and to be present with the Lord.

What? Does the Bible contradict itself? To tell us in one place that there will be a later resurrection, but to say that to be absent from the body is to be present with God? God forbid! The resurrection in Revelation 20:5 talks about a bodily resurrection. 2 Corinthians 5:8 talks about the soul. When we step from this mortal plane, our souls will be present with Christ.

Revelation 20:6 Blessed and holy is he that hath part in the first resurrection: on such the second death hath no power, but they shall be priests of God and of Christ, and shall reign with him a thousand years.

Those who take part in the first resurrection are those who take part in the benefit that Christ gave us through His resurrection. If He had "just" died, He would have been no different from any other man. On the contrary, His resurrection is what makes Him different. He arose from the grave to bodily ascend and sit at the Father's right hand. Taking part in that first resurrection is accomplished by believing on Jesus, the Christ, the only begotten Son of God, who died for our sins and was resurrected on the third day.

Those whose bodies are resurrected can be assured they will be with God. The next time we see a resurrection, it will also bring judgment. Some of those will be experiencing the second death. Born once, die twice. Born twice, die once.

SATAN SET FREE FOR THE BATTLE OF GOG AND MAGOG

Revelation 20:7 And when the thousand years are expired, Satan shall be loosed out of his prison,

We are going to discuss what Satan does and what happens after that.

Revelation 20:8 And shall go out to deceive the nations which are in the four quarters of the Earth, Gog and Magog, to gather them together to battle: the number of whom is as the sand of the sea.

OK, a "Little season". We know that a day is a year. A "time" is 1,000 years. A "season" is 250 years, because there are four seasons in a year. But this is a "little season". It will be less than 250 years. It may be only 125 years, which is half a season.

So, when is this? Some say the thousand years started when Christ died. He defeated Satan and was bound so that the Gospel could be preached. Nevertheless, the thousand years is not a thousand years – it is as long as God determines it should be.

We see in Verse 8 of this Chapter that Satan's job is to gather the nations to war. But then, this battle is going to involve Gog and Magog and the region of the Middle East. Where is Gog and Magog?

Let us look at where the Bible says it is located.

Ezekiel 38:2 Son of man, set thy face against Gog, the land of Magog, the chief prince of Meshech and Tubal, and prophesy against him,

Ezekiel 38:3 And say, Thus saith the Lord GOD; Behold, I am against thee, O Gog, the chief prince of Meshech and Tubal:

Ezekiel 39:1 Therefore, thou son of man, prophesy against Gog, and say, Thus saith the Lord GOD; Behold, I am against thee, O Gog, the chief prince of Meshech and Tubal:

The area now known as Syria was colonized in ancient times by people from Magog, Gomer, Tubal, and Togarmah. [109]

Now notice Ezekiel 38:14 - 16, *"And thou [Gog] shalt come from thy place out of the north parts, thou, and many people with thee, all of them riding upon horses, a great company, and a mighty army."*

According to this verse, where is Gog's "place"? Doesn't the verse expressly state that it is in "the north parts"?

"Scholars generally agree that "Gog" is Russia, and that "the land of Magog" includes China. The descendants of Meshech and Tubal have been found together throughout history. [110] In Assyrian and Greek histories, Meshech appears as Musku, Muski, or Mushki—all names related to the Russian spelling of Moscow, as you can read in the International Standard Bible Encyclopedia. What about Tubal? On the eastern side of the Ural Mountains lies the city of Tobolski, named after the Tobol River, a name derived from Tubal. Tobolski was once the seat of the Russian government over Siberia and was considered Russia's Asian capital. [111]

---

[109] https://kujop221.wordpress.com/2021/11/02/this-terrifying-bible-prophecy-is-unfolding-before-our-eyes-2/ Accessed 5/21/22

[110] https://arkofthecovenantfoundation.files.wordpress.com/2020/03/the-prophesied-prince-of-russia-1.pdf

[111] https://www.cogwriter.com/news/prophecy/vladimir-putin-lord-of-the-world-prince-of-rosh/#:~:text=While%20Gerald%20Flurry%20asserts%20that%20Vladimir%20Putin%20is,Just%20look%20at%20the%20power%20he%20already%20has.

There is also a name for all the Russian people in Ezekiel 38:2, although there is controversy over how the Hebrew word rosh should be translated in this verse. The King James Version uses the adjective "chief," but the correct rendering (used by the Moffatt, New King James, and others) uses the word not as an adjective, but as a proper noun: Rosh. Thus, that verse should read, "The prince of Rosh, Meshech, and Tubal." [112]

"Rosh was the ancient name of Russia, once called Rus. Many encyclopedias and commentaries (such as the Jamieson, Fausset, and Brown Commentary) recognize this. So, who is this "prince" of Russia, Moscow and Tobolsk? The use of all three names shows that this is an individual ruler of all the peoples of Russia, from the west to the east. The reference to the cities of Moscow and Tobolsk helps us see how vast Russian territory is in these latter days." [113] Look at the breadth of Russia today. Vladimir Putin wants the lands once under the old Union of Soviet Socialist Republic back.

Revelation 20:9 And they went up on the breadth of the Earth, and compassed the camp of the Saints about, and the beloved city: and fire came down from God out of Heaven, and devoured them.
The beloved city—notice the fire does not devour the beloved city, just the armies from Gog and Magog.

THE DEVIL CAST INTO THE LAKE OF FIRE

Revelation 20:10 And the devil that deceived them was cast into the lake of fire and brimstone, where the beast and the false prophet are, and shall be tormented day and night for ever and ever.
We saw where the beast and the false prophet were cast into the lake of fire. Now Satan is cast into the lake of fire. Their torment will go on forever.

Verses from Isaiah colored John's point of view:
Isaiah 14:9-27 Hell from beneath is moved for thee to meet thee at thy coming: it stirreth up the dead for thee, even all the chief ones of the Earth; it hath raised up from their thrones all the kings of the nations. 10) All they shall speak and say unto thee, Art thou also become weak as we? art thou become like unto us? 11) Thy pomp is brought down to the grave, and the noise of thy viols: the worm is spread under thee, and the worms cover thee. 12) How art thou fallen from Heaven, O Lucifer,

---

[112] https://www.voanews.com/a/putin-s-gamble-on-ukraine-may-be-anything-but-crazy/6458607.html
[113] revelation - Who is Gog of the land of Magog mentioned in Ezekiel Chapters 38 amd 39 - Biblical Hermeneutics Stack Exchange

son of the morning! how art thou cut down to the ground, which didst weaken the nations! 13) For thou hast said in thine heart, I will ascend into Heaven, I will exalt my throne above the stars of God: I will sit also upon the mount of the congregation, in the sides of the north: 14) I will ascend above the heights of the clouds; I will be like the most High. 15) Yet thou shalt be brought down to hell, to the sides of the pit. 16) They that see thee shall narrowly look upon thee, and consider thee, saying, Is this the man that made the Earth to tremble, that did shake kingdoms; 17) That made the world as a wilderness, and destroyed the cities thereof; that opened not the house of his prisoners? 18) All the kings of the nations, even all of them, lie in glory, every one in his own house. 19) But thou art cast out of thy grave like an abominable branch, and as the raiment of those that are slain, thrust through with a sword, that go down to the stones of the pit; as a carcase trodden under feet. 20) Thou shalt not be joined with them in burial, because thou hast destroyed thy land, and slain thy people: the seed of evildoers shall never be renowned. 21) Prepare slaughter for his children for the iniquity of their fathers; that they do not rise, nor possess the land, nor fill the face of the world with cities. 22) For I will rise up against them, saith the LORD of hosts, and cut off from Babylon the name, and remnant, and son, and nephew, saith the LORD. 23) I will also make it a possession for the bittern, and pools of water: and I will sweep it with the besom of destruction, saith the LORD of hosts. 24) The LORD of hosts hath sworn, saying, Surely as I have thought, so shall it come to pass; and as I have purposed, so shall it stand: 25) That I will break the Assyrian in my land, and upon my mountains tread him under foot: then shall his yoke depart from off them, and his burden depart from off their shoulders. 26) This is the purpose that is purposed upon the whole Earth: and this is the hand that is stretched out upon all the nations. 27) For the LORD of hosts hath purposed, and who shall disannul it? and his hand is stretched out, and who shall turn it back?

The Great White Throne Judgement

Revelation Chapters 20:11 - 15

Revelation 20:11 And I saw a great white throne, and him that sat on it, from whose face the Earth and the Heaven fled away; and there was found no place for them.

John knew the scene from Jeremiah:

Jeremiah 4:22-28 For my people is foolish, they have not known me; they are sottish children, and they have none understanding: they are wise to do evil, but to do good they have no knowledge. I beheld the Earth, and, lo, it was without form, and void; and the Heavens, and they had no light. I beheld the mountains, and, lo, they trembled, and all the hills moved lightly. I beheld, and, lo, there was no man, and all the birds of the Heavens were fled. I beheld, and, lo, the fruitful place was a wilderness, and all the cities thereof were broken down at the presence of the LORD, and by his fierce anger. For thus hath the LORD said, The whole land shall be desolate; yet will I not make a full end. For this shall the Earth mourn, and the Heavens above be black: because I have spoken it, I have purposed it, and will not repent, neither will I turn back from it.

Now we switch to the great white throne judgment in verse eleven. Heaven and Earth have fled away, and there was found no place for them. Earth has been destroyed.

John also knew the reference from Isaiah:

Isaiah 13:13 Therefore I will shake the Heavens, and the Earth shall remove out of her place, in the wrath of the LORD of hosts, and in the day of his fierce anger.

Revelation 20:12 And I saw the dead, small and great, stand before God; and the books were opened: and another book was opened, which is the book of life: and the dead were judged out of those things which were written in the books, according to their works.

There are six Heavenly books mentioned in the Bible:

- Book of Life – Exodus 32:33, Phil. 4:3
- Book of the Living – Psa. 69:28
- Where my members are written – Psa. 139:16
- The Book (the deaf shall hear the words) – Isaiah 29:18

- Book of Remembrance – Mal. 3:16
- Volume of the Book it is written of me – Hebrews 10:7

Some of these books may be the same but just mentioned differently, especially the Book of Life and the Book of Living in which our names can be blotted out.

The dead will be judged according to their works. Notice this is the great white throne judgment. Some say Christians will not be at this judgment, but that is NOT what these verses say.

Revelation 20:13 And the sea gave up the dead which were in it; and death and hell delivered up the dead which were in them: and they were judged every man according to their works.

The scenes of the dead in Heaven John would have recognized from Isaiah:

Isaiah 26:19 Thy dead men shall live, together with my dead body shall they arise. Awake and sing, ye that dwell in dust: for thy dew is as the dew of herbs, and the Earth shall cast out the dead.

Then the judgment of the people who are of the people of the world and death and hell and they are judged according to their works.

DEATH AND HELL CAST INTO THE LAKE OF FIRE

Revelation 20:14 And death and hell were cast into the lake of fire. This is the second death.

The Fourth Horse went out in the beginning of time:

Rev 6:8 And I looked, and behold a pale horse: and his name that sat on him was Death, and Hell followed with him. And power was given unto them over the fourth part of the Earth, to kill with sword, and with hunger, and with death, and with the beasts of the Earth.

Death and hell are now cast into the lake of fire. This is the second death. This is why theologians say that whoever is cast into the lake of fire will burn eternally. Because death has been done away with, and therefore, the torture must go on forever.

And yet God calls it a second death—but this is because this death permanently separates the people from God. Sin was but a temporary, curable separation, but this separates us forever and is permanent.

Revelation 20:15 And whosoever was not found written in the book of life was cast into the lake of fire.

This is where the sheep and goats are separated. Those who are not of God's flock of sheep are cast into the lake of fire.

John would recognize these scenes from Isaiah:

Isaiah 24:19-23 The Earth is utterly broken down, the Earth is clean dissolved, the Earth is moved exceedingly. The Earth shall reel to and fro like a drunkard, and shall be removed like a cottage; and the transgression thereof shall be heavy upon it; and it shall fall, and not rise again. And it shall come to pass in that day, that the LORD shall punish the host of the high ones that are on high, and the kings of the Earth upon the Earth. And they shall be gathered together, as prisoners are gathered in the pit, and shall be shut up in the prison, and after many days shall they be visited. Then the moon shall be confounded, and the sun ashamed, when the LORD of hosts shall reign in mount Zion, and in Jerusalem, and before his ancients gloriously.

New Heaven, New Earth, New Jerusalem

Revelation Chapters 21 – 22

Revelation 21:1 And I saw a new Heaven and a new Earth: for the first Heaven and the first Earth were passed away; and there was no more sea.

John knew the verse from Isaiah:

Isaiah 66:22 For as the new Heavens and the new Earth, which I will make, shall remain before me, saith the LORD, so shall your seed and your name remain.

1 Corinthians 13:12 For now we see through a glass, darkly; but then face to face: now I know in part; but then shall I know even as also I am known.

We saw in Revelation 20:11 that the Earth and Heaven had fled away. This vision picks up with that thought. But how did Heaven and Earth go away?

2 Peter 3:10 But the day of the Lord will come as a thief in the night; in the which the Heavens shall pass away with a great noise, and the elements shall melt with fervent heat, the Earth also and the works that are therein shall be burned up.

Sound like a nuclear bomb? Alternatively, many volcanoes could erupt simultaneously since God controls all the elements.

In this vision, there was no more sea. "Sea" in prophecy is people. So, there were no people on this new Earth nor in the new Heaven. So, what happened to us? The answer can be found in:

2 Corinthians 12:2, where Paul is talking about being caught up to the third Heaven.

2 Corinthians 12:2-4 I knew a man in Christ above fourteen years ago, (whether in the body, I cannot tell; or whether out of the body, I cannot tell: God knoweth;) such an one caught up to the third Heaven. And I knew such a man, (whether in the body, or out of the body, I cannot tell: God knoweth;) How that he was caught up into paradise, and heard unspeakable words, which it is not lawful for a man to utter.

Now, the first Heaven is commonly referred to as the air above the Earth. The second Heaven is commonly referred to as "outer space." [114] The third Heaven is above that, where God resides. As for the confirmation of the answer, we will have to wait, because 1 Corinthians 13:12 says now we see as through a dark glass, but then it will be face to face.

Revelation 21:2 And I John saw the holy city, new Jerusalem, coming down from God out of Heaven, prepared as a bride adorned for her husband.
Notice the new city, New Jerusalem. coming down from God. It is coming from Heaven to the new Earth. It is the Bride, ready for her husband.

Revelation 21:3 And I heard a great voice out of Heaven saying, Behold, the Tabernacle of God is with men, and he will dwell with them, and they shall be his people, and God himself shall be with them, and be their God.
The Tabernacle of God is now with men; they shall be His people, and He shall be their God.

Revelation 21:4 And God shall wipe away all tears from their eyes; and there shall be no more death, neither sorrow, nor crying, neither shall there be any more pain: for the former things are passed away.
God wipes away all tears. There is no more death, sorrow, crying, or pain. The former things are passed away.
John knew this from Isaiah:
Isaiah 25:8 He will swallow up death in victory; and the Lord GOD will wipe away tears from off all faces; and the rebuke of his people shall he take away from off all the Earth: for the LORD hath spoken it.

Revelation 21:5 And he that sat upon the throne said, Behold, I make all things new. And he said unto me, Write: for these words are true and faithful.
Christ makes all things new.
There is a new directive for John: Write, for these words are true and faithful.

Revelation 21:6 And he said unto me, It is done. I am Alpha and Omega, the beginning and the end. I will give unto him that is athirst of the fountain of the water of life freely.
Again, Christ says, "It is done."

---

[114] https://jesusnorway.wordpress.com/tag/roswell/

In John 19:30, He said, "It is finished," as He hung on the cross.

In Revelation 16:17, as the seventh vial was being poured out, a voice from the temple of Heaven, from the throne, said, "It is done."

This is the last time He says, "It is done."

John knew God as the fountain of living waters:

Jeremiah 2:13 For my people have committed two evils; they have forsaken me the fountain of living waters, and hewed them out cisterns, broken cisterns, that can hold no water.

Revelation 21:7 He that overcometh shall inherit all things; and I will be his God, and he shall be my son.

All we must do is overcome. Overcome the world's temptations. Overcome the beast and his image and his mark. Easier said than done. Nevertheless, if we do, we will inherit all things; He will be our God, and we will be his children.

Revelation 21:8 But the fearful, and unbelieving, and the abominable, and murderers, and whoremongers, and sorcerers, and idolaters, and all liars, shall have their part in the lake which burneth with fire and brimstone: which is the second death.

Notice the list of those who will be in the lake of fire. We must overcome these things: being fearful – for we must be bold in proclaiming the Gospel; our unbelief – we must believe and become like children who believe whatever they are told. We must believe only what God and His Word tell us, not what the world or our feelings tell us. According to Webster's Dictionary, the abominable is nasty, disgusting, loathsome (hating), highly unpleasant, or disagreeable. Whoremongers, according to the old Jewish belief, were men who sold themselves for sex with other men. [115] Sorcerers deal with the occult and thus with Satan, idolaters worship other gods, and all liars have their part in the lake of fire. You say you do not have any problems with any of that. What about that "little white lie" to keep from hurting someone's feelings? A lie is a lie. One sin carries no more and no less weight than any other sin. What about a relationship with someone who keeps you from Church? What about being hateful or hurtful toward someone, even though you were "just being honest"? What about those days when your hormones are raging or even non-existent, and you are disagreeable with everyone about everything? We all have things to work on—especially me.

---

[115] Strong's Hebrew and Greek Dictionaries, Published 1890; public domain

THE BRIDE OF THE LAMB

Revelation 21:9 And there came unto me one of the seven Angels which had the seven vials full of the seven last plagues, and talked with me, saying, Come hither, I will shew thee the bride, the Lamb's wife.

A look at the Lamb's wife, the Bride of Christ!

Revelation 21:10 And he carried me away in the spirit to a great and high mountain, and shewed me that great city, the holy Jerusalem, descending out of Heaven from God,

It is the New Jerusalem! The Bride is New Jerusalem!

Colossians 1:22 In the body of his flesh through death, to present you holy and unblameable and unreproveable in his sight:

If Christ is the head of the body, the Church, and we are the Church, we are then the body of Christ. If we are the body of Christ, who is the bridegroom, how can we be the bride?

Colossians 2:17 Which are a shadow of things to come; but the body is of Christ.

Colossians 2:19 And not holding the Head, from which all the body by joints and bands having nourishment ministered, and knit together, increaseth with the increase of God.

Ephesians 5:30 For we are members of his body, of his flesh, and of his bones.

Revelation 21:11 Having the glory of God: and her light was like unto a stone most precious, even like a jasper stone, clear as crystal;

The New Jerusalem had the glory of God, like a Jasper stone, but clear as crystal—no impurities in her.

Revelation 21:12 And had a wall great and high, and had twelve gates, and at the gates twelve Angels, and names written thereon, which are the names of the twelve tribes of the children of Israel:

The names of the twelve tribes of Israel are written on the gates, the same twelve we saw where the 144,000 were being sealed. Jews will tell you that this proves the only ones who can go in and out of New Jerusalem are Jews. They say no gentiles will be allowed.

Romans 11:17 says we are grafted into the olive tree—the Jews— God's people.

Revelation 21:13 On the East three gates; on the north three gates; on the south three gates; and on the west three gates.

Three gates on four sides, making twelve gates.

Revelation 21:14 And the wall of the city had twelve foundations, and in them the names of the twelve apostles of the Lamb.

Ah! The Jews have no comment on this! The city was built upon the twelve foundations of the apostles! Now, who is allowed in the city? Answer: Jew and Gentile. Jews saved by their faith and Gentiles who accept the Grace of Christ and are grafted into the olive tree.

Revelation 21:15 And he that talked with me had a golden reed to measure the city, and the gates thereof, and the wall thereof.

Here is that golden reed to measure the city again.

Revelation 21:16 And the city lieth foursquare, and the length is as large as the breadth: and he measured the city with the reed, twelve thousand furlongs. The length and the breadth and the height of it are equal.

Fifteen hundred miles square! There are 660 feet in a furlong and 5,280 feet in a mile.

Six hundred sixty X 12000 equals 7,920,000 feet / 5,280 equals 1500 miles. The whole of the Holy Land is only two hundred miles long! The length of Earth's equator is 24,860.2 miles. [116] So, New Jerusalem is 1/16 the circumference of our Earth.

Revelation 21:17 And he measured the wall thereof, an hundred and forty and four cubits, according to the measure of a man, that is, of the Angel.

Now, if we knew the height and proportion of an Angel, we would know how high this wall is. Notice that the verse says it is "according to the measure of a man." Then, it says that "man" is the Angel.

Revelation 21:17 in the Complete Jewish Bible (CJB) states that the wall will be 216 feet wide. However, it would take a thicker wall than that to support a wall with a height of 1500 miles. I believe someone calculated 216 feet based on the measurement of a human man, not an angelic man

Revelation 21:18 And the building of the wall of it was of jasper: and the city was pure gold, like unto clear glass.

The city is built of clear crystal and transparent gold. No impurities there!

---

[116] https://education.nationalgeographic.org/resource/equator/

Revelation 21:19 And the foundations of the wall of the city were garnished with all manner of precious stones. The first foundation was jasper; the second, sapphire; the third, a chalcedony; the fourth, an emerald;

Revelation 21:20 The fifth, sardonyx; the sixth, sardius; the seventh, chrysolite; the eighth, beryl; the ninth, a topaz; the tenth, a chrysoprasus; the eleventh, a jacinth; the twelfth, an amethyst.

If you research all the stones, you will see that each is believed to have a property to ward off all manner of ills that are not supposed to be in Heaven. Maybe those properties really DO exist.

The Complete Jewish Bible also says the first stone of the foundation is diamond instead of jasper. Number 6 was also a carnelian instead of a sardius. Number 11 in the Jewish Bible was turquoise instead of jacinth.

1. Diamond – anti-infection (used today) [117]
2. Sapphire – heart disease [118]
3. Chalcedony – Increasing faith [119]
4. Emerald – good eyesight [120]
5. Sardonyx – self-control [121]
6. Carnelian – guards against poverty, gives a sense of humor [122]
7. Chrysolite – same as beryl [123]
8. Beryl – prevents women's diseases [124]
9. Topaz – resolves disputes between fathers and sons [125]
10. Chrysoprasus – hope and joy [126]
11. Jacinth – healing [127]
12. Amethyst – purifying [128]

No wonder there are no diseases in Heaven! The crystals prevent everything one can think of.

[117] https://www.iflscience.com/health-and-medicine/tiny-diamonds-allow-doctors-to-check-wounds-without-removing-the-dressing/

[118] https://www.thenaturalsapphirecompany.com/education/sapphires-101/medicinal-properties-sapphires/

[119] https://meanings.crystalsandjewelry.com/chalcedony/

[120] https://www.crystalvaults.com/crystal-encyclopedia/emerald/

[121] https://crystalstones.com/sardonyx/

[122] www.findyourlucky.com › carnelian-gemstone

[123] http://www.gemcoach.com/magical-properties-chrysolite/

[124] https://www.healingwithcrystals.net.au/beryl.html

[125] https://www.sunnyray.org/Topaz-crystal-properties-and-meaning.htm

[126] https://www.healing-crystals-for-you.com/chrysoprase.html#:~:text=Chrysoprase%20promotes%20joy%20and%20happiness%20and%20brings%20through,stone%20to%20attract%20new%20love%2C%20abundance%20and%20prosperity

[127] https://crystal-dawn.com/2021/12/12/weekly-healing-crystal-jacinth/

[128] https://buddhaandkarma.com/products/amethyst-purifying-bracelet#:~:text=The%20amethyst%20bracelet%20is%20used%20to%20purify%20negative,the%20unwanted%20aura%20that%20causes%20conflict%20and%20misunderstanding

Revelation 21:21 And the twelve gates were twelve pearls; every several gate was of one pearl: and the street of the city was pure gold, as it were transparent glass.

Huge pearls and pure gold for paving material.

Revelation 21:22 And I saw no temple therein: for the Lord God Almighty and the Lamb are the temple of it.

There is no Temple in the new Heaven. We saw the temple mentioned several times in Revelation, but there is no temple with the new Heaven and the new Earth. It is said that we are the Temple of God here on Earth.

Revelation 21:23 And the city had no need of the sun, neither of the moon, to shine in it: for the glory of God did lighten it, and the Lamb is the light thereof.

John would have recognized the reference from Isaiah:

Isaiah 60:19 The sun shall be no more thy light by day; neither for brightness shall the moon give light unto thee: but the LORD shall be unto thee an everlasting light, and thy God thy glory.

Isaiah 60:20 Thy sun shall no more go down; neither shall thy moon withdraw itself: for the LORD shall be thine everlasting light, and the days of thy mourning shall be ended.

No sun or moon, either. God and Christ are the rulers. There is no need for the sun to rule by the day and the moon to the lesser light at night. Teachers do not need to shed light on the teaching of the word. God and Christ take care of that light.

Revelation 21:24 And the nations of them which are saved shall walk in the light of it: and the kings of the Earth do bring their glory and honour into it.

We walk in the light of His Word.

Revelation 21:25 And the gates of it shall not be shut at all by day: for there shall be no night there.

The gates of the cities were always shut at night to keep out thieves, robbers, enemies and their armies, and wild animals. There is no need to shut the gates in the New Jerusalem. No night.

Revelation 21:26 And they shall bring the glory and honour of the nations into it.

In verse twenty-four, the kings of the Earth brought their glory and honor into the new city; now, the glory and honor of the nations are brought into the city.

John also knew this from Isaiah:

Isaiah 26:2 Open ye the gates, that the righteous nation which keepeth the truth may enter in.

Revelation 21:27 And there shall in no wise enter into it any thing that defileth, neither whatsoever worketh abomination, or maketh a lie: but they which are written in the Lamb's book of life.

Only those whose names are written in the Lamb's Book of Life are allowed into the New Jerusalem.

Revelation 22:1 And he shewed me a pure river of water of life, clear as crystal, proceeding out of the throne of God and of the Lamb.

The River of Water of Life. Christ has this water. If we drink of the water of life, we will never thirst, meaning to thirst after the Word of God.

Revelation 22:2 In the midst of the street of it, and on either side of the river, was there the tree of life, which bare twelve manner of fruits, and yielded her fruit every month: and the leaves of the tree were for the healing of the nations.

The tree of life is on either side of the river of water of life. It bears twelve different fruits and gives fruit every month. The leaves are for the healing of the nations—no more war. Healing is accomplished.

There is a passage in Jeremiah which is mindful of this:

Jeremiah 17:7 Blessed is the man that trusteth in the LORD, and whose hope the LORD is.

Jeremiah 17:8 For he shall be as a tree planted by the waters, and that spreadeth out her roots by the river, and shall not see when heat cometh, but her leaf shall be green; and shall not be careful in the year of drought, neither shall cease from yielding fruit.

We saw back in Revelation 7:16 where no heat would come upon those which came out of great tribulation and washed their robes and made them white in the blood of the Lamb. [129]

This, being "as a tree planted by the waters," is what happens when we fully trust in God and make Him our hope. They shall not be careful in the year of drought, neither shall cease from yielding fruit. Those who make God their hope have enough in Him to have no

---

[129] Revelation 7:14

want of rain in a drought. They have seeds in themselves, so they have moisture. They will be fruitful in holiness and all good works. They spread the seed of the Gospel and, in so doing, yield fruit.

Revelation 22:3 And there shall be no more curse: but the throne of God and of the Lamb shall be in it; and his servants shall serve him:
This Greek word, translated as curse, is from a Greek word that means opposition or intensity. [130] All is calm and of one accord.

Revelation 22:4 And they shall see his face; and his name shall be in their foreheads.
He wrote his name on us back in Revelation 3:12. Here, His Name is in our foreheads – in our minds, committed to memory.

Revelation 22:5 And there shall be no night there; and they need no candle, neither light of the sun; for the Lord God giveth them light: and they shall reign for ever and ever.
We need no sun and no candle. Again, our teaching will come straight from God.
Compare this to Revelation 18:23, where the light went out. Not so much as a candle of teaching of the word of God.

JESUS IS TO COME QUICKLY

Revelation 22:6 And he said unto me, These sayings are faithful and true: and the Lord God of the holy prophets sent his Angel to shew unto his servants the things which must shortly be done.
He returns to his command to John to write, "These sayings are faithful and true," and goes back to the beginning to reiterate that these things must be done shortly.
Revelation 1:1 The Revelation of Jesus Christ, which God gave unto him, to shew unto his servants things which must shortly come to pass; and he sent and signified it by his Angel unto his servant John:

Revelation 22:7 Behold, I come quickly: blessed is he that keepeth the sayings of the prophecy of this book.
He comes quickly. Notice, again, how we are to keep the sayings of the prophecy of this book. It is not enough to read or hear; we must keep His word.

---

[130] Strong's Hebrew and Greek Dictionaries, Published 1890, Public Domain

161

Revelation 22:8 And I John saw these things, and heard them. And when I had heard and seen, I fell down to worship before the feet of the Angel which shewed me these things.

John consistently falls at the feet of the Angels who talk to him.

Revelation 22:9 Then saith he unto me, See thou do it not: for I am thy fellowservant, and of thy brethren the prophets, and of them which keep the sayings of this book: worship God.

And he is constantly being told not to do it. God is the only one we are to worship. Paul wrote one of his letters to the people in Colossae about their Angel worship.

1 Corinthians 6:3 says we will judge the Angels. How can we judge them if we worship them?

Oh! Satan was originally an Angel. What do we get to say about him?

Revelation 22:10 And he saith unto me, Seal not the sayings of the prophecy of this book: for the time is at hand.

The book of Revelation is not sealed the way Daniel was.

Revelation 22:11 He that is unjust, let him be unjust still: and he which is filthy, let him be filthy still: and he that is righteous, let him be righteous still: and he that is holy, let him be holy still.

At that time, in the future, we are to let people remain as they are. We are to be the example and let our light shine so others will want to have what we have. When they ask us, we can tell them.

Revelation 22:12 And, behold, I come quickly; and my reward is with me, to give every man according as his work shall be.

Again, we will gain rewards according to our works.

Revelation 22:13 I am Alpha and Omega, the beginning and the end, the first and the last.

Christ is the first and the last. He was in the beginning when things were created and He will be at the judgment and then in the new Heaven and new Earth.

Revelation 22:14 Blessed are they that do his commandments, that they may have right to the tree of life, and may enter in through the gates into the city.

We must keep His commandments to have the right to the Tree of Life and even enter the city where the Tree of Life is found. To accept

Christ is one thing. Then, to change and keep His commandments shows we love Him.

Revelation 22:15 For without are dogs, and sorcerers, and whoremongers, and murderers, and idolaters, and whosoever loveth and maketh a lie.

All those things we saw before, with the addition of dogs. This Greek word can mean either literal dogs or figurative dogs. The Book of Enoch refers to the Palestinians as dogs. Matthew 15:26 refers to Canaanites as dogs.

Sorcerers are associated with witchcraft. In Galatians 5:20, the word that is translated as "witchcraft" is the Greek word *pharmakeia,* [131] which is where we get our word pharmacy from, and where the word drug comes from.

Whoremongers are men who sell themselves for sex. [132] —Male prostitutes.

The others are self-explanatory.

Revelation 22:16 I Jesus have sent mine Angel to testify unto you these things in the Churches. I am the root and the offspring of David, and the bright and morning star.

Christ has sent his ministers to tell us of these things. If our ministers are not telling us, they are not doing their jobs.

Revelation 22:17 And the Spirit and the bride say, Come. And let him that heareth say, Come. And let him that is athirst come. And whosoever will, let him take the water of life freely.

The Holy Spirit and the New Jerusalem say, "Come." We are to repeat that to others. We thirst for the word of God and need to come to the river of the water of life and take freely of it.

Revelation 22:18 For I testify unto every man that heareth the words of the prophecy of this book, If any man shall add unto these things, God shall add unto him the plagues that are written in this book:

I pray I have added nothing more than God gave and translated His Word into an understandable explanation.

Revelation 22:19 And if any man shall take away from the words of the book of this prophecy, God shall take away his part out of the book

---

[131] Strong's Hebrew and Greek Dictionaries, Published 1890, Public Domain
[132] Ibid.

of life, and out of the holy city, and from the things which are written in this book.

I further pray I have taken nothing away from the words God gave. Sometimes, I have given more than one plausible explanation and left it that it could be either. God knows. Sometimes, God does not reveal all He knows, for we cannot manage it.

Revelation 22:20 He which testifieth these things saith, Surely I come quickly. Amen. Even so, come, Lord Jesus.

We do say, Come quickly, Lord Jesus. Amen.

Revelation 22:21 The grace of our Lord Jesus Christ be with you all. Amen.

Worth repeating: The grace of our Lord Jesus Christ be with you all. Amen.

Father, we pray that the words of this prophecy will settle in the hearts of each one reading or hearing these words. May they keep the words of Your prophecy and Your commandments. May they be overcomers and reap the rewards You have for them. Draw each one closer to You, and come quickly, Lord Jesus. Amen.

But, What About . . .

OK, we saw where John was aware, if Revelation is a timeline, of everything he saw through the first trumpet (for the destruction of the Temple). Once Jesus, the perfect sacrifice, was offered, there was no need for either the daily sacrifice or the annual sacrifice (Passover). God had given the Jewish people one generation (approximately forty years), from the death of Christ until 70 A.D. to repent, accept Jesus as their Messiah, and begin to live under God's grace instead of God's law, which they had proven they could not keep.

If everything up to that point had been historical, then what about the rest of the Book of Revelation? What transpired in history to cover the second trumpet – the great mountain being cast into the sea and the third part of the sea becoming blood, and a third of the ships being destroyed (Revelation 8:2)? And what about the locusts of Revelation Chapter 9? How do you explain them having the faces of men and the hair of women?

And just where are we in that timeline?

These questions will be answered in the next book:

Revelation: Where Are We?

APPENDIX A - Men's Hearts

Matthew 13:3 And he spake many things unto them in parables, saying, Behold, a sower went forth to sow;

Matthew 13:4 And when he sowed, some seeds fell by the way side, and the fowls came and devoured them up:

Matthew 13:5 Some fell upon stony places, where they had not much Earth: and forthwith they sprung up, because they had no deepness of Earth

Matthew 13:6 And when the sun was up, they were scorched; and because they had no root, they withered away.

Matthew 13:7 And some fell among thorns; and the thorns sprung up, and choked them:

Matthew 13:8 But other fell into good ground, and brought forth fruit, some an hundredfold, some sixtyfold, some thirtyfold.

Matthew 13:9 Who hath ears to hear, let him hear.

Jesus's Explanation:

Matthew 13:19 When any one heareth the word of the kingdom, and understandeth it not, then cometh the wicked one, and catcheth away that which was sown in his heart. This is he which received seed by the way side.

Matthew 13:20 But he that received the seed into stony places, the same is he that heareth the word, and anon with joy receiveth it;

Matthew 13:21 Yet hath he not root in himself, but dureth for a while: for when tribulation or persecution ariseth because of the word, by and by he is offended.

Matthew 13:22 He also that received seed among the thorns is he that heareth the word; and the care of this world, and the deceitfulness of riches, choke the word, and he becometh unfruitful.

Matthew 13:23 But he that received seed into the good ground is he that heareth the word, and understandeth it; which also beareth fruit, and bringeth forth, some an hundredfold, some sixty, some thirty.

APPENDIX B - The Songs of Moses

Song #1

One in Exodus 15:1 - 19, and then in Deuteronomy 31:19 – 32:44, which God gave to him to write.

Exo 15:1 Then sang Moses and the children of Israel this song unto the LORD, and spake, saying, I will sing unto the LORD, for he hath triumphed gloriously: the horse and his rider hath he thrown into the sea.

Exo 15:2 The LORD is my strength and song, and he is become my salvation: he is my God, and I will prepare him an habitation; my father's God, and I will exalt him.

Exo 15:3 The LORD is a man of war: the LORD is his name.

Exo 15:4 Pharaoh's chariots and his host hath he cast into the sea: his chosen captains also are drowned in the Red sea.

Exo 15:5 The depths have covered them: they sank into the bottom as a stone.

Exo 15:6 Thy right hand, O LORD, is become glorious in power: thy right hand, O LORD, hath dashed in pieces the enemy.

Exo 15:7 And in the greatness of thine excellency thou hast overthrown them that rose up against thee: thou sentest forth thy wrath, which consumed them as stubble.

Exo 15:8 And with the blast of thy nostrils the waters were gathered together, the floods stood upright as an heap, and the depths were congealed in the heart of the sea.

Exo 15:9 The enemy said, I will pursue, I will overtake, I will divide the spoil; my lust shall be satisfied upon them; I will draw my sword, my hand shall destroy them.

Exo 15:10 Thou didst blow with thy wind, the sea covered them: they sank as lead in the mighty waters.

Exo 15:11 Who is like unto thee, O LORD, among the gods? who is like thee, glorious in holiness, fearful in praises, doing wonders?

Exo 15:12 Thou stretchedst out thy right hand, the Earth swallowed them.

Exo 15:13 Thou in thy mercy hast led forth the people which thou hast redeemed: thou hast guided them in thy strength unto thy holy habitation.

Exo 15:14 The people shall hear, and be afraid: sorrow shall take hold on the inhabitants of Palestina.

Exo 15:15 Then the dukes of Edom shall be amazed; the mighty men of Moab, trembling shall take hold upon them; all the inhabitants of Canaan shall melt away.

Exo 15:16 Fear and dread shall fall upon them; by the greatness of thine arm they shall be as still as a stone; till thy people pass over, O LORD, till the people pass over, which thou hast purchased.

Exo 15:17 Thou shalt bring them in, and plant them in the mountain of thine inheritance, in the place, O LORD, which thou hast made for thee to dwell in, in the Sanctuary, O Lord, which thy hands have established.

Exo 15:18 The LORD shall reign for ever and ever.

Exo 15:19 For the horse of Pharaoh went in with his chariots and with his horsemen into the sea, and the LORD brought again the waters of the sea upon them; but the children of Israel went on dry land in the midst of the sea.

Song #2

Deu 31:19 Now therefore write ye this song for you, and teach it the children of Israel: put it in their mouths, that this song may be a witness for me against the children of Israel.

Deu 31:20 For when I shall have brought them into the land which I sware unto their fathers, that floweth with milk and honey; and they shall have eaten and filled themselves, and waxen fat; then will they turn unto other gods, and serve them, and provoke me, and break my covenant.

Deu 31:21 And it shall come to pass, when many evils and troubles are befallen them, that this song shall testify against them as a witness; for it shall not be forgotten out of the mouths of their seed: for I know their imagination which they go about, even now, before I have brought them into the land which I sware.

Deu 31:22 Moses therefore wrote this song the same day, and taught it the children of Israel.

Deu 31:23 And he gave Joshua the son of Nun a charge, and said, Be strong and of a good courage: for thou shalt bring the children of Israel into the land which I sware unto them: and I will be with thee.

Deu 31:24 And it came to pass, when Moses had made an end of writing the words of this law in a book, until they were finished,

Deu 31:25 That Moses commanded the Levites, which bare the ark of the covenant of the LORD, saying,

Deu 31:26 Take this book of the law, and put it in the side of the ark of the covenant of the LORD your God, that it may be there for a witness against thee.

Deu 31:27 For I know thy rebellion, and thy stiff neck: behold, while I am yet alive with you this day, ye have been rebellious against the LORD; and how much more after my death?

Deu 31:28 Gather unto me all the elders of your tribes, and your officers, that I may speak these words in their ears, and call Heaven and Earth to record against them.

Deu 31:29 For I know that after my death ye will utterly corrupt yourselves, and turn aside from the way which I have commanded you; and evil will befall you in the latter days; because ye will do evil in the sight of the LORD, to provoke him to anger through the work of your hands.

The Song of Moses

Deu 31:30 And Moses spake in the ears of all the congregation of Israel the words of this song, until they were ended.

Deu 32:1 Give ear, O ye Heavens, and I will speak; and hear, O Earth, the words of my mouth.

Deu 32:2 My doctrine shall drop as the rain, my speech shall distil as the dew, as the small rain upon the tender herb, and as the showers upon the grass:

Deu 32:3 Because I will publish the name of the LORD: ascribe ye greatness unto our God.

Deu 32:4 He is the Rock, his work is perfect: for all his ways are judgment: a God of truth and without iniquity, just and right is he.

Deu 32:5 They have corrupted themselves, their spot is not the spot of his children: they are a perverse and crooked generation.

Deu 32:6 Do ye thus requite the LORD, O foolish people and unwise? is not he thy father that hath bought thee? hath he not made thee, and established thee?

Deu 32:7 Remember the days of old, consider the years of many generations: ask thy father, and he will shew thee; thy elders, and they will tell thee.

Deu 32:8 When the most High divided to the nations their inheritance, when he separated the sons of Adam, he set the bounds of the people according to the number of the children of Israel.

Deu 32:9 For the LORD'S portion is his people; Jacob is the lot of his inheritance.

Deu 32:10 He found him in a desert land, and in the waste howling wilderness; he led him about, he instructed him, he kept him as the apple of his eye.

Deu 32:11 As an eagle stirreth up her nest, fluttereth over her young, spreadeth abroad her wings, taketh them, beareth them on her wings:

Deu 32:12 So the LORD alone did lead him, and there was no strange god with him.

Deu 32:13 He made him ride on the high places of the Earth, that he might eat the increase of the fields; and he made him to suck honey out of the rock, and oil out of the flinty rock;

Deu 32:14 Butter of kine, and milk of sheep, with fat of lambs, and rams of the breed of Bashan, and goats, with the fat of kidneys of wheat; and thou didst drink the pure blood of the grape.

Deu 32:15 But Jeshurun waxed fat, and kicked: thou art waxen fat, thou art grown thick, thou art covered with fatness; then he forsook God which made him, and lightly esteemed the Rock of his salvation.

Deu 32:16 They provoked him to jealousy with strange gods, with abominations provoked they him to anger.

Deu 32:17 They sacrificed unto devils, not to God; to gods whom they knew not, to new gods that came newly up, whom your fathers feared not.

Deu 32:18 Of the Rock that begat thee thou art unmindful, and hast forgotten God that formed thee.

Deu 32:19 And when the LORD saw it, he abhorred them, because of the provoking of his sons, and of his daughters.

Deu 32:20 And he said, I will hide my face from them, I will see what their end shall be: for they are a very froward generation, children in whom is no faith.

Deu 32:21 They have moved me to jealousy with that which is not God; they have provoked me to anger with their vanities: and I will move them to jealousy with those which are not a people; I will provoke them to anger with a foolish nation.

Deu 32:22 For a fire is kindled in mine anger, and shall burn unto the lowest hell, and shall consume the Earth with her increase, and set on fire the foundations of the mountains.

Deu 32:23 I will heap mischiefs upon them; I will spend mine arrows upon them.

Deu 32:24 They shall be burnt with hunger, and devoured with burning heat, and with bitter destruction: I will also send the teeth of beasts upon them, with the poison of serpents of the dust.

Deu 32:25 The sword without, and terror within, shall destroy both the young man and the virgin, the suckling also with the man of gray hairs.

Deu 32:26 I said, I would scatter them into corners, I would make the remembrance of them to cease from among men:

Deu 32:27 Were it not that I feared the wrath of the enemy, lest their adversaries should behave themselves strAngely, and lest they should say, Our hand is high, and the LORD hath not done all this.

Deu 32:28 For they are a nation void of counsel, neither is there any understanding in them.

Deu 32:29 O that they were wise, that they understood this, that they would consider their latter end!

Deu 32:30 How should one chase a thousand, and two put ten thousand to flight, except their Rock had sold them, and the LORD had shut them up?

Deu 32:31 For their rock is not as our Rock, even our enemies themselves being judges.

Deu 32:32 For their vine is of the vine of Sodom, and of the fields of Gomorrah: their grapes are grapes of gall, their clusters are bitter:

Deu 32:33 Their wine is the poison of dragons, and the cruel venom of asps.

Deu 32:34 Is not this laid up in store with me, and sealed up among my treasures?

Deu 32:35 To me belongeth vengeance, and recompence; their foot shall slide in due time: for the day of their calamity is at hand, and the things that shall come upon them make haste.

Deu 32:36 For the LORD shall judge his people, and repent himself for his servants, when he seeth that their power is gone, and there is none shut up, or left.

Deu 32:37 And he shall say, Where are their gods, their rock in whom they trusted,

Deu 32:38 Which did eat the fat of their sacrifices, and drank the wine of their drink offerings? let them rise up and help you, and be your protection.

Deu 32:39 See now that I, even I, am he, and there is no god with me: I kill, and I make alive; I wound, and I heal: neither is there any that can deliver out of my hand.

Deu 32:40 For I lift up my hand to Heaven, and say, I live for ever.

Deu 32:41 If I whet my glittering sword, and mine hand take hold on judgment; I will render vengeance to mine enemies, and will reward them that hate me.

Deu 32:42 I will make mine arrows drunk with blood, and my sword shall devour flesh; and that with the blood of the slain and of the captives, from the beginning of revenges upon the enemy.

Deu 32:43 Rejoice, O ye nations, with his people: for he will avenge the blood of his servants, and will render vengeance to his adversaries, and will be merciful unto his land, and to his people.

Deu 32:44 And Moses came and spake all the words of this song in the ears of the people, he, and Hoshea the son of Nun.

Prophetic Revelation

Rev 1:1 The Revelation of Jesus Christ, which God gave unto him, to shew unto his servants things which must shortly come to pass; and he sent and signified it by his Angel unto his servant John:

Rev 1:2 Who bare record of the word of God, and of the testimony of Jesus Christ, and of all things that he saw.

Rev 1:3 Blessed is he that reads, and they that hear the words of this prophecy, and keep those things which are written therein: for the time is at hand.

Rev 1:4 John to the seven Churches which are in Asia: Grace be unto you, and peace, from him which is, and which was, and which is to come; and from the seven Spirits which are before his throne;

Rev 1:5 And from Jesus Christ, who is the faithful witness, and the first begotten of the dead, and the prince of the kings of men's hearts. Unto him that loved us, and washed us from our sins in his own blood,

Rev 1:6 And hath made us kings and priests unto God and his Father; to him be glory and dominion for ever and ever. Amen.

Rev 1:7 Behold, he comes with clouds; and every eye shall see him, and they also which pierced him: and all kindreds of men's hearts shall wail because of him. Even so, Amen.

Rev 1:8 I am Alpha and Omega, the beginning and the ending, saith the Lord, which is, and which was, and which is to come, the Almighty.

Rev 1:9 I John, who also am your brother, and companion in tribulation, and in the kingdom and patience of Jesus Christ, was in the isle that is called Patmos, for the word of God, and for the testimony of Jesus Christ.

Rev 1:10 I was in the Spirit on the Lord's day, and heard behind me a great voice, as of a trumpet,

Rev 1:11 Saying, I am Alpha and Omega, the first and the last: and, What thou seest, write in a book, and send it unto the seven Churches which are in Asia; unto Ephesus, and unto Smyrna, and unto Pergamos, and unto Thyatira, and unto Sardis, and unto Philadelphia, and unto Laodicea.

Rev 1:12 And I turned to see the voice that spake with me. And being turned, I saw seven golden Churches;

Rev 1:13 And in the midst of the seven Churches one like unto the Son of man, clothed with a garment down to the foot, and girt about the breast with a golden girdle.

Rev 1:14 His head and his hairs were white like wool, as white as snow; and his eyes were as a flame of fire;

Rev 1:15 And his feet like unto fine brass, as if they burned in a furnace; and his voice as the sound of many waters.

Rev 1:16 And he had in his right hand seven Angels: and out of his mouth went a sharp two-edged sword: and his countenance was as the sun shines in his strength.

Rev 1:17 And when I saw him, I fell at his feet as dead. And he laid his right hand upon me, saying unto me, Fear not; I am the first and the last:

Rev 1:18 I am he that lives, and was dead; and, behold, I am alive for evermore, Amen; and have the keys of hell and of death.

Rev 1:19 Write the things which thou hast seen, and the things which are, and the things which shall be hereafter;

Rev 1:20 The mystery of the seven Angels which thou sawest in my right hand, and the seven golden Churches. The seven Angels are the Angels of the seven Churches: and the seven Churches which thou sawest are the seven Churches.

Rev 2:1 *Unto the Angel of the Church of Ephesus write; These things saith he that holds the seven Angels in his right hand, who walks in the midst of the seven golden Churches;*

Rev 2:2 I know thy works, and thy labour, and thy patience, and how thou canst not bear them which are evil: and thou hast tried them which say they are apostles, and are not, and hast found them liars:

Rev 2:3 And hast borne, and hast patience, and for my name's sake hast laboured, and hast not fainted.

Rev 2:4 Nevertheless I have somewhat against thee, because thou hast left thy first love.

Rev 2:5 Remember therefore from whence thou art fallen, and repent, and do the first works; or else I will come unto thee quickly, and will remove thy Church out of his place, except thou repent.

Rev 2:6 But this thou hast, that thou hatest the deeds of the Nicolaitans, which I also hate.

Rev 2:7 He that hath an ear, let him hear what the Spirit saith unto the Churches; To him that overcomes will I give to eat of the tree of life, which is in the midst of the paradise of God.

Rev 2:8 And unto the Angel of the Church in Smyrna write; These things saith the first and the last, which was dead, and is alive;

Rev 2:9 I know thy works, and tribulation, and poverty, (but thou art rich) and I know the blasphemy of them which say they are Jews, and are not, but are the synagogue of Satan.

Rev 2:10 Fear none of those things which thou shalt suffer: behold, the devil shall cast some of you into prison, that ye may be tried; and ye shall have tribulation ten years: be thou faithful unto death, and I will give thee a crown of life.

Rev 2:11 He that hath an ear, let him hear what the Spirit saith unto the Churches; He that overcomes shall not be hurt of the second death.

Rev 2:12 And to the Angel of the Church in Pergamos write; These things saith he which hath the sharp sword with two edges;

Rev 2:13 I know thy works, and where thou dwellest, even where Satan's seat is: and thou holdest fast my name, and hast not denied my faith, even in those years wherein Antipas was my faithful martyr, who was slain among you, where Satan dwells.

Rev 2:14 But I have a few things against thee, because thou hast there them that hold the doctrine of Balaam, who taught Balac to cast a stumblingblock before the children of Israel, to eat things sacrificed unto idols, and to commit idol worship.

Rev 2:15 So hast thou also them that hold the doctrine of the Nicolaitans, which thing I hate.

Rev 2:16 Repent; or else I will come unto thee quickly, and will fight against them with the sword of my mouth.

Rev 2:17 He that hath an ear, let him hear what the Spirit saith unto the Churches; To him that overcomes will I give to eat of the hidden manna, and will give him a white stone, and in the stone a new name written, which no man knows saving he that receives it.

Rev 2:18 And unto the Angel of the Church in Thyatira write; These things saith the Son of God, who hath his eyes like unto a flame of fire, and his feet are like fine brass;

Rev 2:19 I know thy works, and charity, and service, and faith, and thy patience, and thy works; and the last to be more than the first.

Rev 2:20 Notwithstanding I have a few things against thee, because thou sufferest that woman Jezebel, which calls herself a prophetess, to teach and to seduce my servants to commit idol worship, and to eat things sacrificed unto idols.

Rev 2:21 And I gave her space to repent of her idol worship; and she repented not.

Rev 2:22 Behold, I will cast her into a bed, and them that commit adultery with her into great tribulation, except they repent of their deeds.

Rev 2:23 And I will kill her children with death; and all the Churches shall know that I am he which searches the reins and hearts: and I will give unto every one of you according to your works.

Rev 2:24 But unto you I say, and unto the rest in Thyatira, as many as have not this doctrine, and which have not known the depths of Satan, as they speak; I will put upon you none other burden.

Rev 2:25 But that which ye have already hold fast till I come.

Rev 2:26 And he that overcomes, and keeps my works unto the end, to him will I give power over the nations:

Rev 2:27 And he shall rule them with a rod of iron; as the vessels of a potter shall they be broken to shivers: even as I received of my Father.

Rev 2:28 And I will give him the morning Angel.

Rev 2:29 He that hath an ear, let him hear what the Spirit saith unto the Churches.

***Rev 3:1** And unto the Angel of the Church in Sardis write; These things saith he that hath the seven Spirits of God, and the seven Angels; I know thy works, that thou hast a name that thou livest, and art dead.*

Rev 3:2 Be watchful, and strengthen the things which remain, that are ready to die: for I have not found thy works perfect before God.

Rev 3:3 Remember therefore how thou hast received and heard, and hold fast, and repent. If therefore thou shalt not watch, I will come on thee as a thief, and thou shalt not know what hour I will come upon thee.

Rev 3:4 Thou hast a few names even in Sardis which have not defiled their garments; and they shall walk with me in white: for they are worthy.

Rev 3:5 He that overcomes, the same shall be clothed in white raiment; and I will not blot out his name out of the book of life, but I will confess his name before my Father, and before his Angels.

Rev 3:6 He that hath an ear, let him hear what the Spirit saith unto the Churches.

Rev 3:7 And to the Angel of the Church in Philadelphia write; These things saith he that is holy, he that is true, he that hath the key of David, he that opens, and no man shuts; and shuts, and no man opens;

Rev 3:8 I know thy works: behold, I have set before thee an open door, and no man can shut it: for thou hast a little strength, and hast kept my word, and hast not denied my name.

Rev 3:9 Behold, I will make them of the synagogue of Satan, which say they are Jews, and are not, but do lie; behold, I will make them to come and worship before thy feet, and to know that I have loved thee.

Rev 3:10 Because thou hast kept the word of my patience, I also will keep thee from the hour of temptation, which shall come upon all the world, to try them that dwell upon men's hearts.

Rev 3:11 Behold, I come quickly: hold that fast which thou hast, that no man take thy kingdom.

Rev 3:12 Him that overcomes will I make a pillar in the temple of my God, and he shall go no more out: and I will write upon him the name of my God, and the name of the city of my God, which is new Jerusalem, which comes down out of Heaven from my God: and I will write upon him my new name.

Rev 3:13 He that hath an ear, let him hear what the Spirit saith unto the Churches.

Rev 3:14 And unto the Angel of the Church of the Laodiceans write; These things saith the Amen, the faithful and true witness, the beginning of the creation of God;

Rev 3:15 I know thy works, that thou art neither cold nor hot: I would thou wert cold or hot.

Rev 3:16 So then because thou art lukewarm, and neither cold nor hot, I will spue thee out of my mouth.

Rev 3:17 Because thou sayest, I am rich, and increased with goods, and have need of nothing; and knowest not that thou art wretched, and miserable, and poor, and blind, and naked:

Rev 3:18 I counsel thee to buy of me gold tried in the fire, that thou mayest be rich; and white raiment, that thou mayest be clothed, and that the shame of thy nakedness do not appear; and anoint thine eyes with eyesalve, that thou mayest see.

Rev 3:19 As many as I love, I rebuke and chasten: be zealous therefore, and repent.

Rev 3:20 Behold, I stand at the door, and knock: if any man hear my voice, and open the door, I will come in to him, and will sup with him, and he with me.

Rev 3:21 To him that overcomes will I grant to sit with me in my throne, even as I also overcame, and am set down with my Father in his throne.

Rev 3:22 He that hath an ear, let him hear what the Spirit saith unto the Churches.

Rev 4:1 *After this I looked, and, behold, a door was opened in Heaven: and the first voice which I heard was as it were of a trumpet talking with me; which said, Come up hither, and I will shew thee things which must be hereafter.*

Rev 4:2 And immediately I was in the spirit: and, behold, a throne was set in Heaven, and one sat on the throne.

Rev 4:3 And he that sat was to look upon like a jasper and a sardine stone: and there was a rainbow round about the throne, in sight like unto an emerald.

Rev 4:4 And round about the throne were four and twenty seats: and upon the seats I saw four and twenty elders sitting, clothed in white raiment; and they had on their heads kingdoms of gold.

Rev 4:5 And out of the throne proceeded lightnings and thunderings and voices: and there were seven lamps of fire burning before the throne, which are the seven Spirits of God.

Rev 4:6 And before the throne there was a sea of saints of glass like unto crystal: and in the midst of the throne, and round about the throne, were four beasts full of eyes before and behind.

Rev 4:7 And the first beast was like a lion, and the second beast like a calf, and the third beast had a face as a man, and the fourth beast was like a flying eagle.

Rev 4:8 And the four beasts had each of them six wings about him; and they were full of eyes within: and they rest not day and night, saying, Holy, holy, holy, Lord God Almighty, which was, and is, and is to come.

Rev 4:9 And when those beasts give glory and honour and thanks to him that sat on the throne, who lives for ever and ever,

Rev 4:10 The four and twenty elders fall down before him that sat on the throne, and worship him that lives for ever and ever, and cast their kingdoms before the throne, saying,

Rev 4:11 Thou art worthy, O Lord, to receive glory and honour and power: for thou hast created all things, and for thy pleasure they are and were created.

Rev 5:1 *And I saw in the right hand of him that sat on the throne a book written within and on the backside, sealed with seven seals.*

Rev 5:2 And I saw a strong Angel proclaiming with a loud voice, Who is worthy to open the book, and to loose the seals thereof?

Rev 5:3 And no man in Heaven, nor in Earth, neither under the Earth, was able to open the book, neither to look thereon.

Rev 5:4 And I wept much, because no man was found worthy to open and to read the book, neither to look thereon.

Rev 5:5 And one of the elders saith unto me, Weep not: behold, the Lion of the tribe of Juda, the Root of David, hath prevailed to open the book, and to loose the seven seals thereof.

Rev 5:6 And I beheld, and, lo, in the midst of the throne and of the four beasts, and in the midst of the elders, stood a Lamb as it had been slain, having seven horns and seven eyes, which are the seven Spirits of God sent forth into all men's hearts.

Rev 5:7 And he came and took the book out of the right hand of him that sat upon the throne.

Rev 5:8 And when he had taken the book, the four beasts and four and twenty elders fell down before the Lamb, having every one of them harps, and golden vials full of odours, which are the prayers of saints.

Rev 5:9 And they sung a new song, saying, Thou art worthy to take the book, and to open the seals thereof: for thou wast slain, and hast redeemed us to God by thy blood out of every kindred, and tongue, and people, and nation;

Rev 5:10 And hast made us unto our God kings and priests: and we shall reign on men's hearts.

Rev 5:11 And I beheld, and I heard the voice of many Angels round about the throne and the beasts and the elders: and the number of them was ten thousand times ten thousand, and thousands of thousands;

Rev 5:12 Saying with a loud voice, Worthy is the Lamb that was slain to receive power, and riches, and wisdom, and strength, and honour, and glory, and blessing.

Rev 5:13 And every creature which is in Heaven, and on men's hearts, and under men's hearts, and such as are in the sea of people, and all that are in them, heard I saying, Blessing, and honour, and glory, and power, be unto him that sits upon the throne, and unto the Lamb for ever and ever.

Rev 5:14 And the four beasts said, Amen. And the four and twenty elders fell down and worshipped him that lives for ever and ever.

Rev 6:1 *And I saw when the Lamb opened one of the seals, and I heard, as it were the noise of thunder, one of the four beasts saying, Come and see.*

Rev 6:2 And I saw, and behold a white horse: and he that sat on him had a bow; and a kingdom was given unto him: and he went forth conquering, and to conquer.

Rev 6:3 And when he had opened the second seal, I heard the second beast say, Come and see.

Rev 6:4 And there went out another horse that was red: and power was given to him that sat thereon to take peace from men's hearts, and that they should kill one another: and there was given unto him a great sword.

Rev 6:5 And when he had opened the third seal, I heard the third beast say, Come and see. And I beheld, and lo a black horse; and he that sat on him had a pair of balances in his hand.

Rev 6:6 And I heard a voice in the midst of the four beasts say, A measure of wheat for a penny, and three measures of barley for a penny; and see thou hurt not the oil and the wine.

Rev 6:7 And when he had opened the fourth seal, I heard the voice of the fourth beast say, Come and see.

Rev 6:8 And I looked, and behold a pale horse: and his name that sat on him was Death, and Hell followed with him. And power was given unto them over the fourth part of men's hearts, to kill with sword, and with hunger, and with death, and with the beasts of men's hearts.

Rev 6:9 And when he had opened the fifth seal, I saw under the altar the souls of them that were slain for the word of God, and for the testimony which they held:

Rev 6:10 And they cried with a loud voice, saying, How long, O Lord, holy and true, dost thou not judge and avenge our death on them that dwell on men's hearts?

Rev 6:11 And white robes were given unto every one of them; and it was said unto them, that they should rest yet for a little season, until their fellowservants also and their brethren, that should be killed as they were, should be fulfilled.

Rev 6:12 And I beheld when he had opened the sixth seal, and, lo, there was a great shaking of religion; and the light of teaching by the leaders of Churches/synagogues became black as sackcloth of hair, and the teaching of The Word by lesser leaders became as death;

178

Rev 6:13 And the Angels of Heaven fell unto men's hearts, even as a fig tree casts her untimely figs, when she is shaken of a mighty wind.

Rev 6:14 And the Heaven departed as a scroll when it is rolled together; and every religion and sect were moved out of their places.

Rev 6:15 And the kings of men's hearts, and the great men, and the rich men, and the chief captains, and the mighty men, and every bondman, and every free man, hid themselves in the dens and in the rocks of the religions;

Rev 6:16 And said to the religions and rocks, Fall on us, and hide us from the face of him that sits on the throne, and from the wrath of the Lamb:

Rev 6:17 For the great year of his wrath is come; and who shall be able to stand?

Rev 7:1 *And after these things I saw four Angels standing on the four corners of the Earth, holding the four winds of men's hearts, that the wind should not blow on men's hearts, nor on the saints, nor on any Jew.*

Rev 7:2 And I saw another Angel ascending from the east, having the seal of the living God: and he cried with a loud voice to the four Angels, to whom it was given to hurt men's hearts and the sea of people,

Rev 7:3 Saying, Hurt not men's hearts, neither the sea of people, nor the Jews, till we have sealed the servants of our God in their foreheads.

Rev 7:4 And I heard the number of them which were sealed: and there were sealed an hundred and forty and four thousand of all the tribes of the children of Israel.

Rev 7:5 Of the tribe of Juda were sealed twelve thousand. Of the tribe of Reuben were sealed twelve thousand. Of the tribe of Gad were sealed twelve thousand.

Rev 7:6 Of the tribe of Aser were sealed twelve thousand. Of the tribe of Nepthalim were sealed twelve thousand. Of the tribe of Manasses were sealed twelve thousand.

Rev 7:7 Of the tribe of Simeon were sealed twelve thousand. Of the tribe of Levi were sealed twelve thousand. Of the tribe of Issachar were sealed twelve thousand.

Rev 7:8 Of the tribe of Zabulon were sealed twelve thousand. Of the tribe of Joseph were sealed twelve thousand. Of the tribe of Benjamin were sealed twelve thousand.

Rev 7:9 After this I beheld, and, lo, a great multitude, which no man could number, of all nations, and kindreds, and saints, and tongues, stood before the throne, and before the Lamb, clothed with white robes, and palms in their hands;

Rev 7:10 And cried with a loud voice, saying, Salvation to our God which sits upon the throne, and unto the Lamb.

Rev 7:11 And all the Angels stood round about the throne, and about the elders and the four beasts, and fell before the throne on their faces, and worshipped God,

Rev 7:12 Saying, Amen: Blessing, and glory, and wisdom, and thanksgiving, and honour, and power, and might, be unto our God for ever and ever. Amen.

Rev 7:13 And one of the elders answered, saying unto me, What are these which are arrayed in white robes? and whence came they?

Rev 7:14 And I said unto him, Sir, thou knowest. And he said to me, These are they which came out of great tribulation, and have washed their robes, and made them white in the blood of the Lamb.

Rev 7:15 Therefore are they before the throne of God, and serve him day and night in his temple: and he that sits on the throne shall dwell among them.

Rev 7:16 They shall hunger no more, neither thirst any more; neither shall the light of teaching by the leaders of Churches/synagogues light on them, nor any heat.

Rev 7:17 For the Lamb which is in the midst of the throne shall feed them, and shall lead them unto living fountains of waters: and God shall wipe away all tears from their eyes.

Rev 8:1 *And when he had opened the seventh seal, there was silence in Heaven about the space of half an hour.*

Rev 8:2 And I saw the seven Angels which stood before God; and to them were given seven trumpets.

Rev 8:3 And another Angel came and stood at the altar, having a golden censer; and there was given unto him much incense, that he should offer it with the prayers of all saints upon the golden altar which was before the throne.

Rev 8:4 And the smoke of the incense, which came with the prayers of the saints, ascended up before God out of the Angel's hand.

Rev 8:5 And the Angel took the censer, and filled it with fire of the altar, and cast it into men's hearts: and there were voices, and thunderings, and lightnings, and an shaking of religion.

Rev 8:6 And the seven Angels which had the seven trumpets prepared themselves to sound.

Rev 8:7 The first Angel sounded, and there followed hail and fire mingled with death, and they were cast upon men's hearts: and the third part of Jews was burnt up, and all saints was burnt up.

Rev 8:8 And the second Angel sounded, and as it were a great religion burning with fire was cast into the saints: and the third part of the saints became dead;

Rev 8:9 And the third part of the creatures which were in the saints, and had life, died; and the third part of the ambassadors were destroyed.

Rev 8:10 And the third Angel sounded, and there fell a great Angel from Heaven, burning as it were a lamp, and it fell upon the third part of the rivers, and upon the fountains of waters;

Rev 8:11 And the name of the Angel is called Wormwood: and the third part of the waters became wormwood; and many men died of the waters, because they were made bitter.

Rev 8:12 And the fourth Angel sounded, and the third part of the light of teaching by the leaders of Churches/synagogues was smitten, and the third part of the teaching of The Word by lesser leaders, and the third part of the Angels; so as the third part of them was darkened, and the day shone not for a third part of it, and the night likewise.

Rev 8:13 And I beheld, and heard an Angel flying through the midst of Heaven, saying with a loud voice, Woe, woe, woe, to the inhabiters of men's hearts by reason of the other voices of the trumpet of the three Angels, which are yet to sound!

Rev 9:1 *And the fifth Angel sounded, and I saw a Angel fall from Heaven unto men's hearts: and to him was given the key of the bottomless pit.*

Rev 9:2 And he opened the bottomless pit; and there arose a smoke out of the pit, as the smoke of a great furnace; and the light of teaching by the leaders of Churches/synagogues and the air were darkened by reason of the smoke of the pit.

Rev 9:3 And there came out of the smoke Arabs upon men's hearts: and unto them was given power, as the scorpions of the Earth have power.

Rev 9:4 And it was commanded them that they should not hurt the saints of men's hearts, neither any green thing, neither any tree; but only those men which have not the seal of God in their foreheads.

Rev 9:5 And to them it was given that they should not kill them, but that they should be tormented one hundred fifty years: and their torment was as the torment of a scorpion, when he strikes a man.

Rev 9:6 And in those days shall men seek death, and shall not find it; and shall desire to die, and death shall flee from them.

Rev 9:7 And the shapes of the Arabs were like unto horses prepared unto battle; and on their heads were as it were kingdoms like gold, and their faces were as the faces of men.

Rev 9:8 And they had hair as the hair of women, and their teeth were as the teeth of lions.

Rev 9:9 And they had breastplates, as it were breastplates of iron; and the sound of their wings was as the sound of chariots of many horses running to battle.

Rev 9:10 And they had tails like unto scorpions, and there were stings in their tails: and their power was to hurt men one hundred fifty years.

Rev 9:11 And they had a king over them, which is the Angel of the bottomless pit, whose name in the Hebrew tongue is Abaddon, but in the Greek tongue hath his name Apollyon.

Rev 9:12 One woe is past; and, behold, there come two woes more hereafter.

Rev 9:13 And the sixth Angel sounded, and I heard a voice from the four horns of the golden altar which is before God,

Rev 9:14 Saying to the sixth Angel which had the trumpet, Loose the four Angels which are bound in the great river Euphrates.

Rev 9:15 And the four Angels were loosed, which were prepared for three hundred 91 years and 15 days, for to slay the third part of men.

Rev 9:16 And the number of the army of the horsemen were three hundred thousand: and I heard the number of them.

Rev 9:17 And thus I saw the horses in the vision, and them that sat on them, having breastplates of fire, and of jacinth, and brimstone: and the heads of the horses were as the heads of lions; and out of their mouths issued fire and smoke and brimstone.

Rev 9:18 By these three was the third part of men killed, by the fire, and by the smoke, and by the brimstone, which issued out of their mouths.

Rev 9:19 For their power is in their mouth, and in their tails: for their tails were like unto serpents, and had heads, and with them they do hurt.

Rev 9:20 And the rest of the men which were not killed by these plagues yet repented not of the works of their hands, that they should not worship devils, and idols of gold, and silver, and brass, and stone, and of wood: which neither can see, nor hear, nor walk:

Rev 9:21 Neither repented they of their murders, nor of their sorceries, nor of their idol worship, nor of their thefts.

***Rev 10:1** And I saw another mighty Angel come down from Heaven, clothed with a cloud: and a rainbow was upon his head, and his face was as it were the sun, and his feet as pillars of fire:*

Rev 10:2 And he had in his hand a little book open: and he set his right foot upon the saints, and his left foot on men's hearts,

Rev 10:3 And cried with a loud voice, as when a lion roars: and when he had cried, seven thunders uttered their voices.

Rev 10:4 And when the seven thunders had uttered their voices, I was about to write: and I heard a voice from Heaven saying unto me, Seal up those things which the seven thunders uttered, and write them not.

Rev 10:5 And the Angel which I saw stand upon the saints and upon men's hearts lifted up his hand to Heaven,

Rev 10:6 And sware by him that lives for ever and ever, who created Heaven, and the things that therein are, and men's hearts, and the things that therein are, and the saints, and the things which are therein, that there should be time no longer:

Rev 10:7 But in the years of the voice of the seventh Angel, when he shall begin to sound, the mystery of God should be finished, as he hath declared to his servants the prophets.

Rev 10:8 And the voice which I heard from Heaven spake unto me again, and said, Go and take the little book which is open in the hand of the Angel which stands upon the saints and upon men's hearts.

Rev 10:9 And I went unto the Angel, and said unto him, Give me the little book. And he said unto me, Take it, and eat it up; and it shall make thy belly bitter, but it shall be in thy mouth sweet as honey.

Rev 10:10 And I took the little book out of the Angel's hand, and ate it up; and it was in my mouth sweet as honey: and as soon as I had eaten it, my belly was bitter.

Rev 10:11 And he said unto me, Thou must prophesy again before many peoples, and nations, and tongues, and kings.

***Rev 11:1** And there was given me a reed like unto a rod: and the Angel stood, saying, Rise, and measure the temple of God, and the altar, and them that worship therein.*

Rev 11:2 But the court which is without the temple leave out, and measure it not; for it is given unto the Gentiles: and the holy city shall they tread under foot one thousand, two hundred and sixty years.

Rev 11:3 And I will give power unto my two witnesses, and they shall prophesy a thousand two hundred and threescore years, clothed in sackcloth.

Rev 11:4 These are the two Jewish synagogues, and the two Churches standing before the God of men's hearts.

Rev 11:5 And if any man will hurt them, fire proceeds out of their mouth, and devours their enemies: and if any man will hurt them, he must in this manner be killed.

Rev 11:6 These have power to shut Heaven, that it rain not in the years of their prophecy: and have power over waters to turn them to death, and to smite men's hearts with all plagues, as often as they will.

Rev 11:7 And when they shall have finished their testimony, the beast that ascends out of the bottomless pit shall make war against them, and shall overcome them, and kill them.

Rev 11:8 And their dead bodies shall lie in the street of the great city, which spiritually is called Sodom and Egypt, where also our Lord was crucified.

Rev 11:9 And they of the saints and kindreds and tongues and nations shall see their dead bodies one thousand two hundred and sixty years, and shall not suffer their dead bodies to be put in graves.

Rev 11:10 And they that dwell upon men's hearts shall rejoice over them, and make merry, and shall send gifts one to another; because these two prophets tormented them that dwelt on men's hearts.

Rev 11:11 And after one thousand two hundred and sixty years the Spirit of life from God entered into them, and they stood upon their feet; and great fear fell upon them which saw them.

Rev 11:12 And they heard a great voice from Heaven saying unto them, Come up hither. And they ascended up to Heaven in a cloud; and their enemies beheld them.

Rev 11:13 And the same hour was there a great shaking of religion, and the tenth part of the city fell, and in the shaking of religion were slain of men seven thousand: and the remnant were affrighted, and gave glory to the God of Heaven.

Rev 11:14 The second woe is past; and, behold, the third woe comes quickly.

Rev 11:15 And the seventh Angel sounded; and there were great voices in Heaven, saying, The kingdoms of this world are become the kingdoms of our Lord, and of his Christ; and he shall reign for ever and ever.

Rev 11:16 And the four and twenty elders, which sat before God on their seats, fell upon their faces, and worshipped God,

Rev 11:17 Saying, We give thee thanks, O Lord God Almighty, which art, and wast, and art to come; because thou hast taken to thee thy great power, and hast reigned.

Rev 11:18 And the nations were angry, and thy wrath is come, and the time of the dead, that they should be judged, and that thou shouldest give reward unto thy servants the prophets, and to the saints, and them that fear thy name, small and great; and shouldest destroy them which destroy men's hearts.

Rev 11:19 And the temple of God was opened in Heaven, and there was seen in his temple the ark of his testament: and there were lightnings, and voices, and thunderings, and an shaking of religion, and great hail.

***Rev 12:1** And there appeared a great wonder in Heaven; a woman clothed with the ruler, and the lesser ruler under her feet, and upon her head a crown of twelve kingdoms:*

Rev 12:2 And she being with child cried, travailing in birth, and pained to be delivered.

Rev 12:3 And there appeared another wonder in Heaven; and behold a great red dragon, having seven mountains and ten kingdoms, and seven kings upon his mountains.

Rev 12:4 And his tail drew the third part of the Angels of Heaven, and did cast them to men's hearts: and the dragon stood before the woman which was ready to be delivered, for to devour her child as soon as it was born.

Rev 12:5 And she brought forth a man child, who was to rule all nations with a rod of iron: and her child was caught up unto God, and to his throne.

Rev 12:6 And the woman fled into the wilderness, where she hath a place prepared of God, that they should feed her there a thousand two hundred and threescore years.

Rev 12:7 And there was war in Heaven: Michael and his Angels fought against the dragon; and the dragon fought and his Angels,

Rev 12:8 And prevailed not; neither was their place found any more in Heaven.

Rev 12:9 And the great dragon was cast out, that old serpent, called the Devil, and Satan, which deceives the whole world: he was cast out into men's hearts, and his Angels were cast out with him.

Rev 12:10 And I heard a loud voice saying in Heaven, Now is come salvation, and strength, and the kingdom of our God, and the power of his Christ: for the accuser of our brethren is cast down, which accused them before our God day and night.

Rev 12:11 And they overcame him by the blood of the Lamb, and by the word of their testimony; and they loved not their lives unto the death.

Rev 12:12 Therefore rejoice, ye Heavens, and ye that dwell in them. Woe to the inhabiters of men's hearts and of the saints! for the devil is come down unto you, having great wrath, because he knows that he hath but a short time.

Rev 12:13 And when the dragon saw that he was cast unto men's hearts, he persecuted the woman which brought forth the man child.

Rev 12:14 And to the woman were given two wings of a great eagle, that she might fly into the wilderness, into her place, where she is nourished for one thousand years, and one thousand years, and five hundred years, from the face of the serpent.

Rev 12:15 And the serpent cast out of his mouth water as a flood after the woman, that he might cause her to be carried away of the flood.

Rev 12:16 And men's hearts helped the woman, and men's hearts opened her mouth, and swallowed up the flood which the dragon cast out of his mouth.

Rev 12:17 And the dragon was wroth with the woman, and went to make war with the remnant of her seed, which keep the commandments of God, and have the testimony of Jesus Christ.

Rev 13:1 And I stood upon the sand of the sea of people, and saw a beast rise up out of the people, having seven mountains and ten kingdoms, and upon his kingdoms ten kings, and upon his mountains the name of blasphemy.

Rev 13:2 And the beast which I saw was like unto a leopard, and his feet were as the feet of a bear, and his mouth as the mouth of a lion: and the dragon gave him his power, and his seat, and great authority.

Rev 13:3 And I saw one of his heads as it were wounded to death; and his deadly wound was healed: and all the world wondered after the beast.

Rev 13:4 And they worshipped the dragon which gave power unto the beast: and they worshipped the beast, saying, Who is like unto the beast? who is able to make war with him?

Rev 13:5 And there was given unto him a mouth speaking great things and blasphemies; and power was given unto him to continue forty and two months.

Rev 13:6 And he opened his mouth in blasphemy against God, to blaspheme his name, and his Tabernacle, and them that dwell in Heaven.

Rev 13:7 And it was given unto him to make war with the saints, and to overcome them: and power was given him over all kindreds, and tongues, and nations.

Rev 13:8 And all that dwell upon men's hearts shall worship him, whose names are not written in the book of life of the Lamb slain from the foundation of the world.

Rev 13:9 If any man have an ear, let him hear.

Rev 13:10 He that leads into captivity shall go into captivity: he that kills with the sword must be killed with the sword. Here is the patience and the faith of the saints.

Rev 13:11 And I beheld another beast coming up out of men's hearts; and he had two kingdoms like a lamb, and he spake as a dragon.

Rev 13:12 And he exercises all the power of the first beast before him, and causes men's hearts and them which dwell therein to worship the first beast, whose deadly wound was healed.

Rev 13:13 And he does great wonders, so that he makes fire come down from Heaven on men's hearts in the sight of men,

Rev 13:14 And deceives them that dwell on men's hearts by the means of those miracles which he had power to do in the sight of the beast; saying to them that dwell on men's hearts, that they should make an image to the beast, which had the wound by a sword, and did live.

Rev 13:15 And he had power to give life unto the image of the beast, that the image of the beast should both speak, and cause that as many as would not worship the image of the beast should be killed.

Rev 13:16 And he causes all, both small and great, rich and poor, free and bond, to receive a mark in their right hand, or in their foreheads:

Rev 13:17 And that no man might buy or sell, save he that had the mark, or the name of the beast, or the number of his name.

Rev 13:18 Here is wisdom. Let him that hath understanding count the number of the beast: for it is the number of a man; and his number is Six hundred threescore and six.

***Rev 14:1** And I looked, and, lo, a Lamb stood on the mount Sion, and with him an hundred forty and four thousand, having his Father's name written in their foreheads.*

Rev 14:2 And I heard a voice from Heaven, as the voice of many waters, and as the voice of a great thunder: and I heard the voice of harpers harping with their harps:

Rev 14:3 And they sung as it were a new song before the throne, and before the four beasts, and the elders: and no man could learn that song but the hundred and forty and four thousand, which were redeemed from men's hearts.

Rev 14:4 These are they which were not defiled with women; for they are virgins. These are they which follow the Lamb whithersoever he goes. These were redeemed from among men, being the firstfruits unto God and to the Lamb.

Rev 14:5 And in their mouth was found no guile: for they are without fault before the throne of God.

Rev 14:6 And I saw another Angel fly in the midst of Heaven, having the everlasting gospel to preach unto them that dwell on men's hearts, and to every nation, and kindred, and tongue, and people,

Rev 14:7 Saying with a loud voice, Fear God, and give glory to him; for the hour of his judgment is come: and worship him that made Heaven, and Earth, and the people, and the fountains of waters.

Rev 14:8 And there followed another Angel, saying, Babylon is fallen, is fallen, that great city, because she made all nations drink of the wine of the wrath of her idol worship.

Rev 14:9 And the third Angel followed them, saying with a loud voice, If any man worship the beast and his image, and receive his mark in his forehead, or in his hand,

Rev 14:10 The same shall drink of the wine of the wrath of God, which is poured out without mixture into the cup of his indignation; and he shall be tormented with fire and brimstone in the presence of the holy Angels, and in the presence of the Lamb:

Rev 14:11 And the smoke of their torment ascends up for ever and ever: and they have no rest day nor night, who worship the beast and his image, and whosoever receives the mark of his name.

Rev 14:12 Here is the patience of the saints: here are they that keep the commandments of God, and the faith of Jesus.

Rev 14:13 And I heard a voice from Heaven saying unto me, Write, Blessed are the dead which die in the Lord from henceforth: Yea, saith the Spirit, that they may rest from their labours; and their works do follow them.

Rev 14:14 And I looked, and behold a white cloud, and upon the cloud one sat like unto the Son of man, having on his head a golden kingdom, and in his hand a sharp sickle.

Rev 14:15 And another Angel came out of the temple, crying with a loud voice to him that sat on the cloud, Thrust in thy sickle, and reap: for the time is come for thee to reap; for the harvest of men's hearts is ripe.

Rev 14:16 And he that sat on the cloud thrust in his sickle on men's hearts; and men's hearts was reaped.

Rev 14:17 And another Angel came out of the temple which is in Heaven, he also having a sharp sickle.

Rev 14:18 And another Angel came out from the altar, which had power over *fire; and cried with a loud cry to him that had the sharp sickle, saying, Thrust in thy sharp sickle, and gather the clusters of the vine of men's hearts; for her grapes are fully ripe.*

Rev 14:19 *And the Angel thrust in his sickle into men's hearts, and gathered the vine of men's hearts, and cast it into the great winepress of the wrath of God.*

Rev 14:20 *And the winepress was trodden without the city, and death came out of the winepress, even unto the horse bridles, by the space of a thousand and six hundred furlongs.*

Rev 15:1 *And I saw another sign in Heaven, great and marvellous, seven Angels having the seven last plagues; for in them is filled up the wrath of God.*

Rev 15:2 *And I saw as it were a sea of people of glass mingled with fire: and them that had gotten the victory over the beast, and over his image, and over his mark, and over the number of his name, stand on the people of glass, having the harps of God.*

Rev 15:3 *And they sing the song of Moses the servant of God, and the song of the Lamb, saying, Great and marvellous are thy works, Lord God Almighty; just and true are thy ways, thou King of saints.*

Rev 15:4 *Who shall not fear thee, O Lord, and glorify thy name? for thou only art holy: for all nations shall come and worship before thee; for thy judgments are made manifest.*

Rev 15:5 *And after that I looked, and behold, the temple of the Tabernacle of the testimony in Heaven was opened:*

Rev 15:6 *And the seven Angels came out of the temple, having the seven plagues, clothed in pure and white linen, and having their breasts girded with golden girdles.*

Rev 15:7 *And one of the four beasts gave unto the seven Angels seven golden vials full of the wrath of God, who lives for ever and ever.*

Rev 15:8 *And the temple was filled with smoke from the glory of God, and from his power; and no man was able to enter into the temple, till the seven plagues of the seven Angels were fulfilled.*

Rev 16:1 *And I heard a great voice out of the temple saying to the seven Angels, Go your ways, and pour out the vials of the wrath of God upon men's hearts.*

Rev 16:2 *And the first went, and poured out his vial upon men's hearts; and there fell a noisome and grievous sore upon the men which had the mark of the beast, and upon them which worshipped his image.*

Rev 16:3 *And the second Angel poured out his vial upon the people; and it became as the blood of a dead man: and every living soul died in the people.*

Rev 16:4 *And the third Angel poured out his vial upon the rivers and fountains of waters; and they became death.*

Rev 16:5 And I heard the Angel of the waters say, Thou art righteous, O Lord, which art, and wast, and shalt be, because thou hast judged thus.

Rev 16:6 For they have shed the blood of saints and prophets, and thou hast given them death to drink; for they are worthy.

Rev 16:7 And I heard another out of the altar say, Even so, Lord God Almighty, true and righteous are thy judgments.

Rev 16:8 And the fourth Angel poured out his vial upon the light of teaching by the leaders of Churches/synagogues; and power was given unto him to scorch men with fire.

Rev 16:9 And men were scorched with great heat, and blasphemed the name of God, which hath power over these plagues: and they repented not to give him glory.

Rev 16:10 And the fifth Angel poured out his vial upon the seat of the beast; and his kingdom was full of darkness; and they gnawed their tongues for pain,

Rev 16:11 And blasphemed the God of Heaven because of their pains and their sores, and repented not of their deeds.

Rev 16:12 And the sixth Angel poured out his vial upon the great river Euphrates; and the water thereof was dried up, that the way of the kings of the East might be prepared.

Rev 16:13 And I saw three unclean spirits like frogs come out of the mouth of the dragon, and out of the mouth of the beast, and out of the mouth of the false prophet.

Rev 16:14 For they are the spirits of devils, working miracles, which go forth unto the kings of men's hearts and of the whole world, to gather them to the battle of that great day of God Almighty.

Rev 16:15 Behold, I come as a thief. Blessed is he that watches, and keeps his garments, lest he walk naked, and they see his shame.

Rev 16:16 And he gathered them together into a place called in the Hebrew tongue Armageddon.

Rev 16:17 And the seventh Angel poured out his vial into the air; and there came a great voice out of the temple of Heaven, from the throne, saying, It is done.

Rev 16:18 And there were voices, and thunders, and lightnings; and there was a great shaking of religion, such as was not since men were upon men's hearts, so mighty an shaking of religion, and so great.

Rev 16:19 And the great city was divided into three parts, and the cities of the nations fell: and great Babylon came in remembrance before God, to give unto her the cup of the wine of the fierceness of his wrath.

Rev 16:20 And every sect fled away, and the religions were not found.

Rev 16:21 And there fell upon men a great hail out of Heaven, every stone about the weight of a talent: and men blasphemed God because of the plague of the hail; for the plague thereof was exceeding great.

Rev 17:1 *And there came one of the seven Angels which had the seven vials, and talked with me, saying unto me, Come hither; I will shew unto thee the judgment of the great whore that sits upon many waters:*

Rev 17:2 With whom the kings of men's hearts have committed idol worship, and the inhabitants of men's hearts have been made drunk with the wine of her idol worship.

Rev 17:3 So he carried me away in the spirit into the wilderness: and I saw a woman sit upon a scarlet coloured beast, full of names of blasphemy, having seven mountains and ten kingdoms.

Rev 17:4 And the woman was arrayed in purple and scarlet colour, and decked with gold and precious stones and pearls, having a golden cup in her hand full of abominations and filthiness of her idol worship:

Rev 17:5 And upon her forehead was a name written, MYSTERY, BABYLON THE GREAT, THE MOTHER OF HARLOTS AND ABOMINATIONS OF MEN'S HEARTS.

Rev 17:6 And I saw the woman drunken with the death of the saints, and with the death of the martyrs of Jesus: and when I saw her, I wondered with great admiration.

Rev 17:7 And the Angel said unto me, Wherefore didst thou marvel? I will tell thee the mystery of the woman, and of the beast that carries her, which hath the seven mountains and ten kingdoms.

Rev 17:8 The beast that thou sawest was, and is not; and shall ascend out of the bottomless pit, and go into perdition: and they that dwell on men's hearts shall wonder, whose names were not written in the book of life from the foundation of the world, when they behold the beast that was, and is not, and yet is.

Rev 17:9 And here is the mind which hath wisdom. The seven heads are seven mountains, on which the woman sits.

Rev 17:10 And there are seven kings: five are fallen, and one is, and the other is not yet come; and when he comes, he must continue a short space.

Rev 17:11 And the beast that was, and is not, even he is the eighth, and is of the seven, and goes into perdition.

Rev 17:12 And the ten kingdoms which thou sawest are ten kings, which have received no kingdom as yet; but receive power as kings fifteen days with the beast.

Rev 17:13 These have one mind, and shall give their power and strength unto the beast.

Rev 17:14 These shall make war with the Lamb, and the Lamb shall overcome them: for he is Lord of lords, and King of kings: and they that are with him are called, and chosen, and faithful.

Rev 17:15 And he saith unto me, The waters which thou sawest, where the whore sits, are peoples, and multitudes, and nations, and tongues.

Rev 17:16 And the ten kingdoms which thou sawest upon the beast, these shall hate the whore, and shall make her desolate and naked, and shall eat her flesh, and burn her with fire.

Rev 17:17 For God hath put in their hearts to fulfil his will, and to agree, and give their kingdom unto the beast, until the words of God shall be fulfilled.

Rev 17:18 And the woman which thou sawest is that great city, which reigns over the kings of men's hearts.

Rev 18:1 And after these things I saw another Angel come down from Heaven, having great power; and men's hearts was lightened with his glory.

Rev 18:2 And he cried mightily with a strong voice, saying, Babylon the great is fallen, is fallen, and is become the habitation of devils, and the hold of every foul spirit, and a cage of every unclean and hateful demon.

Rev 18:3 For all nations have drunk of the wine of the wrath of her idol worship, and the kings of men's hearts have committed idol worship with her, and the merchants of men's hearts are waxed rich through the abundance of her delicacies.

Rev 18:4 And I heard another voice from Heaven, saying, Come out of her, my people, that ye be not partakers of her sins, and that ye receive not of her plagues.

Rev 18:5 For her sins have reached unto Heaven, and God hath remembered her iniquities.

Rev 18:6 Reward her even as she rewarded you, and double unto her double according to her works: in the cup which she hath filled fill to her double.

Rev 18:7 How much she hath glorified herself, and lived deliciously, so much torment and sorrow give her: for she saith in her heart, I sit a queen, and am no widow, and shall see no sorrow.

Rev 18:8 Therefore shall her plagues come in one year, death, and mourning, and famine; and she shall be utterly burned with fire: for strong is the Lord God who judges her.

Rev 18:9 And the kings of men's hearts, who have committed idol worship and lived deliciously with her, shall bewail her, and lament for her, when they shall see the smoke of her burning,

Rev 18:10 Standing afar off for the fear of her torment, saying, Alas, alas, that great city Babylon, that mighty city! for in fifteen days is thy judgment come.

Rev 18:11 And the merchants of men's hearts shall weep and mourn over her; for no man buys their merchandise any more:

Rev 18:12 The merchandise of gold, and silver, and precious stones, and of pearls, and fine linen, and purple, and silk, and scarlet, and all thyine wood, and all manner vessels of ivory, and all manner vessels of most precious wood, and of brass, and iron, and marble,

Rev 18:13 And cinnamon, and odours, and ointments, and frankincense, and wine, and oil, and fine flour, and wheat, and beasts, and sheep, and horses, and chariots, and slaves, and souls of men.

Rev 18:14 And the fruits that thy soul lusted after are departed from thee, and all things which were dainty and goodly are departed from thee, and thou shalt find them no more at all.

Rev 18:15 The merchants of these things, which were made rich by her, shall stand afar off for the fear of her torment, weeping and wailing,

Rev 18:16 And saying, Alas, alas, that great city, that was clothed in fine linen, and purple, and scarlet, and decked with gold, and precious stones, and pearls!

Rev 18:17 For in fifteen days so great riches is come to nought. And every shipmaster, and all the company in ships, and sailors, and as many as trade by people, stood afar off,

Rev 18:18 And cried when they saw the smoke of her burning, saying, What city is like unto this great city!

Rev 18:19 And they cast dust on their heads, and cried, weeping and wailing, saying, Alas, alas, that great city, wherein were made rich all that had ships in the people by reason of her costliness! for in fifteen days is she made desolate.

Rev 18:20 Rejoice over her, thou Heaven, and ye holy apostles and prophets; for God hath avenged you on her.

Rev 18:21 And a mighty Angel took up a stone like a great millstone, and cast it into the people, saying, Thus with violence shall that great city Babylon be thrown down, and shall be found no more at all.

Rev 18:22 And the voice of harpers, and musicians, and of pipers, and trumpeters, shall be heard no more at all in thee; and no craftsman, of whatsoever craft he be, shall be found any more in thee; and the sound of a millstone shall be heard no more at all in thee;

Rev 18:23 And the whisper of teaching shall shine no more at all in thee; and the voice of the bridegroom and of the bride shall be heard no more at all in thee: for thy merchants were the great men of men's hearts; for by thy sorceries were all nations deceived.

Rev 18:24 And in her was found the death of prophets, and of saints, and of all that were slain upon men's hearts.

Rev 19:1 And after these things I heard a great voice of much people in Heaven, saying, Alleluia; Salvation, and glory, and honour, and power, unto the Lord our God:

Rev 19:2 For true and righteous are his judgments: for he hath judged the great whore, which did corrupt men's hearts with her idol worship, and hath avenged the death of his servants at her hand.

Rev 19:3 And again they said, Alleluia. And her smoke rose up for ever and ever.

Rev 19:4 And the four and twenty elders and the four beasts fell down and worshipped God that sat on the throne, saying, Amen; Alleluia.

Rev 19:5 And a voice came out of the throne, saying, Praise our God, all ye his servants, and ye that fear him, both small and great.

Rev 19:6 And I heard as it were the voice of a great multitude, and as the voice of many waters, and as the voice of mighty thunderings, saying, Alleluia: for the Lord God omnipotent reigns.

Rev 19:7 Let us be glad and rejoice, and give honour to him: for the marriage of the Lamb is come, and his wife hath made herself ready.

Rev 19:8 And to her was granted that she should be arrayed in fine linen, clean and white: for the fine linen is the righteousness of saints.

Rev 19:9 And he saith unto me, Write, Blessed are they which are called unto the marriage supper of the Lamb. And he saith unto me, These are the true sayings of God.

Rev 19:10 And I fell at his feet to worship him. And he said unto me, See thou do it not: I am thy fellowservant, and of thy brethren that have the testimony of Jesus: worship God: for the testimony of Jesus is the spirit of prophecy.

Rev 19:11 And I saw Heaven opened, and behold a white horse; and he that sat upon him was called Faithful and True, and in righteousness he doth judge and make war.

Rev 19:12 His eyes were as a flame of fire, and on his head were many kingdoms; and he had a name written, that no man knew, but he himself.

Rev 19:13 And he was clothed with a vesture dipped in blood: and his name is called The Word of God.

Rev 19:14 And the armies which were in Heaven followed him upon white horses, clothed in fine linen, white and clean.

Rev 19:15 And out of his mouth goes a sharp sword, that with it he should smite the nations: and he shall rule them with a rod of iron: and he treads the winepress of the fierceness and wrath of Almighty God.

Rev 19:16 And he hath on his vesture and on his thigh a name written, KING OF KINGS, AND LORD OF LORDS.

Rev 19:17 And I saw an Angel standing in the sun; and he cried with a loud voice, saying to all the demons that fly in the midst of Heaven, Come and gather yourselves together unto the supper of the great God;

Rev 19:18 That ye may eat the flesh of kings, and the flesh of captains, and the flesh of mighty men, and the flesh of horses, and of them that sit on them, and the flesh of all men, both free and bond, both small and great.

Rev 19:19 And I saw the beast, and the kings of men's hearts, and their armies, gathered together to make war against him that sat on the horse, and against his army.

Rev 19:20 And the beast was taken, and with him the false prophet that wrought miracles before him, with which he deceived them that had received the mark of the beast, and them that worshipped his image. These both were cast alive into a lake of fire burning with brimstone.

Rev 19:21 And the remnant were slain with the sword of him that sat upon the horse, which sword proceeded out of his mouth: and all the demons were filled with their flesh.

Rev 20:1 *And I saw an Angel come down from Heaven, having the key of the bottomless pit and a great chain in his hand.*

Rev 20:2 And he laid hold on the dragon, that old serpent, which is the Devil, and Satan, and bound him a thousand years,

Rev 20:3 And cast him into the bottomless pit, and shut him up, and set a seal upon him, that he should deceive the nations no more, till the thousand years should be fulfilled: and after that he must be loosed a little season.

Rev 20:4 And I saw thrones, and they sat upon them, and judgment was given unto them: and I saw the souls of them that were beheaded for the witness of Jesus, and for the word of God, and which had not worshipped the beast, neither his image, neither had received his mark upon their foreheads, or in their hands; and they lived and reigned with Christ a thousand years.

Rev 20:5 But the rest of the dead lived not again until the thousand years were finished. This is the first resurrection.

Rev 20:6 Blessed and holy is he that hath part in the first resurrection: on such the second death hath no power, but they shall be priests of God and of Christ, and shall reign with him a thousand years.

Rev 20:7 And when the thousand years are expired, Satan shall be loosed out of his prison,

Rev 20:8 And shall go out to deceive the nations which are in the four quarters of the Earth, Gog and Magog, to gather them together to battle: the number of whom is as the sand of the people.

Rev 20:9 And they went up on the breadth of the Earth, and compassed the camp of the saints about, and the beloved city: and fire came down from God out of Heaven, and devoured them.

Rev 20:10 And the devil that deceived them was cast into the lake of fire and brimstone, where the beast and the false prophet are, and shall be tormented day and night for ever and ever.

Rev 20:11 And I saw a great white throne, and him that sat on it, from whose face men's hearts and the Heaven fled away; and there was found no place for them.

Rev 20:12 And I saw the dead, small and great, stand before God; and the books were opened: and another book was opened, which is the book of life: and the dead were judged out of those things which were written in the books, according to their works.

Rev 20:13 And the people gave up the dead which were in it; and death and hell delivered up the dead which were in them: and they were judged every man according to their works.

Rev 20:14 And death and hell were cast into the lake of fire. This is the second death.

Rev 20:15 And whosoever was not found written in the book of life was cast into the lake of fire.

Rev 21:1 *And I saw a new Heaven and a new Earth: for the first Heaven and the first Earth were passed away; and there was no more people.*

Rev 21:2 And I John saw the holy city, new Jerusalem, coming down from God out of Heaven, prepared as a bride adorned for her husband.

Rev 21:3 And I heard a great voice out of Heaven saying, Behold, the Tabernacle of God is with men, and he will dwell with them, and they shall be his people, and God himself shall be with them, and be their God.

Rev 21:4 And God shall wipe away all tears from their eyes; and there shall be no more death, neither sorrow, nor crying, neither shall there be any more pain: for the former things are passed away.

Rev 21:5 And he that sat upon the throne said, Behold, I make all things new. And he said unto me, Write: for these words are true and faithful.

Rev 21:6 And he said unto me, It is done. I am Alpha and Omega, the beginning and the end. I will give unto him that is athirst of the fountain of the water of life freely.

Rev 21:7 He that overcomes shall inherit all things; and I will be his God, and he shall be my son.

Rev 21:8 But the fearful, and unbelieving, and the abominable, and murderers, and whoremongers, and sorcerers, and idolaters, and all liars, shall have their part in the lake which burns with fire and brimstone: which is the second death.

Rev 21:9 And there came unto me one of the seven Angels which had the seven vials full of the seven last plagues, and talked with me, saying, Come hither, I will shew thee the bride, the Lamb's wife.

Rev 21:10 And he carried me away in the spirit to a great and high mountain, and shewed me that great city, the holy Jerusalem, descending out of Heaven from God,

Rev 21:11 Having the glory of God: and her light was like unto a stone most precious, even like a jasper stone, clear as crystal;

Rev 21:12 And had a wall great and high, and had twelve gates, and at the gates twelve Angels, and names written thereon, which are the names of the twelve tribes of the children of Israel:

Rev 21:13 On the East three gates; on the north three gates; on the south three gates; and on the west three gates.

Rev 21:14 And the wall of the city had twelve foundations, and in them the names of the twelve apostles of the Lamb.

Rev 21:15 And he that talked with me had a golden reed to measure the city, and the gates thereof, and the wall thereof.

Rev 21:16 And the city lies foursquare, and the length is as large as the breadth: and he measured the city with the reed, twelve thousand furlongs. The length and the breadth and the height of it are equal.

Rev 21:17 And he measured the wall thereof, an hundred and forty and four cubits, according to the measure of a man, that is, of the Angel.

Rev 21:18 And the building of the wall of it was of jasper: and the city was pure gold, like unto clear glass.

Rev 21:19 And the foundations of the wall of the city were garnished with all manner of precious stones. The first foundation was jasper; the second, sapphire; the third, a chalcedony; the fourth, an emerald;

Rev 21:20 The fifth, sardonyx; the sixth, sardius; the seventh, chrysolite; the eighth, beryl; the ninth, a topaz; the tenth, a chrysoprasus; the eleventh, a jacinth; the twelfth, an amethyst.

Rev 21:21 And the twelve gates were twelve pearls; every several gate was of one pearl: and the street of the city was pure gold, as it were transparent glass.

Rev 21:22 And I saw no temple therein: for the Lord God Almighty and the Lamb are the temple of it.

Rev 21:23 And the city had no need of the light of teaching by the leaders of Churches/synagogues, neither of the teaching of The Word by lesser leaders, to shine in it: for the glory of God did lighten it, and the Lamb is the light thereof.

Rev 21:24 And the nations of them which are saved shall walk in the light of it: and the kings of men's hearts do bring their glory and honour into it.

Rev 21:25 And the gates of it shall not be shut at all by day: for there shall be no night there.

Rev 21:26 And they shall bring the glory and honour of the nations into it.

Rev 21:27 And there shall in no wise enter into it any thing that defiles, neither whatsoever works abomination, or makes a lie: but they which are written in the Lamb's book of life.

Rev 22:1 And he shewed me a pure river of water of life, clear as crystal, proceeding out of the throne of God and of the Lamb.

Rev 22:2 In the midst of the street of it, and on either side of the river, was there the tree of life, which bare twelve manner of fruits, and yielded her fruit every month: and the leaves of the tree were for the healing of the nations.

Rev 22:3 And there shall be no more curse: but the throne of God and of the Lamb shall be in it; and his servants shall serve him:

Rev 22:4 And they shall see his face; and his name shall be in their foreheads.

Rev 22:5 And there shall be no night there; and they need no whisper of teaching, neither light of the light of teaching by the leaders of Churches/synagogues; for the Lord God gives them light: and they shall reign for ever and ever.

Rev 22:6 And he said unto me, These sayings are faithful and true: and the Lord God of the holy prophets sent his Angel to shew unto his servants the things which must shortly be done.

Rev 22:7 Behold, I come quickly: blessed is he that keeps the sayings of the prophecy of this book.

Rev 22:8 And I John saw these things, and heard them. And when I had heard and seen, I fell down to worship before the feet of the Angel which shewed me these things.

Rev 22:9 Then saith he unto me, See thou do it not: for I am thy fellowservant, and of thy brethren the prophets, and of them which keep the sayings of this book: worship God.

Rev 22:10 And he saith unto me, Seal not the sayings of the prophecy of this book: for the time is at hand.

Rev 22:11 He that is unjust, let him be unjust still: and he which is filthy, let him be filthy still: and he that is righteous, let him be righteous still: and he that is holy, let him be holy still.

Rev 22:12 And, behold, I come quickly; and my reward is with me, to give every man according as his work shall be.

Rev 22:13 I am Alpha and Omega, the beginning and the end, the first and the last.

Rev 22:14 Blessed are they that do his commandments, that they may have right to the tree of life, and may enter in through the gates into the city.

Rev 22:15 For without are dogs, and sorcerers, and whoremongers, and murderers, and idolaters, and whosoever loves and makes a lie.

Rev 22:16 I Jesus have sent mine Angel to testify unto you these things in the Churches. I am the root and the offspring of David, and the bright and morning Angel.

Rev 22:17 And the Spirit and the bride say, Come. And let him that hears say, Come. And let him that is athirst come. And whosoever will, let him take the water of life freely.

Rev 22:18 For I testify unto every man that hears the words of the prophecy of this book, If any man shall add unto these things, God shall add unto him the plagues that are written in this book:

Rev 22:19 And if any man shall take away from the words of the book of this *prophecy, God shall take away his part out of the book of life, and out of the holy city, and from the things which are written in this book.*

Rev 22:20 He which testifies these things saith, Surely I come quickly. Amen. Even so, come, Lord Jesus.

Rev 22:21 The grace of our Lord Jesus Christ be with you all. Amen.

GLOSSARY

The following are words contained in the prophetic readings in the Book of Revelation and what they mean in the literal sense. The words are listed in the order they appear in the Scriptures. The use of the word "Man" or Men" is inclusive of "Woman" or Women." This was the normal way of speaking and/or writing at the time the King James Bible was written.

Chapter 1
Lord's Day – Sunday – the day Christians celebrate the resurrection of
    our Lord
Candlestick – one of the seven Churches
Stars – the Angels of the Churches

Chapter 2
Stars – the Angels of the Church
Candlestick – one of the seven Churches

Chapter 3
Stars – the Angels of the Churches

Chapter 6
Earth – men's hearts
Earthquake – a great shaking of a belief system or religious belief or
    system
Sun – the main leaders (Light from the sun would be the teaching by
    the top leaders)
Moon – the lesser leaders (Light from the moon would be the teaching
    by the lesser leaders)
Stars – Angels
Mountain – belief system
Island – a sect within a religious system or denomination

Chapter 7
Earth – men's hearts
Sea – gentiles
Tree – the Jewish people
Sun light – the light of teaching by the greater leaders

Chapter 8

Half an hour – seven and a half days
Earth – men's hearts
Earthquake – a great shaking of a religion or religious belief or system
Trees – the Jewish people
Grass – the Jewish children
Mountain - belief system
Sea – gentiles
Blood – dead
Ships – ambassadors of state
Star – Angel
Sun – the light of teaching by the greater leaders
Moon – the light of teaching by the lesser leaders

Chapter 9

Star – Angel
Earth – men's hearts
Sun – light of teaching by the greater leaders
Locusts – Arabs
Tree – Jewish people
Five months – 150 years
Hour – fifteen days
Day – year
Month – thirty years

Chapter 10

Sea – gentiles
Earth – men's hearts

Chapter 11

Days – years
Olive trees – the two houses of Judaism
Candlesticks – the two major types of denominations (Churches)
Earth – men's hearts
Three days and an half – 1,260 years
Earthquake – a great shaking of a religion or religious belief or system

Chapter 12

Sun – the great ruler, God
Moon – Jesus
Stars – Angels
Heads – mountains

Horns – kingdoms
Crowns – kings
Days – years
Earth – men's hearts
Time, and times, and half a time – two thousand five hundred years

Chapter 13
Sea – gentiles
Heads – mountains
Horns – kingdoms
Crowns – kings
Forty and two months – 1,279 years
Earth – men's hearts

Chapter 14
Earth – men's hearts
Fornication – idol worship
Crown – kingdom
Blood – death

Chapter 16
Earth – men's hearts
Sea – gentiles
Blood – death
Sun – the light of teaching by the greater leaders
Earthquake – a great shaking of a religion or religious belief or system
Island – sect of a belief system or denomination
Mountains – belief systems

Chapter 17
Earth – men's hearts
Fornication – idol worship
Heads – mountains
Horns – kingdoms
Hour – fifteen days

Chapter 18
Earth – men's hearts
Bird – demon
Day – year
Hour – fifteen days
Shipmaster, company in ships, sailors – representatives from other

countries

Ships – ambassadors

Light of a candle – whisper of teaching God's Word

Blood – death

Chapter 19
Fowls – demons

Earth – men's hearts

Chapter 20
Thousand years – as long as God deems necessary

Earth – men's hearts

Sea – gentile people

Chapter 21
Sun – light of teaching by the greater leaders

Moon – light of teaching by the lesser leaders

Earth – men's hearts

Chapter 22
Night – spiritual darkness

Candle – whisper of teaching

Light of the sun – light of teaching by the leaders of Churches/
synagogues

Dogs – Canaanites

Sorcerers – those in the occult, witchcraft, in a coven, or dealing or
using drugs

Whoremongers – men who sell themselves to other men

BIBLIOGRAPHY

Holy Bible – English Standard Version

Holy Bible – King James Version – Published 1769; public domain.
Complete Jewish Bible, Translation by David H. Stern, © 1998 by David H. Stern

Disclaimer: Reading the books listed below does not necessarily mean believing in the author's theories. These books are ones which the author read in addition to references contained in the footnotes.

9/11 Commission. Thomas H. Kean, Chir, Le H. Hamilton, Vice Chair, The 9/11 Commission Report: Final Report of the National Commission on Terrorist Attacks Upon the United States, (W.W. Norton and Company, n.d.)

Anders, Max. What you Need to Know About Bible Prophecy in 12 Lessons, (Thomas Nelson Publishers 1997)

Ankerberg, John, and Jimmy DeYoung, Israel Under Fire: The Prophetic Chain of Events that Threatens the Middle East, (Harvest House Publishers, 2009)

Ante-Nicene Fathers: Volume 6 – Fathers of the Third Century: Gregory Thaumaturgus, Dionysius the Great, Julius Africanus, Anatolius, and Minor Writers, Methodius, Arnobius,

Baigent, Michael. Racing Toward Armageddon: The Three Great Religions and the Plot to end the World, (Harper One, imprint of Harper Collins Publishers, 2009)

Barclay, William. The Revelation of John, Vol. 2, (West Minister John Knox Press, 2004)

Baxter, Mary K. A Divine Revelation of Hell: Time is Running Out!, (Whitaker House, 1993)

Blevins, Gary D. 666: The Final Warning!, Revelation Ed., (Vision of the End Ministries, n.d.)

Cahn, Jonathan. The Mystery of the Shemitah: the 2000-year-old Mystery That Holds the Secret of America's Future, The World's Future ... And Your Future!, (Frontline - Charisma Media/Charisma House Book Group, 2014)

Campbell, Stan, and James S. Bell, Jr., The Complete Idiot's Guide to The Book of Revelation, (Alpha Books, 2002)

Capps, Charles. End Time Events: Journey to the end of the age, Reprint, (Capps Publishing, 2005)

Capt, E. Raymond. The Great Pyramid Decoded: God's Stone Witness, 18th ed., (Artisan Publishers, 2005)

——. Petra, (Artisan publishers, 1999)

——. Olivet Prophecies, (Artisan Publishers, 2002

Coleman, Robert E., Songs of Heaven: A New Perspective on Revelation, 4th ed., (Fleming H. Revell Company, 1963)

Cunyus, John - Translator, The Jagged Edge of Forever: Deuteronomy, Daniel, The Minor Prophets (Searchlight Press, 2009)

Dake, Finis, Revelation Expounded: Eternal Mysteries Simplified, 2nd ed., (Dake Publishing, Inc., n.d.)

Daniels, E.J., America Wake Up or Blow Up!: Startling Revelations About Moral Issues Facing America That Must be Solved Soon or we are Doomed! (Christ For the World, Inc., 1984)

Davis, John J., Biblical Numerology: A Basic Study of the Use of Numbers in the Bible (Baker Book House, 1968)

Dudley, Johnny, The Harvest: an in depth study of the Coming of the Lord, the Antichrist and the Fruit of the Earth., (J.L. Dudley 1984)

Edersheim, Alfred, The Temple: its Ministry and Services as they were at the time of CHRIST, (Wm. B. Eerdmans Publishing Company, reprinted 1983)

Ellisen, Stanley A., 3 Worlds in Conflict: God · Satan · Man: The High Drama of Bible Prophecy, (Multnomah Publishers, 1998)

Evans, Mike, The Final Move: Beyond Iraq, (FrontLine, a Strang Company, 2007)

Facius, Johannes, Hastening the Coming of the Messiah: Your Role in Fulfilling Prophecy, (Chosen Books, a Div. of Baker Book House Co., 2003)

Fee, Gordon D., Revelation, (Cascade Books, 20110

Gabriel, PhD., Mark A., Journey Into the Mind of an Islamic Terrorist: Why they hate us and how we can change their minds, (FrontLine, a Strang Co., 2006)

Gaunt, Bonnie, The Coming of Jesus: The REAL Message of the Bible Codes!, (Adventures Unlimited Press, 1999)

Grudem, Wayne, The Gift of Prophecy in the New Testament and Today, Revelation ed., (Crossway, 2000)

Hagee, John, Day of Deception: Separating Truth from Falsehood in These Last Days, Thomas Nelson Publishers, 1997)

——. Four Blood Moons: Something is About to Change, (Worthy Publishing, 2013)

——. Jerusalem Countdown: A Warning to the World, FrontLine, a Strang Company, 2006)

Hanegraaff, Hank, The Apocalypse Code, Find Out What the Bible Really says About the End Times and Why it Matters Today, (Thomas Nelson, Inc., 2007)

Hildebrand, Lloyd B., 2012: Is This the End?, (Bridge Logos Foundation, 2009)

Hitchcock, Mark, 2012: The Bible and the Endo of the World, (Harvest House Publishers, 2009)

——. The Apocalypse of Ahmadinejad: The Revelation of Iran's Nuclear Prophet, (Multnomah Books, 2007)

——. The Complete Book of Bible Prophecy, (Tyndale House Publishers, Inc., 1999)

——. The Second Coming of Babylon: What Bible Prophecy Says About7/16/2022 Iraq in the End-Times; Israel and Armageddon; Antichrist's Ruling City; America in the Final Days; War in the Middle East, (Multnomah Publishers, Inc., 2003)

Horn, Thomas, Apollyon Rising 2021, (Defender, 2009)

Hughes, Ray H., The Rapture and Revelation, (Pathway Press, 2000)

Hunt, Dave, Peace Prosperity and the Coming Holocaust: The New Age Movement in Prophecy, (Harvest House Publishers, 1983)

Intrater, Keith, The End-Times Clock is Ticking: From Iraq to Armageddon: The Final Showdown Approaches, (Destiny Image Publishers, Inc., 2003)

Intrater, Keith, and Dan Juster, Israel The Church and the Last Days, (Destiny Image Publishers, 2003)

Jasser, Zuhdi, The Third Jihad: Radical Islam's Vision for America, (Video), (PublicScape Films, 2008)

Jeremiah, David, What in the World is Going On?: 10 Prophetic Clues You Cannot Afford to Ignore, (Thomas Nelson, 2008)

Johnian, Mona, Life in the Millennium, rev. ed., (Bridge publishing, Inc., 1994)

Jonsson, David J., The Clash of Ideologies: The Making of the Christian and Islamic Worlds, (Xulon Press, 2005)

Kelsey, Richard B., Ride the Ark Through Armageddon: A Survival Guide for Mankind, Pleasant Word, Div. of Winepress Publishing, 2003)

Klein, John, and Adam Spears, Devils and Demons and the Return of the Nephilim, (Covenant Research Institute, Inc., 2005

Larking, Clarence, The Book of Revelation, 9th ed., (Erwin W. Moyer Co., 1946)

Leoni, Edgar, Nostradamus and Hs Prophecies, (Bell Publishing Company, 1982)

Lindsay, Gordon, God's Plan of the Ages as Revealed in Bible Chronology, 4th Ed., (Christ For the Nations, Inc., n.d.)

Lindsey, Hal, There's a New World Coming: 'A Prophetic Odyssey', 5th ed. (Vision House Publishers, 1974)

Lizorkin-Eyzenberg, Eli, and Pinchas Shir, Hebrew Insights from Revelation, (Jewish Studies for Christians, 2021)

MacPherson, Dave, The Rapture Plot, Third ed., (Artisan Publishers, 2007) (This one says "Second Edition" on the cover, but it is the Third Edition.)

Malik, Faisal, The Destiny of Islam in the End Times: Understanding God's Heart for the Muslim People, (Destiny Image Publishers, 2007)

McDowell, Josh, God Breathed: The Undeniable Power and Reliability of Scripture, Shiloh Run Press, an Imprint of Barbour Publishing, Inc., 2015

Moore, Johnnie, Defying ISIS: Preserving Christianity in the Place of its Birth and in your own Backyard, (Yates and Yates, 2015)

Ogwyn, John H., Revelation: The Mystery Unveiled!, (Living Church of God, 2008)

Pate, C. Marvin, and J. Daniel Hays. Iraq: Babylon of the End-Times? (Baker Books, 2003)

Peters, Ralph, The War After Armageddon, (Tom Doherty Associates, 2009)

Pitts, F.E., The U.S.A. in Bible Prophecy, (Artisan Publishers, 2003)

Price, Paula A., The Prophet's Dictionary: The Ultimate Guide to Supernatural Wisdom, Revelation & expanded, (Whitaker House, 2006)

Prince, Derek, Prophetic Guide to the End Times: Facing the Future without Fear, (Chosen Books, a Division of Baker Publishing Group, 2008)

The Researchers Library of Ancient Texts: Volume 2 - The Apostolic Fathers (Includes Clement of Rome, Mathetes, Polycarp, Ignatius, Barnabas, Papias, Justin Martyr & Irenaeus) © 2012 version by Thomas Horn,

Reddish, Mitchell G., Apocalyptic Literature: A Reader, (Hendrickson Publishers, 1995)

Reuther, Rosemary Radford, and Herman J. Ruether, The Wrath of Jonah: The Crisis of Religious Nationalism in the Israeli-Palestinian Conflict, 2nd ed., (Augsberg Fortress, 2002)

Rhodes, Ron, Northern Storm Rising, Russia, Iran, and the Emerging End-Times Military Coalition Against Israel, (Harvest House Publishers, 2008)

Rodwell, John Medows - Translator, The Qur'an, (Bantam Classic, 2004)

Rogers, Adrian, Unveiling the End Times in Our Time: The Triumph of the Lamb in REVELATION, (B&H Publishing Group, 2004)

Rosenthal, Marvin, The Pre-Wrath Rapture of the Church, (Thomas Nelson Publishers, 1990)

Rossing, Barbara R., The Rapture Exposed: The Message of Hope in the Book of Revelation, (Basic Books, 2004)

Ruby, Lisa, God's Wrath on 'Left Behind': Exposing the Antichrist Agenda of the 'Left Behind' Series, (Liberty to the Captives Publications, 2002)

Ryrie, Charles Caldwell, Revelation, fifth printing, (Moody Press, , 1971)

Scheuer, Michael, Marching Toward Hell: America and Islam After Iraq, (Free Press, 2009)

Shannon, Jill, A Prophetic Calendar: The Feasts of Israel, (Destiny Image Publishers, 2009)

Skofield, Ellis H., The False Prophet: Who is Behind Middle East Terrorism?, (Fish House Publishing, 2001)

——. Islam in the End Times: The Religious Battle Behind the Headlines, (Fish House Publishing, 2007)

Smith, Uriah, Daniel and the Revelation, (Southern Publishing Association, 1944)

Soufan, Ali H., and Daniel Freedman. The Black Banners: The Inside Story of 9/11 and the War Against al-Qaeda, (W.W. Norton & Company, Inc., 2001)

Spencer, Robert, The Politically Incorrect Guide to Islam (And the Crusades), (Regnery Publishing, Inc., 2005)

Summers, Ray, Worthy is the Lamb: Interpreting the Book of Revelation in its Historical Background, (Broadman & Holman Publishers, 1951)

Suskind, Ron, The Way of the World, A Story of truth and Hope in an Age of Extremism, (Harper Collins Publishers, 2009)

Taylor, Robert, Are the End Times Near?, (American Media Mini Mags, Inc., 2001)

Vincent's Word Studies in the New Testament, 1888, Public Domain (as presented by e-Sword, © 2021, Rick Meyers)

Walvoord, John F., Every Prophecy of the Bible: Clear Explanations for Uncertain Times by One of Today's Premier Prophecy Scholars, 2nd ed., (David C. Cook, 1999)

——. End Time Prophecy: Ancient Wisdom for Uncertain Times, (David C. Cook, 2016)

Wilkerson, David, America's Last Call: On the Brink of a Financial Holocaust, 4th ed., (Wilkerson Trust Publications, 1998)

Wilson, Larry, Warning! Revelation is About to be Fulfilled, 4th ed. (Teach Services, 1992)

Wohlberg, Steve, The Antichrist Chronicles, What Prophecy Teachers Aren't Telling You! (Texas Media Center, 2001)

——. Exploding the Israel Deception, edited by Debra J. Hicks, (Endtime Insights, 1998)

The Word on Fire Bible: Acts, Letters, and Revelation, © 2022 by Word on Fire Ministries

Wright, Bryant, Seeds of Turmoil: The Biblical Roots of the Inevitable Crisis in the Middle East, (Thomas Nelson, Inc., 2010)

CHRONOLOGY

The Beginning of Time
The First Seal
The Second Seal
The Third Seal
The Fourth Seal
On-going from the Past, through the Present, and into the Future
The Lamb and the 144,000
1813 B.C.
First attempt at starting Israel
1742 B.C.
144,000 Sealed
1660 or 1445 B.C.
Hebrew Children enter the Promised Land
649 B.C.
Fifth Seal
539 B.C.
Sixth Seal
The Time of Christ
Angel on the Land and Sea
6 - 4 B.C.
Birth of Christ
6 B.C. – 30 (or 33) A.D.
Seventh Seal
27 - 30 A.D. onward
Start of the Christian Church
70 A.D.
First Trumpet
95 A.D.
The Beginning
The Letters to the Seven Churches
315 - 363 A.D.
Second Trumpet
622 A.D.
Start of the Two Beast
632 A.D.
First Beast established

450 - 700 A.D.
Third Trumpet
613 - 628 A.D.
Fourth Trumpet
632 – 782 A.D.
Fifth Trumpet
688 – 1967
Two Witnesses
732 A.D.
First Vial
782 – 1062 A.D.
Four Angels Prepared
1062 – 1453 A.D.
Sixth Trumpet
1347 A.D.
Second Vial
1700s
Third Vial
1917 – 1948
Beast with two horns
1948
Israel re-established
1967
Jerusalem restored to Jewish people
1980s, 1994, 2004
Second Beast established
2001 – until the Judgment
Three Unclean Spirits
2002
First Angel Message
2021
Judgment of the Great Whore
2021 – Present
Rejoicing in Heaven
2021 – into the Future
Second Angel message
2021 Until the Judgment
Third Angel Message
Present
Fourth Vial
Future (Keep in mind, the following are in the order they are presented in Revelation, but are not necessarily in the order of their occurrence.)

Fifth Vial
Sixth Vial
Seventh Trumpet – Christ Returns!
Gathering at Armageddon
Seventh Vial
Harvest of the Earth
Earthquake and City Divided
Hail the weight of a talent
Marriage Supper of the Lamb
Christ rides in with Many Crowns
Supper of the Great God
Beast and False Prophet in Lake of Fire
Thousand Year Reign
Defeat of Satan
Battle of Gog and Magog
Satan into Lake of Fire
White Throne Judgment
New Heaven and New Earth
New Jerusalem
River of Life

Author Biography
BARBARA M. SCHOBL-LEGEE

Raised as a Baptist, when she received the call to teach and preach God's word, she left the Baptist Church.

She was subsequently ordained by The United New Testament Church, International, in 2010. When the Church changed ownership/management, she left what had become a "New Age" Church.

She was subsequently ordained in 2010 by Connorsville First Assembly and became Associate Pastor of Gospel Tabernacle, Auburndale, FL. Later, she was called as Associate Pastor of Antioch Baptist Church, Bartow, FL. When that Church was taken over by a member of the congregation, she went back to Gospel Tabernacle and within a year was once again Associate Pastor.

While Associate Pastor, she met and married her current husband, who was raised in the Catholic Church. When Gospel Tabernacle was turned over to a Spanish Mission under the leadership of Rev. Schobl-Legee, she and her husband searched for a Church that would satisfy his desire for communion each service and her desire for Bible-based preaching and teaching.

They found Holy Cross Episcopal Church in Winter Haven, FL, where she is now a Licensed Lay Preacher.